TILL THE SUN RISES

TILL THE SUN RISES

BIS ZUM SONNENAUFGANG

BIS ZUM SONNEN AUFGANG

CONTENTS

ENTANGLED INTERNATIONALISMS

VERFLOCHTENE INTERNATIONALISMEN

FOREWORD

vinit agarwal

VORWORT

What do the concepts of "Internationalism" and "Internationalism(s)" have to gain from a film that was made by Indian film director Chetna Vora while she was studying film directing at the Film and Television Academy of the GDR in 1980? Why does it matter today that these internationalism(s) were not isolated, that they were in conversation—that they were entangled? This research edition aims to address the above questions via research and archival material. Yet, to subvert the conditions imposed by the concept of the archive itself, I intend to amplify the "poethics" of the film *OYOYO* and the affect it and various other encounters produce in the reader.[1] The aim is not to write a new history of India–GDR relations or even to revise the old one but to allow those who spent various periods of their lives on the India–GDR axis and its para-ontologies (such as Angola–GDR, Bissau–GDR and so on) to meet in this research edition. More often than not, these encounters are not recorded in the meetings of state presidents, in the (over-)historicized exhibitions of famous artists, or in the existing academic discussions, yet—minor, undisciplined, unsettled and unsettling, disruptive, incongruous, and unsuited to any category—they are of key interest here in that they refuse to hold the "Cold War" as the context in which these discussions are more often than not framed. If you must imagine it geometrically, do not imagine a line on both sides of which two almighty superpowers stand and on which the struggle of every other country and people must be defined. Rather imagine a circle, on whose periphery stands all the places that have become newly independent or are still involved in the anti-colonial struggle, all the geographies, soils, water, mountains, and their people who are looking inside the circle and walking toward each other. I call this the interiorization of politics, an internalization that refuses to address the imposed binaries, an internal (de)rationalism, or internationalism. It is ours, it is among us, and it is for us. This "us" also includes people from the GDR and the Eastern Bloc. Therefore, it is important to "feel" sensorially how the fact that these encounters happened via the GDR generates a specific effect. A networked plea that asks for a reconsideration of the politics of the medium of these exchanges, of a carrier of these memories, and of the way the effects of these meetings come alive, especially in our time today.

1. I use the term "poethics" as described by Denise Ferreira Da Silva in "Toward a Black Feminist Poethics: The Quest(ion) of Blackness / Toward the End of the World," *The Black Scholar* 44, no. 2 (Summer 2014): 81–97. She mentions that "a Poethics of Blackness would announce a whole range of possibilities for knowing, doing, and existing." Thus, I try to highlight the possibilities of existing in this film's visual poetry by using this specific notion of poethics.

Wie kann ein Film, den die indische Regisseurin Chetna Vora (1958–1987) während ihres Regie-Studiums an der damaligen Hochschule für Film und Fernsehen der DDR 1980 gedreht hat, unser heutiges Verständnis des „Internationalismus", der „Internationalismen" bereichern? Welche Rolle spielt dabei die Tatsache, dass diese Internationalismen niemals isoliert waren, sondern in Austausch standen, verflochten waren? Die vorliegende Forschungsedition will anhand von Recherchen und Archivmaterialien Antworten auf diese Fragen geben. Um dabei Beschränkungen zu umgehen, die uns bereits der Begriff des Archivs auferlegt, möchte ich hier eine *Poethik*[1] des Films *OYOYO* besonders zur Geltung bringen und ihre Wirkung auf die Leser·innen auch durch weitere Begegnungen verstärken. Es ist nicht meine Absicht, eine neue Geschichte der Beziehungen zwischen Indien und der DDR zu schreiben oder die alte einer Revision zu unterziehen. Vielmehr geht es darum, in diesem Band Stimmen und Personen zu versammeln, deren Leben und Schaffen in unterschiedlichen Phasen auf der Achse Indien – DDR oder entlang ähnlicher geografischer Verflechtungen (Angola – DDR, Bissau – DDR und so weiter) verlief. Solche Begegnungen tauchen in den Protokollen der Staatsbesuche, in den (gar zu) historisierenden Ausstellungen bekannter Künstler, aber auch in akademischen Diskussionen nur selten auf. Dabei sind hier gerade die nebensächlichen, ungeordneten, unerledigten, irritierenden, erschütternden, unpassenden, nicht einfach zu kategorisierenden Begegnungen von Interesse. Auch und gerade, weil sie sich nicht auf den Kontext des Kalten Krieges festlegen lassen, der üblicherweise den Rahmen für diese Diskussionen setzt. Wenn wir uns schon mit einer geometrischen Metapher behelfen müssen, dann nicht mit der einer Linie, die zwei Supermächte voneinander trennt und allen Staaten und Völkern abverlangt, ihren Platz auf der einen oder der anderen Seite zu finden. Stellen wir uns stattdessen lieber einen Kreis vor, von dessen Rand aus all die erst jüngst unabhängig gewordenen oder noch in die Kämpfe der Dekolonialisierung verstrickten Regionen, Landschaften, Gründe, Gewässer und Gebirge mit all ihren Bewohner·innen in die Mitte sehen und aufeinander zugehen. Ich nenne das eine Verinnerlichung des Politischen, welche sich den Zwang zu binären Gegensätzen nicht zu eigen macht, einen inneren (De-)Rationalismus oder Internationalismus. Dieser Prozess gehört zu uns, er geschieht zwischen uns und für uns. Und zu diesem „Wir", das ich meine, gehören auch die Menschen in der DDR, im Ostblock

1. Ich verwende den Begriff „Poethik" gemäß den Überlegungen von Denise Ferreira Da Silva in „Toward a Black Feminist Poethics – The Question of Blackness / Toward the End of the World", in: *The Black Scholar,* 44, 2014, Nr. 2, S. 81–97. Sie spricht von einer „Poethik des Schwarzseins", die „eine ganze Palette von Möglichkeiten des Wissens, Handelns und Existierens eröffnen würde". Anhand ihrer spezifischen Auffassung von Poethik versuche ich im Folgenden, die Möglichkeit aufzuzeigen, uns innerhalb der Bildpoesie und Bildethik dieses Films aufzuhalten.

Like the Cold War binary, the India–GDR axis may also mislead the reader. As is the case in the film *OYOYO* itself, the interaction is never limited to two poles—India and the GDR—but always multifaceted. Students from Guinea-Bissau, Cape Verde, Mongolia, Chile, Cuba, and other places participated in the making of *OYOYO*. And yet this internationalism cannot be understood as a bouquet of interaction between various nation-states. Simply adding "inter" ("in-between") to "nation" (a European ontology of cartographic enclosure) is insufficient to describe what is happening in this film. It is as if the whole film is an attempt at redefining the nature of internationalism and its differences to the multinationalism that is currently a popular concept. This also points to the contemporary relevance this discussion on internationalism holds for our society in which all models of solidarity have either been exhausted or rendered ineffective. These internationalisms are not without a profound relation to Proletarian Internationalism, Afro-Asian solidarity networks and Pan-Africanism. Yet I hope it will become clear on the basis of the various fragments in this research edition that the genealogies of this "coming together" as internationalism in *OYOYO* do not completely fit in the containers of Proletarian Internationalism, Afro-Asian solidarity, or Pan-Africanism. The remains of these historical internationalist movements precipitate today in the osmosis of oral history and minor archives, constituting an "archival leak" that is the very raison d'être of this research edition. The encounters proposed in the film (and new ones that have come about in this research edition) render the category of nation-state porous. In 1978, these anti-colonial nations were still for the most part newly formed, their borders were ever-changing, and their geopolitics was still haunted by colonialism and newly attained freedom. This is why the interaction that occurs in the film between Carmen-Maria Barbosa e Sá and Chetna Vora exceeds the description of an "interaction between medical students from Guinea-Bissau and India in the GDR." This *excess,* this leak, can only reach the reader via an image, a poem, or a song. This research edition consists of songs that we hope the reader will hum along to. This research edition hopes to be a song.

In these pages, you will also find those elements that are not directly and historically related to the biography of Chetna Vora and the film *OYOYO*. The

allgemein. Es ist deshalb wichtig, mit allen Sinnen zu „erspüren“, welch eigentümliche Wirkung es hat, dass diese Begegnungen von der DDR ausgingen. Es ist ein Plädoyer dafür, das Medium dieses Austauschs, die Träger dieser Erinnerungen in ihren politischen Dimensionen neu zu betrachten und zu verfolgen, wie diese Begegnungen – gerade heute – ihre Wirkung entfalten.

Dem binären Schema des Kalten Krieges vergleichbar kann uns aber auch die Achse Indien – DDR auf eine falsche Fährte locken. Denn wie auch im Film *OYOYO* beschränkte sich die Interaktion nie auf ein Hin und Her zwischen Indien und der DDR als zwei Polen, sondern war wesentlich facettenreicher. Studierende aus Guinea-Bissau, Kap Verde, der Mongolischen Volksrepublik, Chile, Kuba und weiteren Ländern waren an der Entstehung von *OYOYO* beteiligt. Doch dieser Internationalismus lässt sich auch nicht als ein bunter Strauß von Beziehungen zwischen Nationalstaaten verstehen. Der Nation (einem europäischen Modell kartografischer Einhegung) einfach ein „Inter“ (zwischen) voranzustellen, wird dem Geschehen in diesem Film nicht gerecht. Denn dieser wirkt wie ein Versuch, das Wesen des Internationalismus neu zu erfassen, ohne beim Konzept eines Multinationalismus zu landen, das derzeit so hoch im Kurs steht. Damit wird zugleich deutlich, worin und wodurch diese Auseinandersetzung mit dem Internationalismus für unsere heutigen Gesellschaften relevant ist – Gesellschaften nämlich, in denen jedes Verständnis von Solidarität verbraucht und wirkungslos geworden ist. Die Internationalismen, die *OYOYO* meint, sind eng verbunden mit dem Proletarischen Internationalismus, den Netzwerken afrikanisch-asiatischer Solidarität und dem Panafrikanismus. Dennoch hoffe ich anhand verschiedener Fragmente in dieser Forschungsedition zu zeigen, dass die Genealogien dieser Zusammenkunft der Internationalismen im Film *OYOYO* in diesen Beziehungen nicht einfach aufgehen. Was von diesen historischen Internationalismen bleibt, dringt osmotisch in die Überlieferung der Oral History ein oder ist in kleinen, unscheinbareren Archiven dokumentiert, wodurch ein archivarischer Durchbruch möglich wird, der den eigentlichen Anlass zum Erscheinen dieser Forschungsedition bietet. Die im Film gezeigten (wie auch die bei der Arbeit an diesem Buch zustande gekommenen) Begegnungen und Gespräche perforieren die Kategorie des Nationalstaats. 1978 waren die aus der Dekolonialisierung hervorgegangenen Nationen größtenteils noch sehr jung. Ihre Grenzen verschoben sich andauernd,

film itself works as a blueprint and a map, a directive principle for internationalism—but not an exact image to be translated. For example, we don't know yet if Meher Rustom Contractor, the Indian puppeteer and president of UNIMA India, ever met or knew Chetna. Meher Contractor taught for several years at Darpana Academy in Ahmedabad, which is in Gujarat, where Chetna also lived. Both of them interacted with the GDR in the same period as their contemporaries and compatriots, yet there is no document or oral account available to ascertain if the two ever met. However, Meher Contractor's presence in this research edition enters the sphere of the "possible," challenging the supremacy of evidentiality as an archival condition that constantly undermines minor and oral histories. There are many such encounters in these pages where *OYOYO* is not directly referred to but rather works as a guiding principle.

It is important to mention that there is also an alternative focus here as the research edition interacts with the first part of the *Entangled Internationalisms* exhibition series, *Till the Sun Rises: Sequence 1* at the Albertinum museum—part of the Dresden State Art Collections (Staatliche Kunstsammlungen Dresden, SKD)—and is laid on by its cross-collection research department. Thus, there are documents, images, and artworks in this edition that are taken from the SKD. The interactions also focus on Dresden as the place of these meetings, Dresden as a caravanserai, Dresden as the "via"—addressing an upheaval in the long

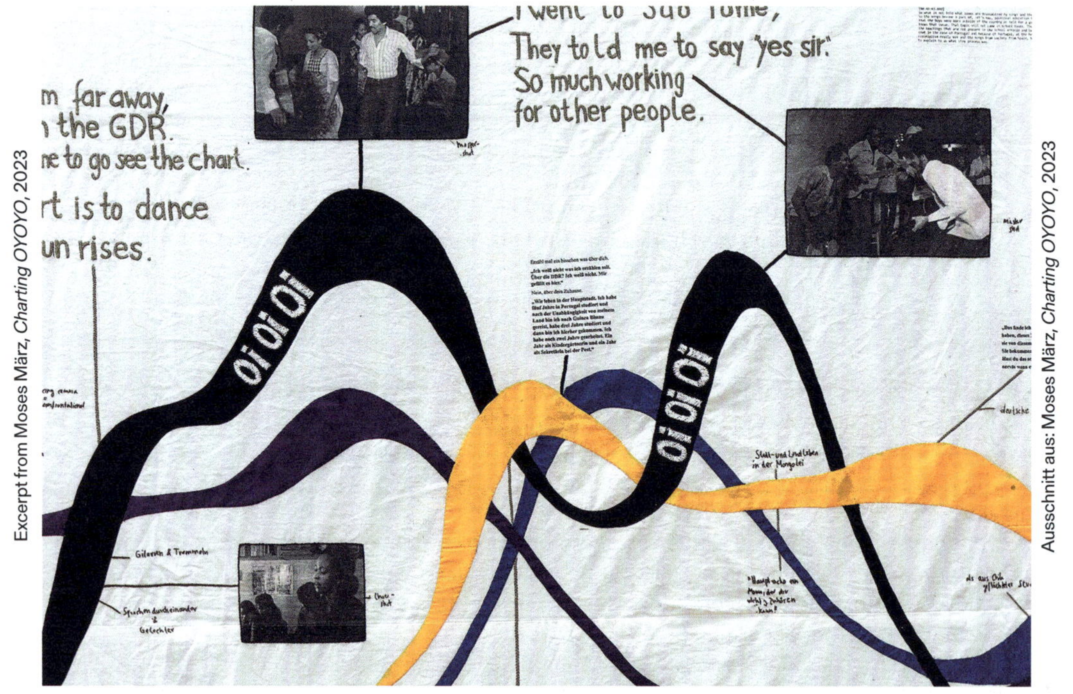

Excerpt from Moses März, *Charting OYOYO*, 2023

Ausschnitt aus: Moses März, *Charting OYOYO*, 2023

geopolitisch standen sie noch unter dem Einfluss der Gespenster des Kolonialismus und der neuen Freiheit. Vor diesem Hintergrund weist der Austausch zwischen Carmen-Maria Barbosa e Sá und Chetna Vora im Film weit über etwas hinaus, das sich als ‚Zusammenkunft von Medizinstudentinnen aus Guinea-Bissau und Indien in der DDR' beschreiben ließe. Dieses Surplus, dieser Durchbruch kann die Leser·innen nur durch ein Bild, Gedicht oder Lied erreichen. Deshalb besteht diese Forschungsedition aus Liedern, die hoffentlich zum Mitsummen anregen. Unser Buch will ein Gesang sein.

Auf den folgenden Seiten finden sich auch Dinge, die nicht direkt mit Leben und Werk von Chetna Vora oder mit dem Film *OYOYO* zu tun haben. Der Film dient dem Buch als Blaupause und Landkarte, als Leitfaden des Internationalismus, nicht als Bildvorlage, die direkt Übersetzung finden soll. So wissen wir beispielsweise nicht, ob die indische Puppenspielerin und UNIMA-Vorsitzende Meher Rustom Contractor Chetna jemals persönlich begegnet ist oder von ihr wusste. Meher Contractor lehrte jedoch mehrere Jahre an der Darpana Academy in Ahmedabad, also im Bundesstaat Gujarat, wo auch Chetna lebte. Beide standen zur selben Zeit im Kontakt mit der DDR. Dennoch gibt es weder einen schriftlichen Beleg noch ein mündliches Zeugnis dafür, dass sie einander je über den Weg gelaufen sind. Meher Contractor ist in diesem Band präsent, weil sie in die Sphäre des Möglichen eintritt – in jenes Vielleicht, das sich der Herrschaft der Belegbarkeit als Bedingung allen Archivierens entgegenstellt und sich so der andauernden Entwertung randständiger und mündlicher Überlieferungen

history of how it came to be what it was and how it became what it is today, and whether what was once possible here—in the city of Dresden during the GDR era—is still possible today.

More than anything else, this edition is a call to manifest—an appeal for the idea of internationalism reflected in Chetna Vora's work, for the participants of the film *OYOYO* and their afterlives, for the lives of artists, singers, poets, and visitors moving between India and the GDR and many other such places to come together as a potent fiction that can affect the bizarre theater of everyday reality that we inhabit.

This document also counters the myth of a single author in the sense conceived with and through the work of Chetna Vora, Meher Behn Contractor, Dr. Krishna Lal, Sushila Rohatgi, and Carmen Maria Barbosa é Sa. This document itself is co-written with Océane Vé-Réveillac, Elisabeth Schmidt, Prof. Sónia Vaz Borges, and Prof. Doreen Mende. None of this research edition could have been written without the close collaboration of Océane Vé-Réveillac, who helped at every stage of the research. I am immensely grateful to Elisabeth Schmidt, who magically coordinated with different departments to procure images, organized research meetings, and actively added to the research with her suggestions.

A special thank you to Vera Wobad, who helped obtain these documents from the SKD archives and generously gave of her precious time. Petra Kuhlmann Hodick gave us access to the Museum of Prints, Drawings, and Photographs (Kupferstich-Kabinett) and allowed us to rediscover the presence of GDR artist Karl Erich Müller's significant contribution to the India–GDR artistic movement through the portraits of his in storage at the Kupferstich-Kabinett. None of these works by Müller have been published or exhibited since their acquisition, and I hope their inclusion here will help the cause of research and scholarship. Prof. Doreen Mende has been a constant support in this research over the years since 2018 through our collaboration in the *Decolonizing Socialism: Entangled Internationalism* project with the Swiss National Science Foundation at HEAD, Geneva; not a single word written here would have been possible without her formative guidance as my professor of curatorial/politics and head of department at

widersetzt. Auf den folgenden Seiten kommt es zu einer Reihe solcher Begegnungen, in denen auf *OYOYO* nicht direkt Bezug genommen wird, der Film aber dennoch eine Richtung vorgibt.

Es muss hier noch ein weiterer Schwerpunkt erwähnt werden. Diese Forschungsedition greift ineinander mit *Bis zum Sonnenaufgang*, der ersten Sequenz der Ausstellungsreihe *Verflochtene Internationalismen* im Albertinum der Staatlichen Kunstsammlungen Dresden, und ist entstanden in Zusammenarbeit mit dem sammlungsübergreifenden Department „Forschung" an den SKD. Dementsprechend finden sich hier Dokumente, Bilder und Kunstwerke aus den Beständen der SKD. Es geht dabei auch um Dresden als Ort dieser Begegnungen, Dresden als Karawanserei, Dresden als das „Über" und das „Durch". Es geht um eine Verwerfung in der langen Geschichte seines Werdens zu dem, was es war und was es heute ist, um die Frage, ob heute hier noch möglich ist, was in Dresden zuzeiten der DDR möglich war.

Vor allem aber ist dieser Band ein Aufruf zur Manifestation, er beschwört die Vorstellungskraft in der Arbeit von Chetna Vora, die am Film *OYOYO* Beteiligten und ihr Nachleben, die Lebensgeschichten von Künstler·innen, Sänger·innen, Dichter·innen, Gästen im Austausch zwischen Indien und der DDR, er ruft sie zusammen zu einer Fiktion, die die Macht hat, dem bizarren Schauspiel der Alltagsrealität, in der wir leben, etwas entgegenzusetzen.

Dieses Dokument tritt zugleich dem Mythos der einsamen Autorschaft entgegen, insofern es entlang und anhand der Arbeit von Chetna Vora, Meher Contractor, Krishna Lal, Sushila Rohatgi und Carmen Maria Barbosa é Sa gedacht wurde. Auch der Text selbst wurde gemeinsam mit Océane Vé-Réveillac, Elisabeth Schmidt, Sónia Vaz Borges und Doreen Mende verfasst. Kein einziger Teil dieser Forschungsedition hätte ohne die enge Mitarbeit von Océane Vé-Réveillac entstehen können, die mich in allen Phasen meiner Recherchen unterstützte. Ein großer Dank geht an Elisabeth Schmidt, die wie von Zauberhand die verschiedenen Abteilungen bei der Bereitstellung von Bildmaterial koordinierte, Recherchetreffen organisierte und selbst mit Anregungen zu unserer Forschung beitrug. Besonderer Dank gebührt auch Vera Wobad, die geholfen hat, diese Dokumente aus dem Archiv der SKD zu besorgen, und dafür viel kostbare Zeit aufwandte. Petra Kuhlmann-Hodick gewährte uns Zugang zum

Critical Curatorial Cybermedia (CCC) during my Masters in Fine Arts at HEAD in Geneva. In preparing this research edition, and throughout my interaction with the exhibition *Till the Sun Rises*, I have constantly thought of the intrepid and fearless work of Hilke Wagner, director of the Albertinum at the SKD, and how she has intervened through public forums and dealt with the forces of colonialism and racial supremacism through her leadership at the Albertinum Museum. Artists and mapmakers Aarti Sunder and Moses März have contributed immensely and directly to the exhibition, and their texts and artworks make this research edition more meaningful.

Kupferstich-Kabinett und ermöglichte es uns, den DDR-Künstler Karl Erich Müller und seinen bedeutenden Beitrag zum künstlerischen Austausch zwischen Indien und der DDR wiederzuentdecken. Kein einziges seiner dort verwahrten Werke wurde nach ihrem Ankauf je publiziert oder ausgestellt, und ich hoffe, dass ihre Aufnahme in die Ausstellung der Wissenschaft in dieser Hinsicht dienlich sein wird. Doreen Mende hat meine Forschung in all den Jahren seit 2018 im Rahmen unserer vom Schweizerischen Nationalfonds geförderten gemeinsamen Arbeit mit der HEAD Genève am Projekt *Decolonizing Socialism: Entangled Internationalism* unterstützt. Kein einziges der hier geschriebenen Worte wäre denkbar ohne ihren prägenden Einfluss als Professorin für Curatorial / Politics und Leiterin des dortigen PhD-Forums CCC (Critical Curatorial Cybernetic Research Practices) während meines Master-Studiums der bildenden Kunst. In Vorbereitung dieser Forschungsedition und in meiner gesamten Auseinandersetzung mit der Ausstellung *Bis zum Sonnenaufgang* musste ich immer wieder an den unbeirrbaren und furchtlosen Einsatz von Hilke Wagner als Direktorin des Albertinums denken, insbesondere daran, wie sie in dieser Funktion die Öffentlichkeit suchte, um kolonialen und rassistischen Kräften entgegenzutreten. Aarti Sunder und Moses März haben sehr viel und direkt zur Ausstellung beigetragen. Ihre Texte und künstlerischen Arbeiten bereichern diese Forschungsedition sehr.

PROLOGUE

oi oi oi oi oi oi o...
Nha guenti forti trabadja p'alguem
Nha guenti forti trabadja p'alguem
Nha guenti forti trabadja p'alguem
Nha rabo dja kria ferida já tem otu rabixo
Nha rabo dja kria ferida já tem otu rabixo
Nha rabo dja kria ferida já tem otu rabixo
Ba São Tomé es fl am pam fl a sim sinhor
M'Ba Lisboa es fl am pam fl a sim sinhor
Quando um tchiga na tchom de Holanda
Nha guenti es fl am pam fl a
Nha guenti es fl am pam fl a sim sinhor so tank iu

PROLOG

At 25′25″ in the film *OYOYO* by Chetna Vora, a slow plucking of strings commences on a guitar. We sense the arrival of a song. Everything is inverted in this fragment. It is like a submarine, an underwater whirlpool that waits in the depths as a potentiality that can come to life the moment you come into contact with this song. The song stays active in this coming together of students from Chile, Guinea-Bissau, the Mongolian Soviet Republic, Cuba, Bulgaria, and many other places. It is called *Forti trabadja p'alguém* (So Much Work for Other People), the title of the film is taken from its opening line, the enunciation of "oi oi oi oi" (a call to gather, which we can understand from the way it is organized in the form of call and response). A voice leads the music, and the song begins in the film. We hear people assembling in the gallery from their respective rooms and dancing together to the accompaniment of this song.

> oi oi oi oi oi oi o...
> My people, so much work for other people
> My people, so much work for other people
> My people, so much work for other people
> My "butt" already has a wound and another one is growing
> My "butt" already has a wound and another one is growing
> My "butt" already has a wound and another one is growing
> I went to SãoTomé (and Príncipe), they told me to say, Yes, sir
> I went to Lisbon, they told me to say, Yes, sir
> When I arrived in the Netherlands,
> My people, they told me to say
> My people, they told me to say, Yes, sir, thank you very much

Bei Minute 25:25 des Films *OYOYO* von Chetna Vora setzt ein langsames Saitenzupfen auf einer Gitarre ein. Ein Lied liegt in der Luft, gleich wird es beginnen. Alles wird in diesem Schnipsel auf den Kopf gestellt. Wie ein Unterseeboot, ein Strudel tief im Wasser wartet alles darauf, zum Leben zu erwachen, sobald wir in Berührung mit diesem Lied geraten. Es zieht sich durch diese Zusammenkunft von Studierenden aus Chile, Guinea-Bissau, der Mongolischen Volksrepublik, Kuba, Bulgarien und etlichen anderen Ländern. Das Lied heißt *Forti trabadja p'alguém* („So viel arbeiten für andere Leute"), und der Titel des Films übernimmt dessen Beginn, nämlich die Laute „oi oi oi oi" (als Appell zur Versammlung, dessen Bedeutung wir aus dem bekannten Muster von Ruf und Antwort erschließen können). Eine Stimme leitet die Musik ein, dann beginnt das Lied im Film. Wir hören, wie Menschen aus ihren Zimmern kommen, sich in einem Flur sammeln und gemeinsam zu der Musik tanzen.

> Oi oi oi oi oi oi o …
> Meine Leute, so viel arbeiten für andere Leute
> Meine Leute, so viel arbeiten für andere Leute
> Meine Leute, so viel arbeiten für andere Leute
> Mein Hintern ist schon wund, eine neue Wunde entsteht
> Mein Hintern ist schon wund, eine neue Wunde entsteht
> Mein Hintern ist schon wund, eine neue Wunde entsteht
> Ich kam nach São Tomé (und Príncipe), man lehrte mich zu sagen:
> Jawohl, mein Herr
> Ich kam nach Lissabon, man lehrte mich zu sagen: Jawohl, mein Herr
> Als ich in Holland ankam
> Meine Leute, sie lehrten mich zu sagen
> Meine Leute, sie lehrten mich zu sagen: Jawohl, mein Herr, danke

OUR CHART IS A SONG

Sónia Vaz Borges in conversation with vinit agarwal and Doreen Mende

Sónia Vaz Borges, Doreen Mende und vinit agarwal im Gespräch

UNSERE TAFEL IST EIN LIED

Excerpts from a conversation that was originally recorded online on August 14, 2020, and edited as "A Transgenerational Commentary of a Song," research video, 25 min., 2020. It was on display as part of the exhibitions *Hidden Labor Across (inter∞note 01)*, KV Verein für zeitgenössische Kunst Leipzig e. V., August 22 – October 17, 2020, and *Till the Sun Rises*, Albertinum, Dresden, February 2 – May 25, 2024.

SVB: In São Tomé and Príncipe, for example, there was a kind of forced migration during colonial times in the 1940s. I say "forced migration" because it had to do with the job market, with training. They didn't learn how to plant, and what they did plant didn't survive because of droughts. And while this was happening in Cape Verde, there was a problem in São Tomé with not having enough people to work in the fields, on the coffee and cacao plantations. One of the strategies of the Portuguese colonial government was to hire Cape Verdean people to go to São Tomé and work on these plantations. In this context, "hired" is a very tricky word, we would say. Yes, they were hired, but it was kind of forced because they could not farm the land and still had to work to make some money in order to survive. So they were paid very little money. It was not too much, but part of the deal was that they went to São Tomé to work in these fields.

And how did they go to São Tomé? They went on a boat. So it replicated a slave ship coming from an island to bring people to the continent to work in this province. My grandparents, for example, went through this process and my dad did too, so I grew up with stories of the exploitation and dehumanization that they faced in the farms on São Tomé and Príncipe. So this is one part of this forced migration that was imposed on Cape Verdean people by colonial regimes, lack of investment in the land and environmental aspects that they could not control, like the lack of rain. And then the second part of the song says he went to Lisbon—i.e., he went to the metropolis, or to the old metropole, depending on the period he's talking about. Cape Verdean people mostly migrated to Lisbon to work in the construction industry (the men) or as domestic workers (the women). And so this is the second part of the migration process, and in both places, in São Tomé and Príncipe and in Lisbon, the historical sites of colonialism, you are obliged to say, "Yes, sir," all the time, no matter what, and that's why he now says, "They told me to say, 'Sim, sinhor,' in São Tomé, they told me to say the same thing in Lisbon; I should bow my head and accept what's given."

And that brings us to another place of migration that is in the Netherlands, in the 1960s and the 1970s. Cape Verdean people were migrating to the Netherlands, especially men, to work as sailors on the Dutch boats. They were registered

SVB: In den 1940er Jahren, während der Kolonialzeit, gab es eine mehr oder weniger erzwungene Migration nach São Tomé und Príncipe. Mit erzwungen meine ich, dass diese Migration mit dem Arbeitsmarkt und mit mangelnder Ausbildung zusammenhing. Die Leute in Kap Verde hatten nicht gelernt, wie man Feldfrüchte anbaut, und was sie anbauten, überstand die Trockenzeiten nicht. Gleichzeitig gab es in São Tomé das Problem, dass man nicht genug Personal für die Arbeit auf den Feldern und den Kaffee- und Kakaoplantagen hatte. Darauf reagierte die portugiesische Kolonialverwaltung unter anderem, indem sie Menschen in Kap Verde für die Feldarbeit in São Tomé anwarb. Von „anwerben" zu sprechen, ist natürlich problematisch. Formell wurden die Leute tatsächlich angestellt, aber aus einer Zwangslage heraus, da sie ihr eigenes Land nicht ertragreich bebauen konnten und daher anderswo Arbeit annehmen mussten, um zu überleben. Die Bezahlung war schlecht, und sie verpflichteten sich, nach São Tomé zu gehen, um dort auf den Feldern zu arbeiten.

Und wie gelangten sie nach São Tomé? Mit dem Schiff. Was wir hier sehen, ist eine Wiederkehr des Sklavenschiffs, nur dass diesmal Menschen von einer Insel zu einer Provinz auf dem Festland gefahren wurden, um dort zu arbeiten. Meine Großeltern haben das mitgemacht, mein Vater ebenso. Und so bin ich mit Erzählungen von der Ausbeutung und Entmenschlichung aufgewachsen, die sie auf den Landgütern von São Tomé und Príncipe erlitten haben. Das ist die eine Seite der Migration, zu der die Menschen in Kap Verde gezwungen waren – durch die Kolonialherrschaft, aber auch aufgrund von mangelnden Investitionen im Land und Umweltbedingungen, die sie nicht beeinflussen konnten, etwa dem ausbleibenden Regen. Im zweiten Teil des Liedes geht es um Lissabon. Der Mann im Lied ist also in die Hauptstadt gereist, vielleicht auch in die ehemalige Hauptstadt, je nachdem, von welcher Zeit er erzählt. Von Kap Verde gingen die Leute nach Lissabon, meist um dort – als Männer – im Baugewerbe oder – wenn sie Frauen waren – als Hausangestellte zu arbeiten. Das ist die andere Seite der Migrationsgeschichte. Doch egal, ob in Lissabon oder in São Tomé und Príncipe: Andauernd hatte man zu allem „Jawohl, mein Herr" zu sagen. Im Lied sagt der Mann, dass man ihm dieses „sim sinhor" in São Tomé und in Lissabon eingebläut hat: Er sollte den Kopf senken und hinnehmen, was auch passiert.

Das führt uns zu einem weiteren Ziel der Migration, nämlich den Niederlanden der 1960er und 1970er Jahre. Viele Kapverdier gingen in die Niederlande,

Auszug aus einem am 14. August 2020 aufgezeichneten Online-Gespräch. Ein Recherche-Video auf Grundlage dieses Gesprächs wurde unter dem Titel „A Transgenerational Commentary of a Song" (2020, 25 min.) im Rahmen der Ausstellungen *Hidden Labor Across (inter∞note 01)*, KV Verein für zeitgenössische Kunst Leipzig e. V. (22. August – 17. Oktober 2020) und *Till the Sun Rises*, Albertinum, Dresden (2. Februar – 25. Mai 2024) gezeigt.

in the Netherlands as Portuguese migrants. That's another aspect of Cape Verdean history, colonial history. So he says when he arrives in the Netherlands, he is not only obliged to say, "Yes, sir," he also has to say, "Thank you." Something else is added in this process of migration: oppression, and exploitation and the kind of labor relations that colonial history and migration give rise to. This is a translation of the song then (or rather the words in the song).

VA: I have two questions. You mentioned these two different versions of the song before. Could you say a bit more about whether there was a difference between these two versions, or what the difference is between the two versions of the song? It also really appealed to me when I was talking about the idea of migration, which is somehow used as an active element in the song. That's how it was in India—albeit in a different time period. In 1857, just after the abolition of slavery, a lot of Indian workers were sent to the Caribbean islands and to Trinidad and Tobago, as well as to Jamaica, as indentured laborers. I was looking into the archives, and most of the people were paid so little that they couldn't return home. So they were somehow obliged to stay there. There were many cases of exploitation too, though they still kept some of their language. Many of them came from Bihar and spoke the Bhojpuri dialect, and they kept some of the language and retained how the language developed in some respect into something else. So they created a version that the older generation still speaks in some homes, which is kind of mix of Bhojpuri that also includes words from other languages, creating a new language to communicate in. This also highlights what the words that are untranslatable are capable of. And the microhistories that are there in those words

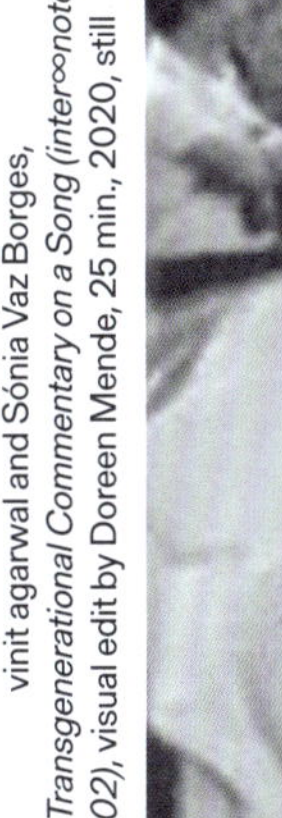

vinit agarwal and Sónia Vaz Borges, *A Transgenerational Commentary on a Song (inter∞note 02)*, visual edit by Doreen Mende, 25 min., 2020, still

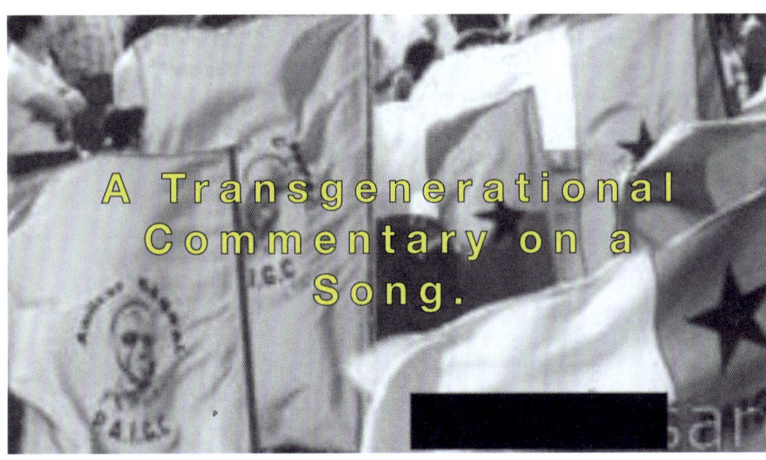

vinit agarwal und Sónia Vaz Borges, *A Transgenerational Commentary on a Song (inter∞note 02)*, visuelle Bearbeitung: Doreen Mende, 25 min., 2020, Videostill

hauptsächlich Männer, die als Matrosen auf niederländischen Schiffen arbeiteten. In den Niederlanden waren sie als portugiesische Wanderarbeiter registriert. Auch das gehört zur kapverdischen Kolonialgeschichte. Und so erzählt der Mann im Lied, dass er in den Niederlanden angekommen nicht nur „Jawohl, mein Herr", sondern obendrein noch „Danke" sagen muss. Das kam noch dazu in diesem Prozess der Migration: Unterdrückung, Ausbeutung und nun eine bestimmte Form von Arbeitsverhältnissen, die sich nur aus kolonialer Geschichte und Arbeitsmigration erklären lassen. Das also wäre eine ungefähre Übersetzung des Liedes (beziehungsweise seines Textes).

VA: Ich habe zwei Fragen. Du hast vorhin zwei verschiedene Fassungen des Liedes erwähnt. Kannst du genauer sagen, worin beide voneinander abweichen? Was ich außerdem bemerkenswert finde ist, dass die Migration in dem Lied gewissermaßen selbst als Akteur erscheint. Auch in Indien war sie das, wenn auch in einer anderen Zeit. Ab 1857, unmittelbar nach Abschaffung der Sklaverei, wurden sehr viele indische Arbeiter·innen als Schuldknechte auf die karibischen Inseln und nach Trinidad und Tobago, aber auch nach Jamaika verschickt. Ich habe mir im Archiv die Quellen angesehen. Diese Menschen bekamen so wenig Geld, dass sie nicht in die Heimat zurückkehren konnten. Also blieben sie notgedrungen in der Fremde. Als Inder·innen wurden sie dort häufig ausgebeutet, dennoch hielten sie an ihrer Sprache fest. Viele stammten aus Bihar und sprachen den Dialekt Bhojpuri, der sich mit der Zeit aber zu etwas Neuem entwickelte. Sie schufen ein Idiom, das manche aus der älteren Generation zu Hause immer noch sprechen: eine Mischung aus Bhojpuri und Wörtern anderer Sprachen, die ein neues Verständigungsmittel ergab. Das zeigt übrigens auch, wie wichtig gerade unübersetzbare Wörter sind. Und es gewährt Einblick in die Mikrohistorie bestimmter

that you have referred to as "pillows." I was thinking of how these microhistories are found in those specific words which refer to very specific objects, and somehow they open up when we get close to these words.

SVB: When the word *rabixo* appears in this song, if you translate it as "pillow," you can see the connection. That's why I translated it as creating another wound in the first version, because if there is another pillow, it should provide protection to stop this wound occurring. Because this *rabixo* is mostly used on donkeys, in this song it might also mean that the man becomes a donkey—he works as a donkey. He works like an animal. So there's a lot of symbolism behind the song. All this is historical symbolism. It's very characteristic of the Cape Verdean songs we know from our childhood that they have this history behind them. But we don't really understand what we are singing until we are confronted with this colonial history. There's a part of the song that is almost impossible to translate if you don't understand the history and the connotations behind it. You can translate the words, but the untranslatable part comes from the emotion behind them. If you don't know this, you lose the meaning of the song. I find it very interesting the way they sing the song because it seems like they are happy. It seems like it's a fun song and has no meaning behind it. You might mistakenly imagine it's just a fun song, when they are actually singing about the pain of migration. They are migrants again, as are many of their ancestors, but they are migrants in a different position. And there's something interesting in the film. Well, you didn't ask me to translate that part, but it also gives a meaning to the song and why they are singing it, because we are in Germany, and Germany . . . let's say, the majority of the population is white, and they are singing this song while they are in the room.

That is the difficult part because I couldn't follow the whole conversation [in the film]. The song is played on top of voices talking. There is someone in the room who says, "So we can deal with all these blonde people," and this relates to the song again—it's another "Yes, sir, thank you." And it is one of the men in the film who says that. But he says it in a funny way. That scene comes before they start singing the song, so you can relate to how they understand their position in the country.

Wörter als Bezeichnungen sehr spezieller Gegenstände, die sich erst erschließen, wenn wir diesen Wörtern auf die Spur gekommen sind.

SVB: Das Wort „rabixo“, das man in diesem Lied als „Kissen“ übersetzen kann, zeigt genau das. Deshalb habe ich es in der ersten Fassung so übersetzt, dass es eine weitere Wunde entstehen lässt, denn wenn es hier ein weiteres Kissen gibt, dann sollte es doch helfen, diese Wunde loszuwerden. Weil ein „rabixo“ meist auf Eseln in Gebrauch war, kann es in diesem Lied auch bedeuten, dass der Mann selbst zum Esel wird, dass er schuftet wie ein Esel, ein Arbeitstier. Das Lied ist voller Symbole und zwar historischer Symbole. Charakteristisch für die Lieder aus Kap Verde, die ich seit meiner frühen Kindheit kenne, ist, dass die Geschichte in ihnen gegenwärtig ist. Allerdings verstehen wir nicht wirklich, was wir da singen, bis wir so weit sind, uns mit der Kolonialgeschichte auseinanderzusetzen. Es gibt eine Stelle in dem Lied, die man ohne Verständnis der Kolonialgeschichte und der entsprechenden Bedeutungsebenen so gut wie nicht übersetzen kann. Man kann wohl Entsprechungen für die einzelnen Worte finden, aber was unübersetzbar bleibt, sind die damit verbundenen Gefühle. Wer davon nichts weiß, an dem geht die eigentliche Bedeutung des Liedes vorbei. Ich finde auch sehr interessant, wie das Lied vorgetragen wird, denn es klingt, als sängen da glückliche Menschen – es wirkt wie ein lustiges Lied, das keine tiefere Bedeutung hat. Man könnte sich von diesem Eindruck leicht täuschen lassen. Tatsächlich geht es um die Leiden der Migration. Man ist wieder Wanderarbeiter wie so viele der Vorfahren, aber man hat eine andere soziale Stellung als sie. Auch im Film gibt es da einen interessanten Moment. Ich habe diese Passage nicht übersetzt, aber die Szene fügt hier dem Lied eine Bedeutungsebene hinzu, da die Beteiligten es in Deutschland singen, wo … nun ja, wo der Großteil der Bevölkerung weiß ist – und zwar in einem Moment, als sie unter sich, in einem Raum sind.

Hier wird es auch für mich unklar, weil ich die Dialoge im Film nicht ganz verstehen konnte. Das Lied ist über die Stimmen der Unterhaltung gelegt. Irgendjemand in dem Raum sagt: „Wir werden schon fertig mit all den blonden Leuten hier“, und das ist eine Anspielung auf das Lied. Eine weitere Variante des „Jawohl, mein Herr, danke“. Einer der Männer im Film sagt das, aber scherzhaft. Diese Szene kommt, bevor sie zu singen beginnen, sie gibt einen Eindruck davon, wie die Beteiligten ihre gesellschaftliche Stellung im Land auffassten.

There is also the fact that these sentences are said in a very casual way, as if we were talking. It's just between us, as if they don't understand what we're saying, so we carry on talking, and he says these things. Then they sing a very short song. And I took the time to go back and forth to try to understand what they were saying and the song that they were singing. It says, "I came from far away. I arrived in the RDA—which is the GDR in Portuguese.[1] And then he said that when he arrived, they told me to go see the chart. I don't know what this chart is, but I played with some ideas about that and said, "This chart, our chart is Guinea-Bissau." The second sentence runs, "Our chart is Cape Verde," and it goes, "How is it?" Then I think they say our chart is to dance till the sun rises. And that's also when, if you relate to the song, they say, "Yes, sir"—you have to say "Yes, sir" all the time. Because they were students from the African Party for the Independence of Guinea Bissau and Cape Verde (PAIGC), it means that no matter what you can't say, it's just a possibility that what we have in the GDR are our itinerary, our schedule, Cape Verde and Guinea-Bissau, and ourselves.[2] If we put together these three aspects, it can be like it's a statement made by these students. We can deal with all these blonde people, we already have our own schedule and our rules. We work with the people we have to work with, which is Guinea-Bissau, Cape Verde, and ourselves. "Yes, sir." It's really interesting to see this in the film, this combination of these three things—it's quite a statement, actually.

But if you take this idea—it's not even two minutes of the scene, the combination of a statement and their voices. That was another aspect that's impossible to translate but if you know the language, you can register the intonation and discern the meaning, which can convey further meaning to other people. It is not a simple translation, because intonation is also very important.

DM: All of this takes place in a student residence in Berlin-Karlshorst, near the school of economics, Hochschule für Ökonomie. It's an important facet of this politics of educational internationalism because the students are studying film, medicine, and agriculture. They are trained in different things. I find that quite compelling in relation to this song, and I would like to ask you, Sónia, how you

1. RDA, GDR, and DDR refer to the East German state in different languages: RDA – República Democrática Alemã; GDR – German Democratic Republic; DDR – Deutsche Demokratische Republik.

2. The PAIGC (Portuguese: Partido Africano para a Independência da Guiné e Cabo Verde) was created in September 1956. Founded by a group of anti-colonialist *militantes* ("militants") primarily from Guinea-Bissau and Cape Verde. The first party congress of the PAIGC, known as the Cassacá Congress, took place between 13 and 17 February 1964 in the liberated southern area of the Guinean forests. Among the resolutions that came out of the congress was the need to enhance knowledge. This took place through the creation of schools, investment in the education of adults and youth, and incentives encouraging individuals to invest in their own education for the betterment of the party cadres.

Zugleich wird all das in einem sehr beiläufigen, unaufgeregten Ton gesagt, als würden wir uns jetzt unter uns unterhalten: Wir sind unter uns. Die anderen verstehen sowieso nicht, was wir sagen, also müssen wir uns auch nicht zurückhalten beim Reden. So spricht er. Und dann singen sie alle ein sehr kurzes Lied. Ich habe mir die Zeit genommen, die Szene mehrmals vor- und zurückzuspulen, um zu verstehen, was genau sie sagen und singen. Es heißt: „Ich komme von weit her. Ich kam in die RDA"[1] – das ist Portugiesisch für DDR. Und weiter: „Als ich ankam, haben sie mir gesagt, ich soll mir die Tafel ansehen." Was diese Tafel sein soll, weiß ich nicht. Ich habe in Gedanken ein paar Möglichkeiten durchgespielt, worum es sich dabei handeln könnte. Weiter: „Diese Tafel, unsere Tafel ist Guinea-Bissau." Die zweite Zeile lautet: „Diese Tafel, unsere Tafel ist Kap Verde." Wenn ich es richtig verstanden habe, singen sie: „Unsere Tafel ist Tanzen bis zum Sonnenaufgang." Das ist auch der Moment, an dem sie – um auf das Lied zurückzukommen – wieder unentwegt „Jawohl, mein Herr" sagen müssen. Immerhin studierte man ja als PAIGC-Delegation,[2] und das bedeutete, dass man zwar alles Mögliche nicht sagen durfte, aber was wir möglicherweise lernen, bestimmt nicht nur die DDR, wir haben auch unsere eigene Tafel, unser Programm in Kap Verde und in Guinea-Bissau und in uns selbst. Wenn wir diese drei Aspekte zusammennehmen, erkennen wir, dass es sich um einen Akt der Selbstbehauptung dieser Studierenden handelt: Wir werden schon zurechtkommen mit all den blonden Leuten hier, wir haben unsere eigenen Pläne und Regeln, an die wir uns halten können. Wir arbeiten, womit wir arbeiten müssen: mit Guinea-Bissau, Kap Verde und mit uns selbst. „Jawohl, mein Herr." Interessant zu beobachten, wie sich diese drei Elemente im Film miteinander verbinden. Das allein ist schon eine starke Aussage.

In der Szene dauert all das keine zwei Minuten und entsteht aus dem Zusammenwirken einer Aussage mit den Stimmen der Singenden. Auch dieser Aspekt bleibt unübersetzbar, aber für diejenigen, die unsere Sprache kennen, gibt er sich in der Sprachmelodie und ihrer Wirkung auf den Inhalt des Gesprochenen zu erkennen. Die Übersetzung ist schwierig, weil die Intonation eine große Rolle spielt.

DM: All das spielt sich in einem Studierendenwohnheim in Berlin-Karlshorst in der Nähe der Hochschule für Ökonomie Berlin ab. Ein wesentlicher Aspekt dieser Bildungsoffensive im Geist des Internationalismus war, dass sie sich an

1. RDA ist die Abkürzung für República Democrática Alemã.

2. Die PAIGC (Partido Africano para a Independência de Guiné e Cabo Verde) wurde im September 1956 von einer Gruppe antikolonialer *militantes*, vor allem aus Guinea-Bissau und Kap Verde, gegründet. Der erste Parteikongress der PAIGC, der sogenannte Cassacá-Kongress, fand vom 13. bis 17. Februar 1964 in den befreiten Gebieten im Süden in den Guineischen Wäldern statt. Zu den Entschlüssen, die bei diesem Kongress gefällt wurden, gehörte der, die Verbreitung von Bildung und Wissen zu fördern. Zu diesem Zweck wurden Schulen geschaffen, in die Bildung von Kindern, Jugendlichen und Erwachsenen investiert und Einzelpersonen ermutigt, ihre individuelle Bildung voranzutreiben, um die Kader der Partei zu stärken.

see this in terms of the social setting and gregariousness it creates. The sonic and the visual language in the film create a social fabric, which is quite specific, since there are not only students from Guinea-Bissau and Cape Verde there but also Indian students and students from Mongolia, Mali, and Ethiopia. So it is quite compelling how this song mobilizes people. What do you think of this song, and as a commentary that bridges generations, was it really important for your generation? Did you hear it as a child? When does this song date from, from the 1960s, the 1970s? Is it an older song that mutated and was transformed over the decades? Is it a song that is transmitted from generation to generation? I would just like to understand the kind of social imaginary that plays a role in the film, a kind of space that is carved out as a path away from the alienation and away from this extremely heavy ideological framework. I think it's difficult for us to imagine what it meant to be a delegate from a political organization like the PAIGC.

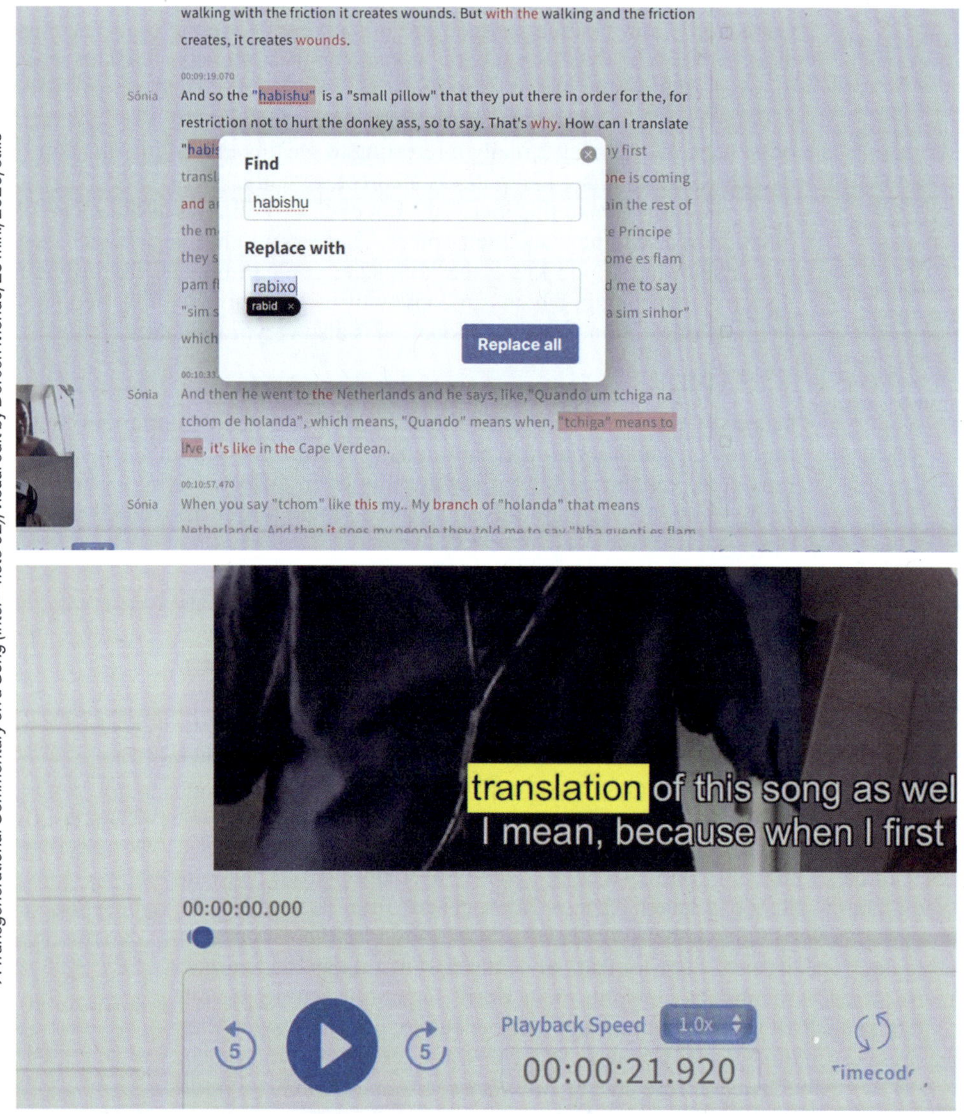

vinit agarwal and Sónia Vaz Borges, *A Transgenerational Commentary on a Song (inter∞note 02)*, visual edit by Doreen Mende, 25 min., 2020, stills

vinit agarwal und Sónia Vaz Borges, *A Transgenerational Commentary on a Song (inter∞note 02)*, visuelle Bearbeitung: Doreen Mende, 25 min., 2020, Videostills

Studierende in verschiedenen Fachbereichen wie Film, Medizin oder Landwirtschaft wandte. Die Beteiligten studierten ganz unterschiedliche Fächer, und gerade das finde ich in Bezug auf das Lied bemerkenswert. Was meinst du, Sónia, bedeutete das für die gemeinschaftsstiftende Funktion des Films? Dessen Bild- und Tonsprache erzeugt ein soziales Gewebe, und das ist insofern etwas Besonderes, als nicht nur Studierende aus Guinea-Bissau und Kap Verde, sondern auch aus Indien, der Mongolei, Mali und Äthiopien beteiligt sind. Mich beeindruckt, wie das Lied dafür eingesetzt wird. Was denkst du? Auch die Generationenfrage interessiert mich: War dieses Lied für deine Generation wirklich von Bedeutung? Hast du es als Kind gehört? Aus welcher Zeit stammt es? Aus den 1960ern, 1970ern? Oder ist es noch älter und wurde im Laufe der Jahre umgeschrieben? Wurde oder wird es von einer Generation an die nächste weitergegeben? Ich möchte einfach besser verstehen, welche gesellschaftlichen Vorstellungen und Fantasien in den Film hineinspielen und darin wirksam sind – in dem Sinn, dass sie einen Raum als Zuflucht aus der Entfremdung schaffen, auch eine Möglichkeit, dem drückend

SVB: Can I ask a question? When was the film made? The bulk of the film happens around 1975, doesn't it?

VA: It was released in 1980.

SVB: I think the song is older. It might be from the 1960s. If we're talking 1980, let's say—my dad was born in 1953 and . . . Or the song might be from the sixties and seventies, it might have been written during that period, or it's just a song from that time, and it's passed on from one generation to the next. In my case, it was passed on within the family. In other words, it became an intergenerational song. I know that my generation is going to pass it on to a new generation because I can remember going to house parties with my friends and their kids. The song was played, it's still played. This means that the generation below me also knows the song. They might not understand the meaning of it, or they understand it later, as in my case—I only understood it later in life.

But they will always have these songs in the background, in the back of their heads. Then the song becomes transgenerational. And that is an important characteristic of Cape Verdean culture, because there are a lot of songs with major historical significance that have been sung since we were young. For example, there is this very famous singer, Cesária Évora, and she has a very famous song called "Sodade," which means "I Miss You" or "I Miss" or "Longing" in English. It's a very Portuguese word, very difficult to translate. And Cesária Évora's song says, "Who showed you this long road, this road to São Tomé," which again brings up the forced migration of contract workers in São Tomé.

This is the reason for making this compilation of songs, If we start to pay attention and put them together, we create a corpus that gives us a kind of history of where we come from. And these histories are not mentioned in schoolbooks.

I was raised in Portugal and the issue of the forced migration of contract workers, the Cape Verdean contract workers in São Tomé, was never brought up. This omission is linked to Portuguese colonialism. What is not recounted, what is not said in the books is transmitted in songs, and it is from songs that you learn.

schweren ideologischen Joch zu entkommen. Mir scheint, dass wir uns nicht ohne Weiteres vorstellen können, was es für die Betreffenden bedeutete, Abgesandte einer politischen Organisation wie der PAIGC zu sein.

SVB: Eine Frage: Wann genau wurde der Film gedreht? Der Großteil der Aufnahmen scheint mir um 1975 entstanden zu sein. Stimmt das?

VA: Er wurde 1980 erstmals gezeigt.

SVB: Ich denke, dass das Lied älter ist. Möglicherweise stammt es aus den 1960er, 1970er Jahren. Es könnte damals geschrieben worden sein, vielleicht ist es aber auch älter und wurde weitergegeben. In meiner Familie wenigstens war es auf jeden Fall so. Mein Vater ist 1953 geboren. Es ist für mich ein Lied, das Generationen verbindet. Ich weiß auch, dass meine Generation es an die nachfolgende weitergeben wird, denn ich erinnere mich, dass ich auf Familienfeiern von meinen Freund·innen und deren Kindern war, bei denen es gespielt wurde, und daran hat sich bis heute nichts geändert. Das heißt, die Generation nach mir kennt es ebenfalls. Sie versteht vielleicht nicht, worum es in dem Lied geht, aber auch ich habe das ja erst später im Leben begriffen, also kommt das vielleicht noch.

Zumindest werden die Jüngeren dieses und andere Lieder im Hinterkopf behalten. Das genügt schon, damit es den Sprung von einer Generation zur nächsten schafft. Das ist charakteristisch für die kapverdische Kultur, dass es viele solche Lieder mit tiefer historischer Bedeutung gibt, die man von frühester Kindheit an hört und mitsingt. Ich erinnere mich an eine berühmte Sängerin namens Cesária Évora und ein ebenso berühmtes Lied namens *Sodade*, was „Du fehlst mir“ oder auch „Ich vermisse“ oder „Sehnsucht“ bedeuten kann – ein sehr portugiesisches Wort, das sich nur schwer übersetzen lässt. Im Text zu diesem Lied von Cesária Évora heißt es: „Wer zeigte euch, wer zeigte euch den weiten Weg, den Weg nach São Tomé …“ Womit wir wieder bei der erzwungenen Migration von Vertragsarbeiter·innen nach São Tomé sind.

Deshalb lohnt es sich, solche Lieder zu sammeln. Indem wir genau hinhören und sie zusammenstellen, schaffen wir ein Korpus, das die Geschichte unserer Herkunft erzählt. Es ist eine Geschichte, die in den Schulbüchern nicht vorkommt.

3. Sónia Vaz Borges, *Militant Education, Liberation Struggle, Consciousness: The PAIGC Education in Guinea Bissau, 1963–1978* (Peter Lang, 2019).

Thus the songs become a part of people's education in politics or cultural history, for those who are born outside of the country or for a generation that is familiar with this issue; this topic is not dealt with in schoolbooks. The songs are a way to create genealogies and develop the teachings that are not covered in school. They tell the story of Portugal, at the height of colonialism and the songs from the circle of Cesária Évora, from this man, from Frank Mimita, explain to us what this process was. In this way, intergenerational and transgenerational transmission takes place through the songs that our parents passed to us. Because we can ask about the meaning, and they can tell us what the meaning is. So this becomes yet more work carried out by our parents, a kind of historical education, so to speak, a militant education. The song creates this *world of linking*, of teaching, too. I am almost sure that this song had the meaning that it had for these students because it reminds them of where they come from. It might remind them of the struggles that people go through in the process of migration, and it can also create this idea of empowering themselves.

DM: Thank you, Sónia—also for the way you elaborate and conceptualize a militant education in your book and the practices and politics of liberation.[3] I really appreciate the way you elaborate in the book on the complexity of what liberation is. I mean, understanding this, on the one hand, as a decolonizing process and the right to self-determination that is, however, informed by a set of practices you define as an individual response to a collective process, which you further elaborate. This includes violent acts like guerrilla warfare and the armed struggle as well as nonviolent actions like strikes, educational projects and programs, cultural and civil resistance, or any combination thereof. And very importantly, it is compelling. How does this sit with the question and with the violence of internationalism in this kind of educational internationalism? I think this also brings us to the question of who got delegated, who the students were that were nominated by the party, and I can imagine that this happened. It's a whole protocol of bigger political and ideological processes. I know this from East Germany. The people who got delegated had to have a clear ideological reputation. Do you know anything

Ich bin in Portugal aufgewachsen, dort war die unfreiwillige Migration der Vertragsarbeiter·innen von Kap Verde nach São Tomé nie ein Thema. Diese Lücke hat mit dem portugiesischen Kolonialismus zu tun. Was in den Büchern nicht steht, davon handeln die Lieder, aus den Liedern lernt man. Damit sind die Lieder Teil einer politischen oder kulturgeschichtlichen Bildung. In Schulbüchern werden diejenigen, die außer Landes geboren wurden, nichts davon erfahren, auch nicht eine Generation, die um diese Problematik weiß. Es sind die Gesänge, die Genealogien herstellen und lehren, was man in der Schule niemals lernt. Sie erzählen die Geschichte, die im Fall Portugals auf den Punkt bringt, was der Kolonialismus wirklich war, und so erklären uns die Lieder von Cesária Évora und Frank Mimita, was geschehen ist. Zur transgenerationellen Weitergabe wurde dieses Wissen dadurch, dass die Eltern uns die Lieder beigebracht haben. Wir konnten sie fragen, worum es darin geht, und sie konnten es uns erklären. So entstand daraus, als ein Werk unserer Eltern, in gewissem Sinn eine historische Aufklärung, eine militante Bildung. Auch unser Lied hier stiftet eine Welt der Verbindungen, um Wissen weiterzugeben. Ich bin mir fast sicher, dass es für die Studierenden eine solche Bedeutung hatte, weil es sie an ihre Herkunft erinnerte. Es stand für die Kämpfe, die Menschen im Verlauf der Migration durchstehen mussten, und es nährte in ihnen womöglich eine Vorstellung von der eigenen Handlungsmacht.

DM: Danke für diese Erläuterung, Sónia – und auch dafür, wie du in deinem Buch eine militante Bildung, eine Praxis und Politik der Befreiung entwickelst.[3] Mir gefällt besonders, dass du darin herausarbeitest, was für ein komplexer Prozess Befreiung ist, dass es sich dabei einerseits um einen Dekolonisierungsprozess und ein Recht auf Selbstbestimmung handelt, der Widerstand andererseits aber erst durch eine Reihe von Praktiken gebildet und von ihnen geprägt wird, also, wie du es beschreibst, individuellen Entscheidungen in einem kollektiven Prozess. Dazu gehören Akte des Guerillakampfs, bewaffnete Auseinandersetzungen ebenso wie gewaltloses Handeln in Form von Streiks, Aufklärungsprojekten, Bildungsprogrammen, kulturellem und zivilgesellschaftlichem Widerstand sowie Kombinationen all dessen. Und das Entscheidende daran ist, es war überzeugend. Wie verhält sich das nun zum Ansatz und zur Gewalt des politischen Internationalismus, zu dem diese internationalistische politische Bildung

3. Sónia Vaz Borges, *Militant Education, Liberation Struggle, Consciousness: The PAIGC Education in Guinea Bissau, 1963–1978*, Frankfurt am Main: Peter Lang 2019.

about how the delegation system worked in this educational framework? I'm sure the GDR was not the only country. You mention in the book that Yugoslavia and Poland, Bulgaria, the Soviet Union, and Cuba also played an important role. I mean, we've just been watching the other thing in Cuba, an African odyssey by Jihan El-Tahri, who writes about how Fidel Castro and the Cuban revolution were very close to and invested in the liberation movement and revolutionary process in Guinea-Bissau. What do you think about this framework of internationalism in this context? Because it may seem contradictory to some extent. How does militant education, the individual response to collective process relate to the rather hefty infrastructure in the party?

SVB: In the case of the PAIGC?

DM: Yes, in terms of the delegation system, they had to have a contract with the East German government, I think, with the party organization. I know this a bit from working with Palestinian solidarity. This was orchestrated on a more macro political kind of level. I am just trying to understand the infrastructure. How did these collaborations and coalitions and this educational internationalism come about, and how was all this implemented?

SVB: All I know is from oral history, from the stories that the students and teachers told me about the process. Focusing on oral history is one of the things that the PAIGC asked some of the countries to do as a token of solidarity in the areas of education and health and health products, and among doctors.

In Portuguese you say *ajuda civil*, civil aid. Education was part of this process. And as for the selection of the students, I don't think the PAIGC had a very strict method for saying who went and who didn't. For example, there is one story of a very good student and in one of Amílcar Cabral's visits to the school, he asked her: "What do you want to do? What do you want to do?" To which the student replied, "I want to be a nun." Cabral said: "I don't think you can be a nun because there are so many other things to do." And she said: "I want to be a

gehörte? Damit stellt sich auch die Frage, wer eigentlich entsandt wurde, welche Studierenden von der Partei, wie ich vermute, dafür ausgewählt wurden. Dahinter stand, wie ich aus dem ostdeutschen Zusammenhang weiß, ein ganzes Protokoll übergeordneter politischer und ideologischer Entscheidungsverfahren. Abgesandt wurde nur, wer eine lupenreine ideologische Reputation vorweisen konnte. Weißt du etwas darüber, wie die Delegationen im Bildungsbereich zustande kamen? Sehr wahrscheinlich war die DDR nicht das einzige Land, mit dem man zusammengearbeitet hat. Du erwähnst in deinem Buch, dass Jugoslawien und Polen, Bulgarien, die Sowjetunion und Kuba eine wichtige Rolle spielten. Wir haben uns auch den Prozess in Kuba angesehen, den die Filmemacherin Jihan El-Thari in *Cuba, an African Odyssey* (2007) beschreibt: Fidel Castros revolutionäres Kuba stand den Befreiungsbewegungen in Guinea-Bissau sehr nahe und war auch unmittelbar darin involviert. Wie betrachtest du diese Rahmenbedingungen internationalistischer Politik in unserem Zusammenhang? Immerhin ergibt sich das Bild eines gewissen Widerspruchs. Wie verträgt sich eine Erziehung zur Militanz, zu individuellem Handeln in einem kollektiven Prozess, mit der ziemlich drückenden Infrastruktur der Partei?

SVB: Du meinst die PAIGC?

DM: Ja, denn was die Organisation der Delegationen anging, wird sie mit Sicherheit einen Vertrag mit der ostdeutschen Regierung geschlossen haben, mit den Organen der SED. Ich kenne das ein wenig aus deren Palästina-Solidarität, die auf einer höheren Ebene der Politik koordiniert wurde. Mir geht es hier nur darum, diese Infrastruktur zu verstehen. Wie sind diese Kooperationen, Koalitionen, internationalistischen Bildungsprogramme zustande gekommen und wie lief das alles ab?

SVB: Ich weiß davon nur, was ich aus mündlichen Berichten habe, was mir die damaligen Studierenden und Lehrenden über diesen Ablauf erzählt haben. Und ausgehend von dieser Oral History kann ich sagen, dass die PAIGC einige Länder um solidarische Unterstützung in den Bereichen der Bildung, Gesundheitsvorsorge, der medizinischen Produkte und ärztlichen Betreuung gebeten hat.

nun in order to help people and to help the struggle." And then Cabral said, yes, you can still help people, but, you know, rather than becoming a nun, there are several other professions you can choose. Then at some point, he mentioned that you can go into medicine, you can be a doctor, you can be a nurse, you can be a pharmacist. These are other ways that you can help people without being a nun. When she grew up and was in sixth grade, she was asked what kind of profession she would like to pursue, and she was offered scholarships because that's how things functioned.

The scholarships were awarded to the PAIGC by countries like Bulgaria, Czechoslovakia, Yugoslavia, Hungary, the GDR, and Cuba, and they were defined according to the particular specialist field. The scholarships had quotas—for example, let's say ten for medicine, ten for civil engineering, ten for what you'd call teachers, ten for engineers, ten for, say, agronomists, and ten for architecture. So there was a series of scholarships that were given or proposed. And then there was the work of the PAIGC: based on the teacher's evaluation of the student, and taking into consideration sometimes what the student wanted to do, they would give scholarships to students and send them to this country to continue their studies. But it was always a matter of what courses they could do, for example, because if you're talking about militant training, it was divided into three parts:[4] the political training that they received from the PAIGC; the technical training that they could receive in the country if there was a school there—I'm talking about the period of the liberation struggle and at least up until 1980. So there was political training, there was technical training, and then there were changing behaviors, collective and individual behaviors. When it comes to the technical

4. "The pedagogical role of the militant school comprised three aspects. Political learning, technical training and the shaping of individual and collective behaviors. Rooted in its community, the school was the privileged site where the armed militant's farmers and young students gathered together and learned among the people and their daily life, everything that could be useful to the progress of the struggle." Sónia Vaz Borges, *Militant Education, Liberation Struggle, Consciousness: The PAIGC Education in Guinea Bissau 1963–1978* (Peter Lang, 2019), 106.

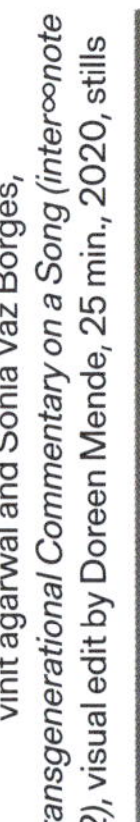
vinit agarwal and Sónia Vaz Borges, *A Transgenerational Commentary on a Song (inter∞note 02)*, visual edit by Doreen Mende, 25 min., 2020, stills

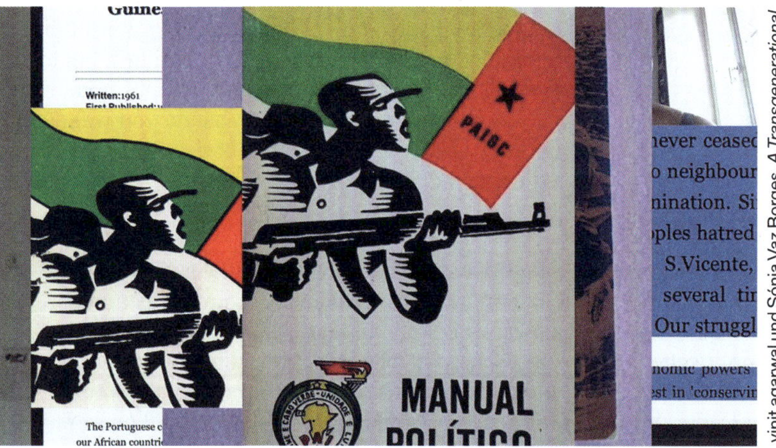

vinit agarwal und Sónia Vaz Borges, *A Transgenerational Commentary on a Song (inter∞note 02)*, visuelle Bearbeitung: Doreen Mende, 25 min., 2020, Videostills

Im Portugiesischen nennt man das „ajuda civil", also Zivilhilfe. Bildung war ein Bestandteil davon. Und was die Vorauswahl der entsandten Studierenden anging, glaube ich eher nicht, dass es vonseiten der PAIGC strikte Vorgaben gab, wer fahren durfte und wer nicht. Es gibt zum Beispiel eine Geschichte von einer herausragenden Schülerin: Bei einem Besuch ihrer Schule fragte Amílcar Cabral sie, was sie denn tun, welchen Weg sie einschlagen wolle. Die Schülerin antwortete, dass sie Nonne werden wolle. Cabral erwiderte: „Ich denke nicht, dass du Nonne werden solltest, es gibt so viel anderes zu tun." Und sie antwortete: „Ich will Nonne werden, um den Menschen zu helfen und unseren Kampf voranzubringen." „Ja, sicher", sagte Cabral, „du kannst Menschen helfen, aber dazu musst du keine Nonne werden, es stehen dir andere Berufswege offen, um genau das zu tun." Im weiteren Verlauf des Gesprächs erwähnte er nebenbei, dass man Medizin studieren und Ärztin oder Krankenschwester oder Apothekerin werden könne, dass auch das Möglichkeiten seien, Menschen zu helfen, ohne Nonne zu werden. Das Mädchen wurde älter, und in der sechsten Klasse wurde sie gefragt, welchen Beruf sie ausüben wolle. Ihr wurde ein Stipendium angeboten. So lief das damals.

Diese Stipendien wurden von Ländern wie Bulgarien, der Tschechoslowakei, Jugoslawien, Ungarn, der DDR und Kuba vergeben. Sie gingen an die PAIGC und waren nach Berufen unterteilt. Es gab Quoten für diese Stipendien, beispielsweise gab es zehn für Medizin, zehn für Bauingenieurswesen, zehn für das, was bei euch ein Lehramtsstudium ist, zehn für Maschinenbau, zehn für Agronomie, zehn für Architektur. Es wurde also eine bestimmte Anzahl von Stipendien vergeben oder angeboten. Aufgabe der PAIGC war es dann, anhand von Bewertungen der Interessenten durch Lehrkräfte und manchmal auch unter Berücksichtigung ihrer Berufswünsche die Stipendien an Studierende zu vergeben, damit diese im betreffenden Land ihre Ausbildung fortsetzen konnten. Aber es

training, most of it was received abroad, within the solidarity network, and the political training was provided by the PAIGC, from a very early age, from the first class, so to speak. This was the first step and began in the second grade, and then came the political education from the third to the sixth grade. This means that, ideologically, these students were already prepared or trained in the PAIGC ideology—the way we also understand this concept of understanding, solidarity, and internationalism, because that was part of the problem.

DM: I have the impression that this double helix of education, as a political training and as your study subject, was continued. I mean, this explains why in *OYOYO*, we see the students in this building that houses . . . you call this a dormitory, where students probably didn't sleep over all the time, but they had ongoing courses of one kind or another on political Marxism-Leninism. And this happened in collaboration with the Ghanaian government, when Kwame Nkrumah came to power: teachers from East Germany would teach Marxism/Leninism in the ideological institute in Ghana. This political economy, continuously engaging with the ideology or philosophy of Marxism-Leninism, was also part of the education of Palestinian freedom fighters. Then students went to study medicine, film, and agriculture. Obviously, in the regular universities.

SVB: I remember talking to students who were studying in the GDR and going to seminars on Marxism-Leninism. Leninism was also being taught in schools during the liberation struggle. It was part of the program of militant education. So there is this trail that is followed at the international level, the ideology of Marxism-Leninism. In the GDR, they had to go through a year or a couple of months of this training in Marxism-Leninism.

There was a network of schools in the territory of Guinea-Bissau during the liberation struggle. Most of the schools were located in Guinea-Bissau, in the jungles—in what were called the bunkers, which means the village school. The boarding schools were located there with the exception of two that were in Guinea and Senegal.

ging auch darum, welche Lehrveranstaltungen sie belegen konnten, denn im Rahmen der ideologischen Ausrichtung kam es zu einer Gliederung der Angebote[4] in die politische Schulung, die man von der PAIGC erhielt, und die fachliche Ausbildung in dem Land, wo sich die jeweilige Hochschule befand. Das gilt für die Zeit vom Befreiungskampf bis mindestens 1980. Politische Schulung, fachliche Ausbildung und eine Verhaltensänderung auf individueller und kollektiver Ebene waren die drei Säulen des Modells, wobei die Ausbildung größtenteils im Ausland und im Rahmen der internationalen Solidarität erfolgte, die politische Schulung jedoch im Inland durch die PAIGC, und das von früher Jugend an, also im Prinzip mit der Einschulung. Erste Schritte gab es im zweiten Schuljahr, vom dritten bis zum sechsten Schuljahr folgte die politische Bildung im engeren Sinn. Das heißt also, dass die Stipendiat·innen durch die Erziehung der PAIGC längst ideologisch geschult waren. Das entsprach unserer Wahrnehmung, nämlich dass die Verzahnung zwischen dem Verstehen der Zusammenhänge, der Solidarität und dem Internationalismus einen Teil der Schwierigkeiten darstellte.

DM: Ich habe den Eindruck, dass diese Doppelhelix aus Bildung im Sinne von politischer Schulung und dem eigentlichen Studienfach noch länger bestand. Das würde erklären, warum wir in *OYOYO* Studierende in diesem Gebäude sehen, diesem Wohnheim, wo sie wahrscheinlich nicht die ganze Zeit über wohnten, aber immer wieder, wenn sie irgendwelche Kurse in Marxismus-Leninismus absolvierten. Darum ging es auch wesentlich in der Kooperation mit dem Staat Ghana, seit Kwame Nkrumah dort an die Macht gelangt war, und so unterrichteten tatsächlich Lehrende aus der DDR Marxismus-Leninismus an der Universität in Accra oder dem Kwame Nkrumah Ideological Institute in Winneba in Ghana. Politische Ökonomie, immer der Ideologie oder Philosophie des Marxismus-Leninismus verpflichtet, war auch Teil der Ausbildungsprogramme der DDR im Kontext der Unterstützung der PLO.

Danach setzte man sein Studium, ob Medizin, Film oder Landwirtschaft, weiter fort, und das naturgemäß an der regulären Hochschule.

SVB: Ich erinnere mich an Gespräche mit ehemaligen Studierenden, die in die DDR gingen und dort Seminare in Marxismus-Leninismus besuchten. Der

4. „Die pädagogische Aufgabe der politischen Schulung umfasste drei Aspekte: politische Erziehung, technische Ausbildung und die Formung des individuellen und kollektiven Verhaltens. Die Schule war in der Gemeinschaft verwurzelt und ein privilegierter Ort, an dem Milizen, Bauern und junge Schüler·innen gemeinsam alles lernten, was dem Fortschritt des Kampfes und des Alltags dienen konnte." Ebd., S. 106.

The PAIGC had an educational system that ran from the first grade to the sixth grade. And that was what they could do under the prevailing conditions. After that, in order to continue their post-secondary school education, they had to travel abroad. Then came the professional training and/or university training in other socialist countries. That was the structure of the school network within the organization during the liberation struggle.

Leninismus wurde in der Phase des Freiheitskampfs auch an Schulen gelehrt. Das gehörte zum Programm einer Ausbildung in Militanz. Auf internationaler Ebene folgte man also diesem Weg der marxistisch-leninistischen Ideologie. Wer in der DDR studierte, musste ein Jahr oder wenigstens ein paar Monate dieser Schulung in Marxismus-Leninismus mitmachen.

Auf dem Gebiet von Guinea-Bissau gab es während des Befreiungskampfs einen Verbund von Schulen, Dorfschulen, die häufig in Dschungeldörfern lagen und „Bunker“ genannt wurden. Die Internate befanden sich bis auf je eines in Guinea und Senegal ebenfalls in Guinea-Bissau.

Die PAIGC betrieb ein Bildungssystem, das die Zeit vom ersten bis zum sechsten Schuljahr abdeckte. Das war das, was sich unter den gegebenen Umständen realisieren ließ. Wer danach noch eine Hochschulbildung anstrebte, musste im Ausland studieren. So kam die Praxis auf, Berufsausbildungen oder Hochschulstudien im sozialistischen Ausland zu absolvieren. Das war Bestandteil der Bildungs- und Ausbildungsstruktur in den Jahren des Befreiungskampfes.

with Tungalag Sodnomgombyn (Ulaanbaatar, Mongolian People's Republic), Emilio Fernandez (Concepción, Chile), Carlos Neto (Bolama, Guinea-Bissau), Irene Blanc (La Habana, Cuba), Ansoumane Mané and Emma Korouma (Ségou, Mali), Manuel Coelho Mendonça (Varela, Guinea-Bissau), Carmen Maria Barbosa e Sá and José Júlio Delgado (Bissau, Guinea-Bissau), Theodros Alemu (Addis Ababa, Ethiopia), Monica Mateluna (Santiago, Chile), and many more

OYOYO

mit Tungalag Sodnomgombyn (Ulaanbaatar / Mongolische Volksrepublik), Emilio Fernandez (Concepción / Chile), Carlos Neto (Bolama / Guinea-Bissau), Irene Blanc (La Habana / Kuba), Ansoumane Mané und Emma Korouma (Ségou / Mali), Manuel Coelho Mendonça (Vorela), Carmen Maria Barbosa e Sá und Jose Júlio Delgado (Bissau / Guinea-Bissau), Theodros Alemu (Addis Abeba / Äthiopien), Monica Mateluna (Santiago / Chile) und anderen.

Chetna Vora (director) and Lars Barthel (cinematographer): *OYOYO*, film for submission in the penultimate year of study, 48 min. version; a production of the Film and Television Academy of the GDR 1980. Digitisation and restoration of the Film University Babelsberg KONRAD WOLF, supported by the Film Heritage Funding Programme, financed by BKM, Länder and FFA.

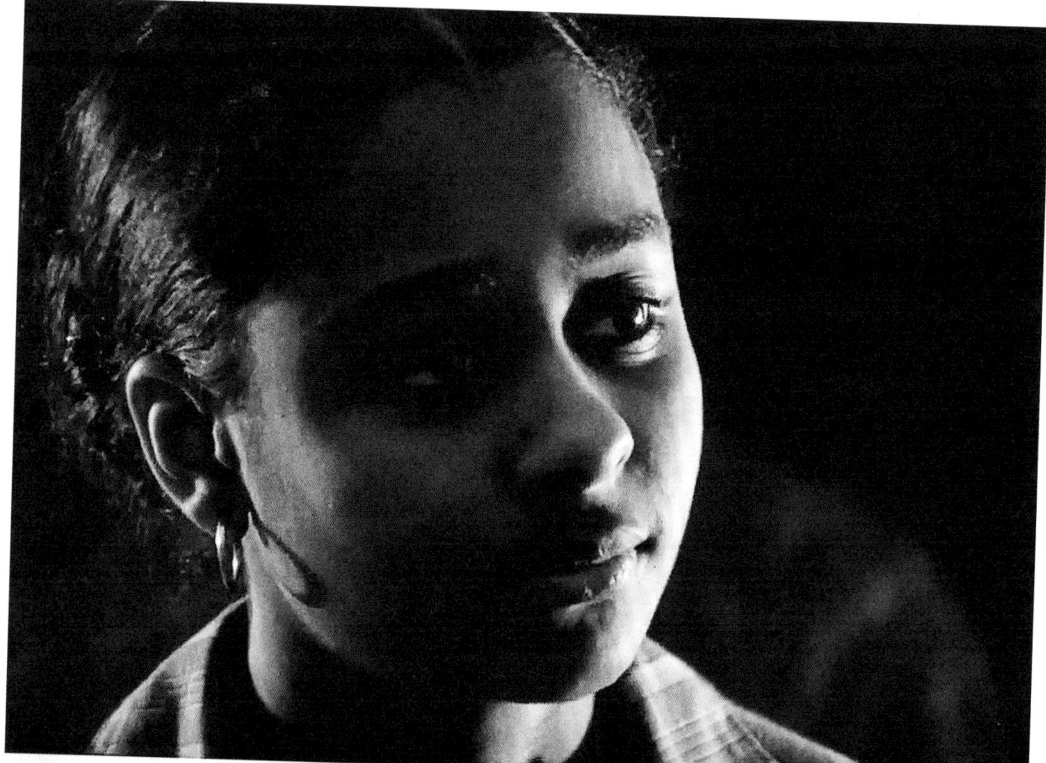

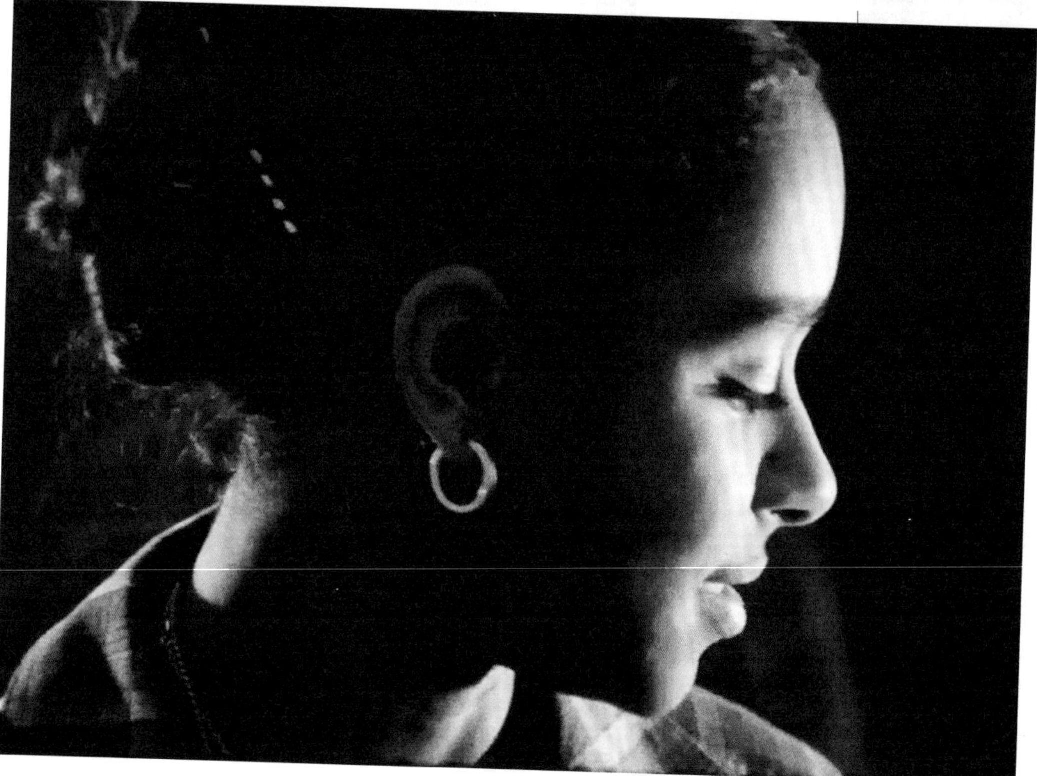

Chetna Vora (Regie) und Lars Barthel (Kamera), *OYOYO*, zur Einreichung im vorletzten Studienjahr, 48-minütige Fassung, eine Produktion der Hochschule für Film und Fernsehen der DDR, 1980. Digitalisierung und Restaurierung der Filmuniversität Babelsberg KONRAD WOLF, unterstützt durch das Förderprogramm Filmerbe, finanziert durch BKM, Länder und FFA.

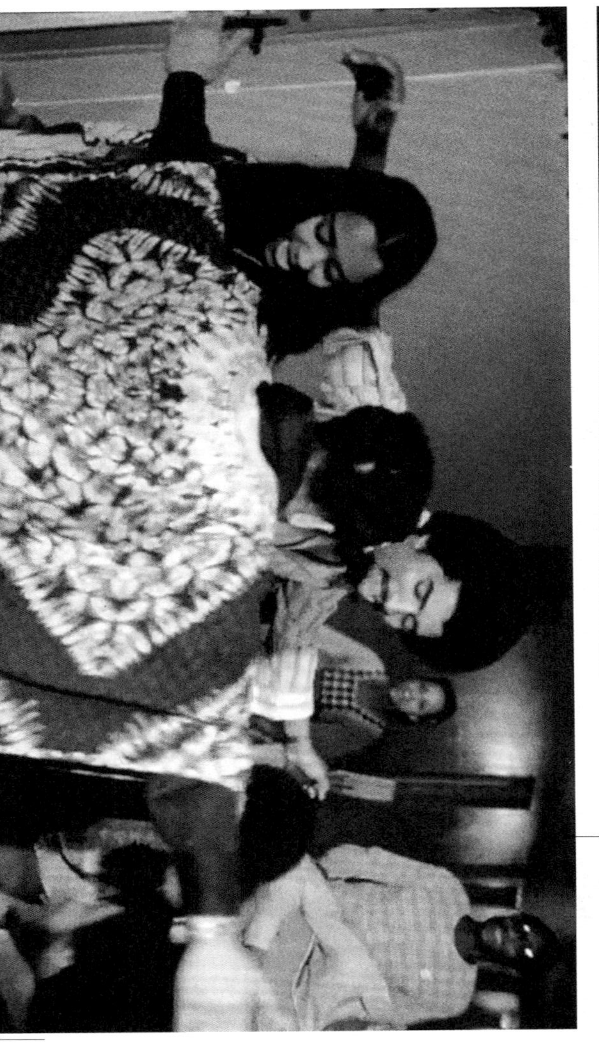

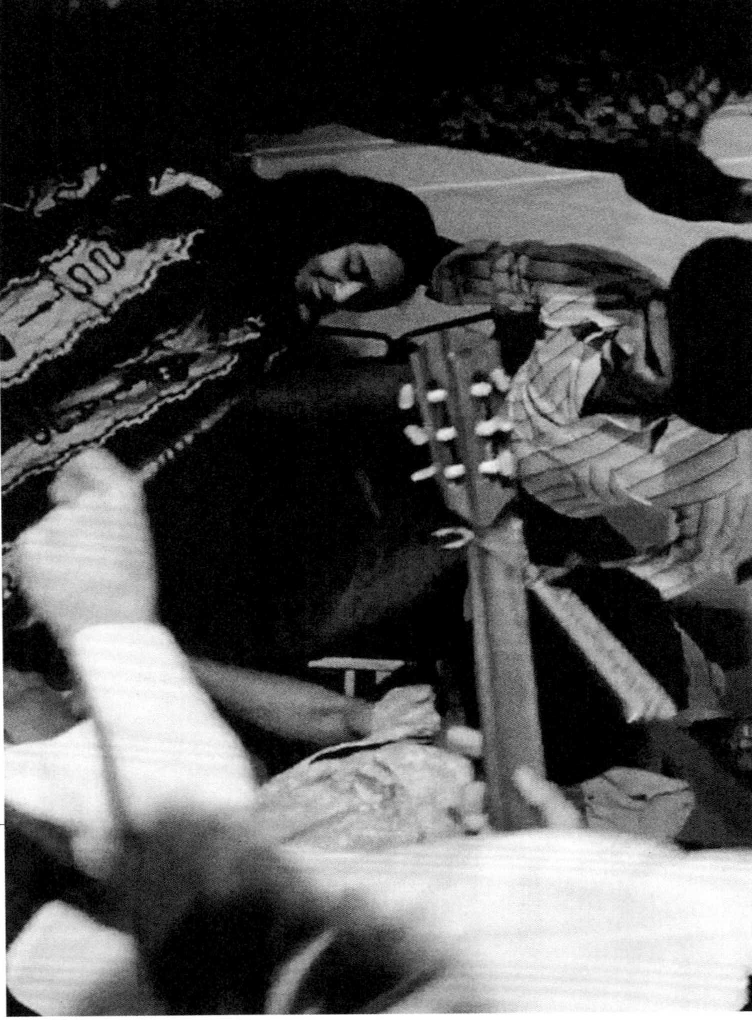

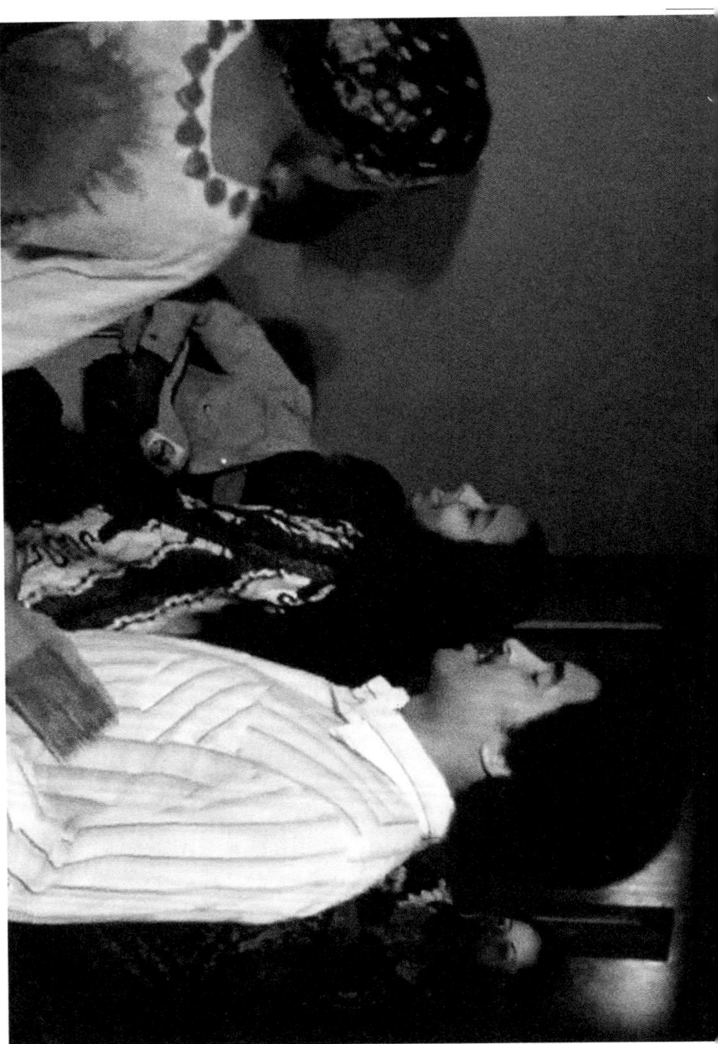

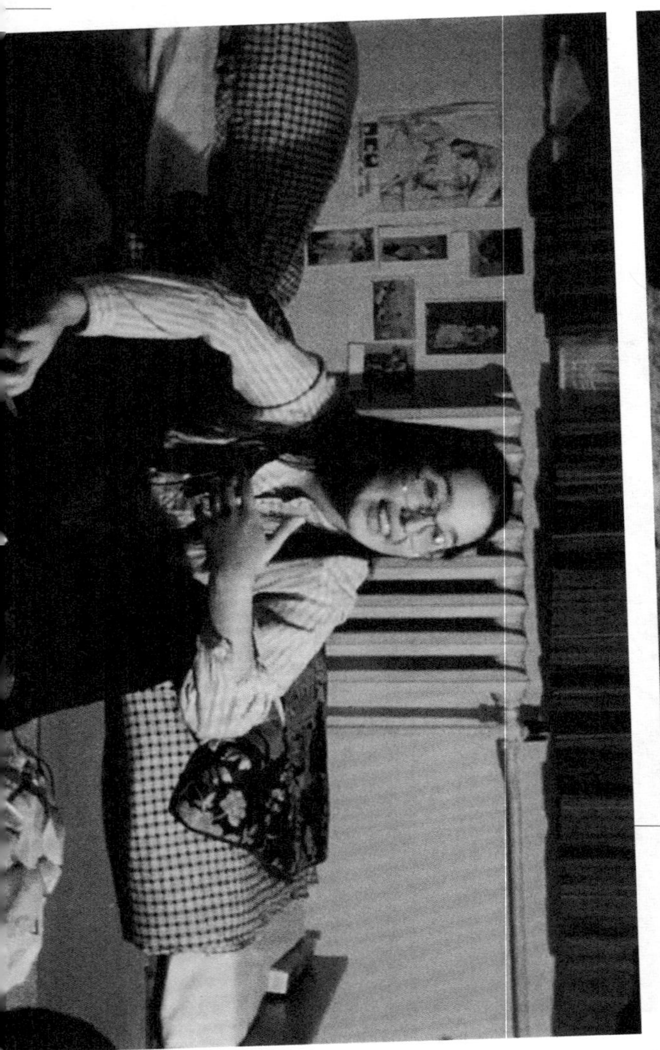

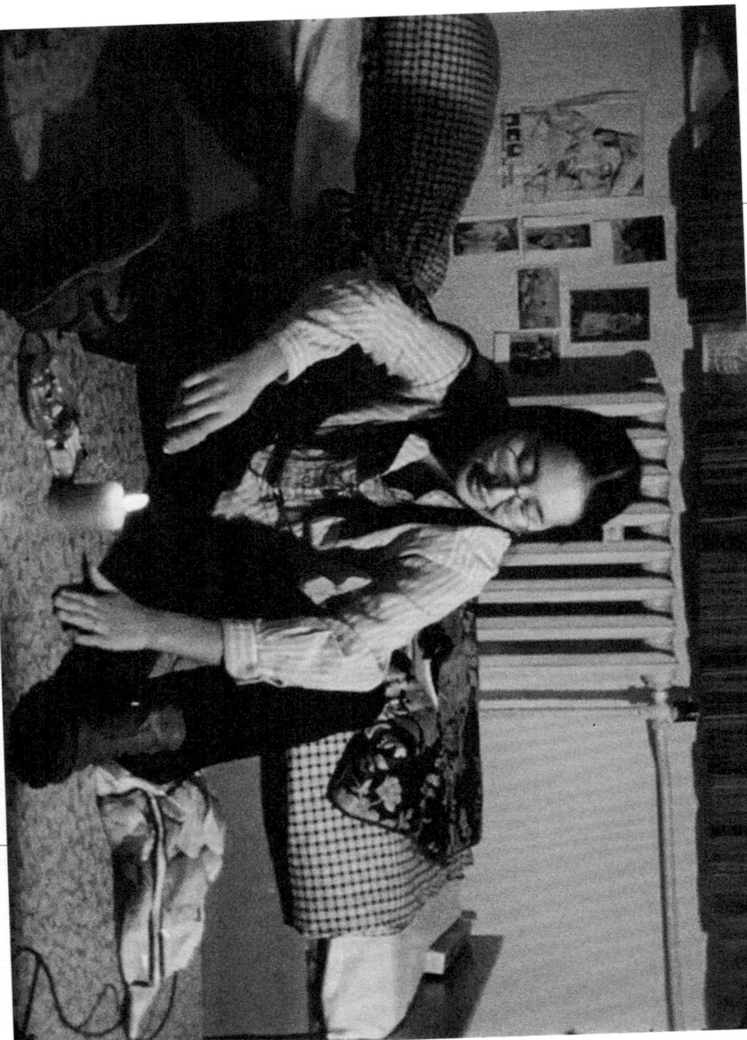

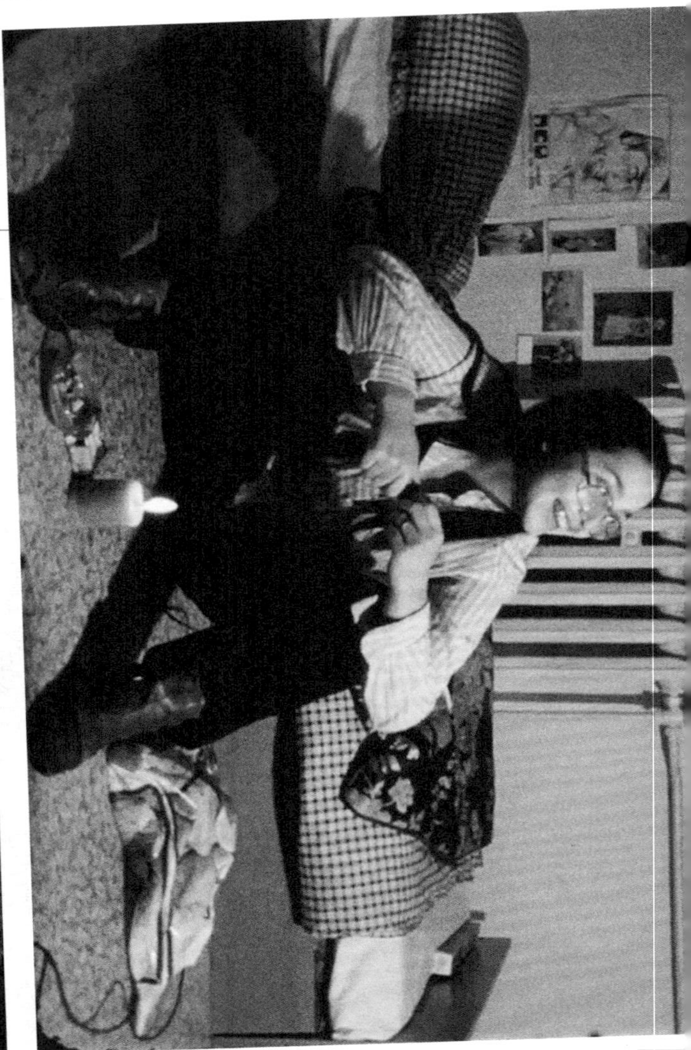

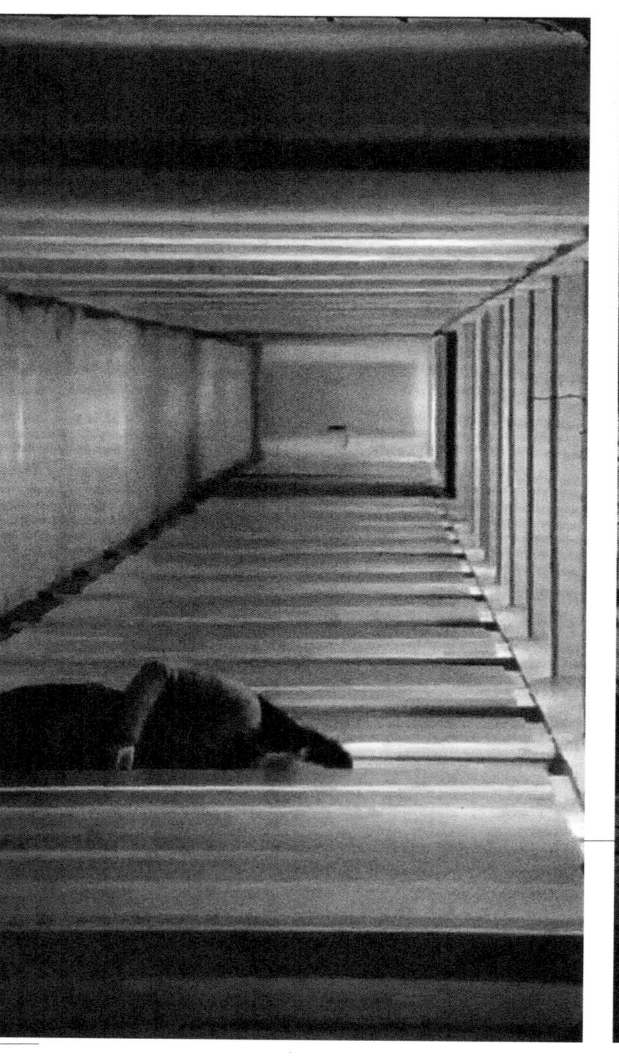

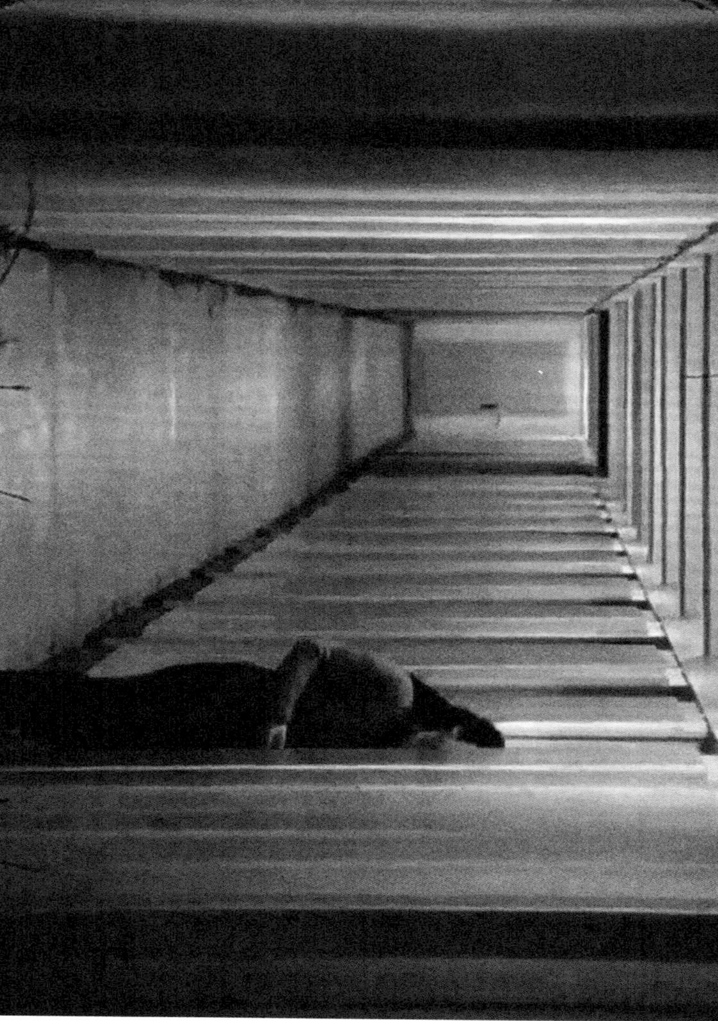

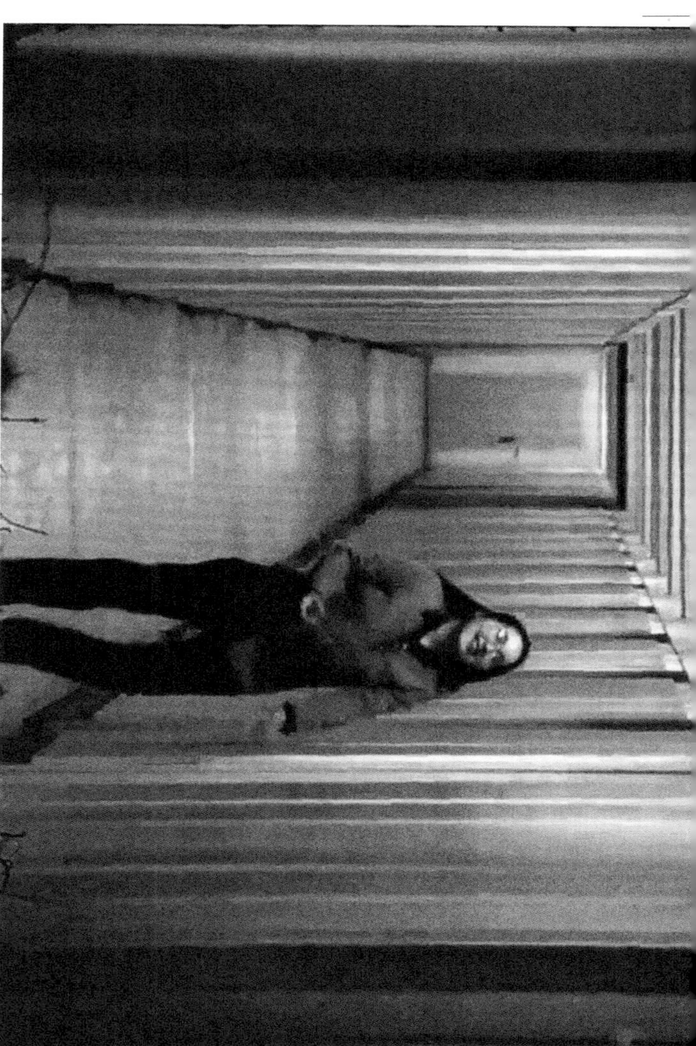

OBJECT TO ABSTRACTION: PANORAMA OF A SONG

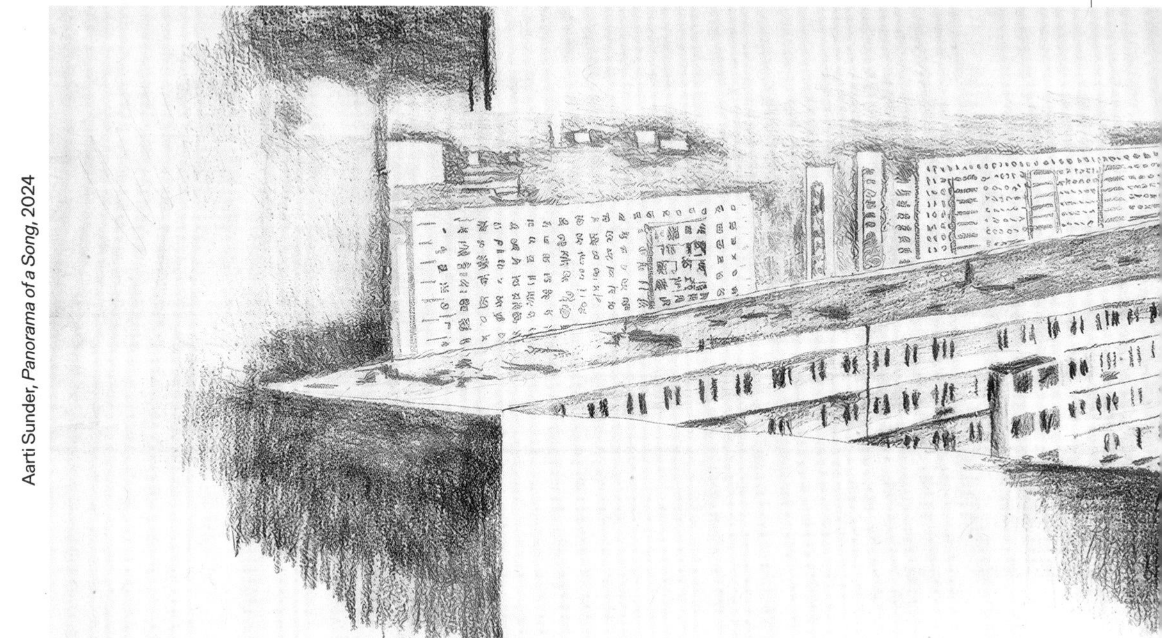

Aarti Sunder, *Panorama of a Song*, 2024

Aarti Sunder

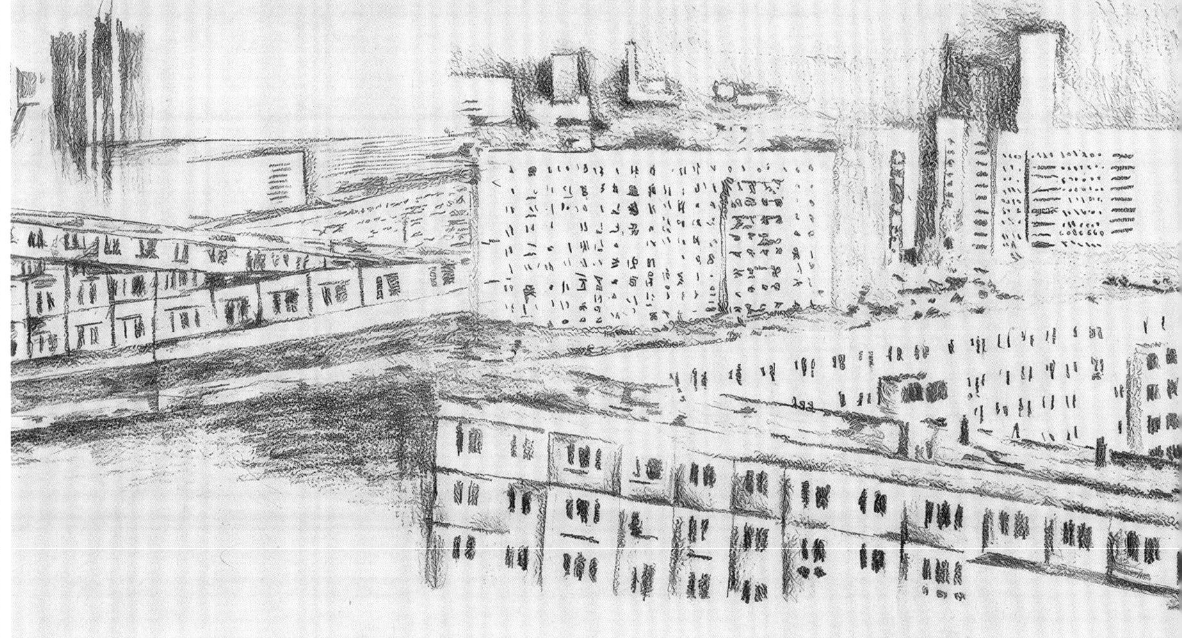

VOM OBJEKT ZUR ABSTRAKTION: PANORAMA EINES LIEDES

This is the long drawing—I followed the film from beginning to end and picked up interesting images, textures, and shapes and contours that I thought would help tell the story of the film, its feeling, and the way the participants interacted with each other. As I began stacking these images, I noticed that the body language of the participants was slowly morphing from acquaintance-like to more and more friend-like: we are introduced to the architecture at the beginning, and when we enter the building, many worlds collide and in that collision and overlap, friendships, politics, and realignments are set in motion. The song starts playing; there is dancing, converging, and the realignments continue.

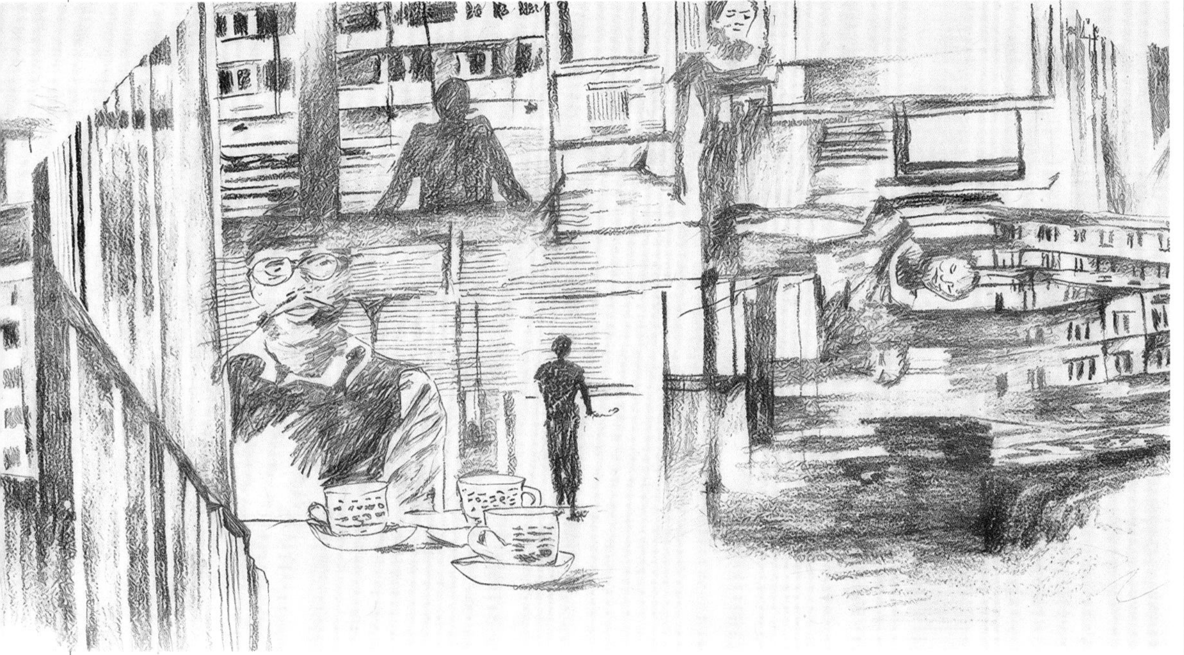

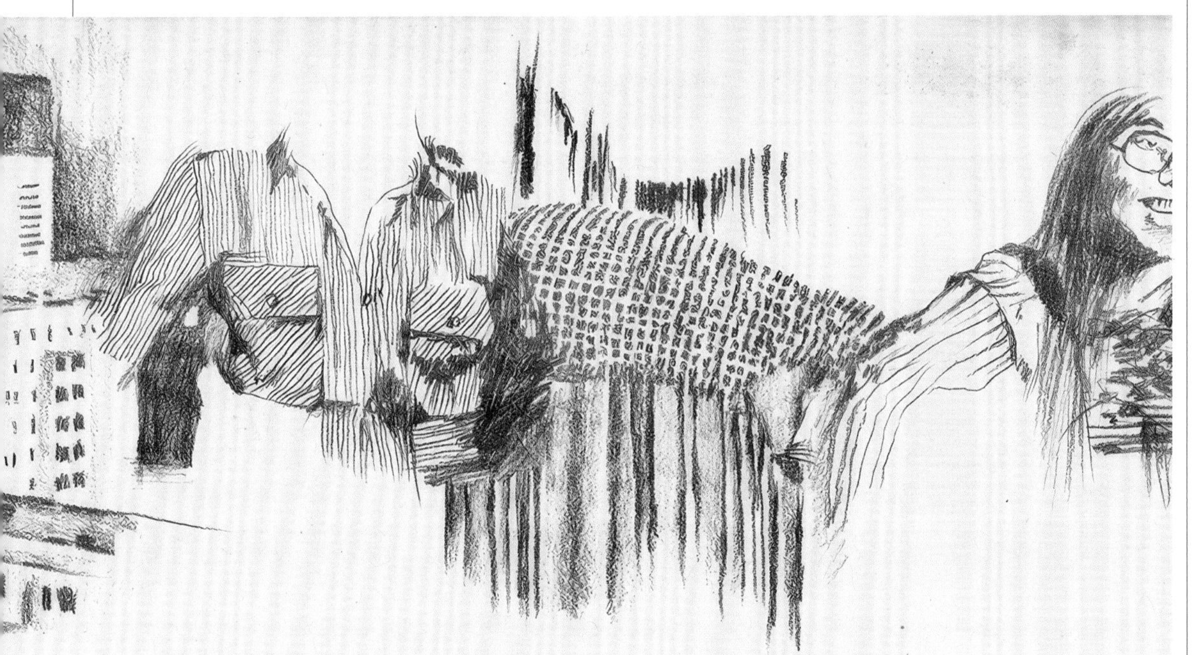

Für diese bandförmig langgestreckte Zeichnung habe ich den Film von Anfang bis Ende durchgesehen und interessante Bilder, Texturen, Formen und Konturen aufgegriffen, bei denen ich den Eindruck hatte, dass sie etwas über die Geschichte des Films, über seine Grundstimmung und den Umgang der Beteiligten miteinander erzählen. Als ich daranging, die Bilder zusammenzulegen, fiel mir auf, dass sich die Körpersprache der Personen im Film allmählich ändert: Aus einem Verhalten unter Bekannten wird eines der Freundschaft, Vertrautheit. Am Beginn des Films lernen wir das Gebäude kennen und können mit ansehen, wie dort viele Welten aufeinanderprallen und ineinander übergehen. Dabei entstehen Freundschaften, es kommt zu politischen Auseinandersetzungen und Schulterschlüssen. Das Lied klingt an, es wird getanzt, Menschen kommen zusammen und bilden immer neue Verbindungen.

The drawing follows this movement: from the architecture to the definition of the object (the object of history, the object of the human, the person embedded within a context from a specific country); it then continues into abstraction, where ideas and alignments collide, and there is an active search for a common ethic. How do we get into the position where we can contemplate pacifism? (Here, I am not referring to the dishonest pacifism that ultimately serves to increase GDP or win an election, or one that helps push for unjust policies).

To even consider a pacifist politics requires a willingness to completely change the manner in which we live today and do away with GDP as the sole

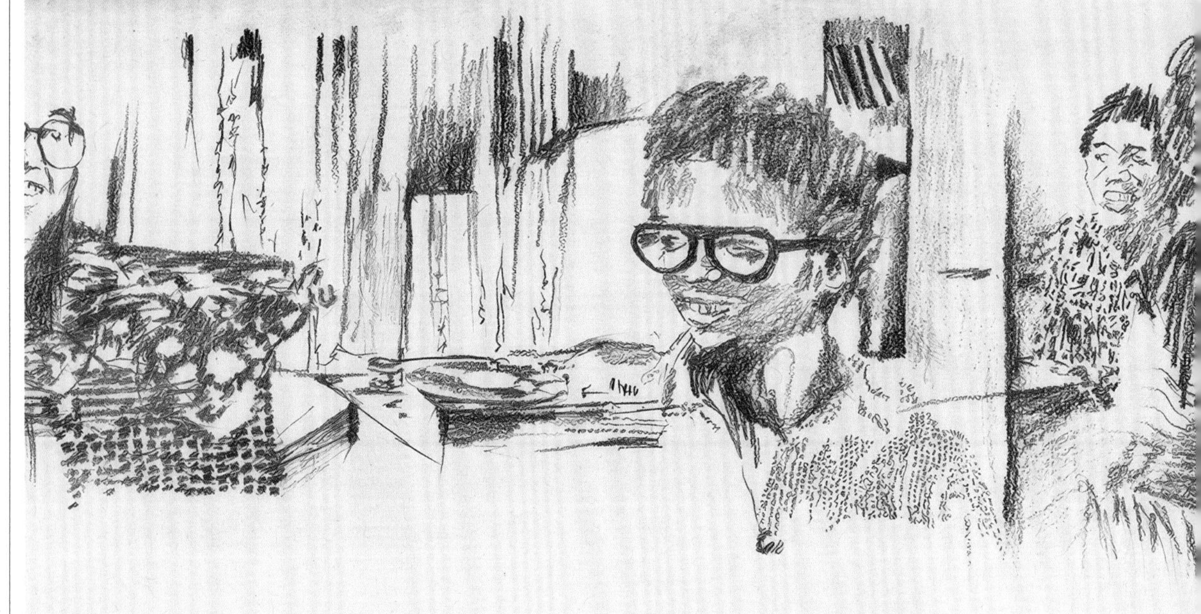

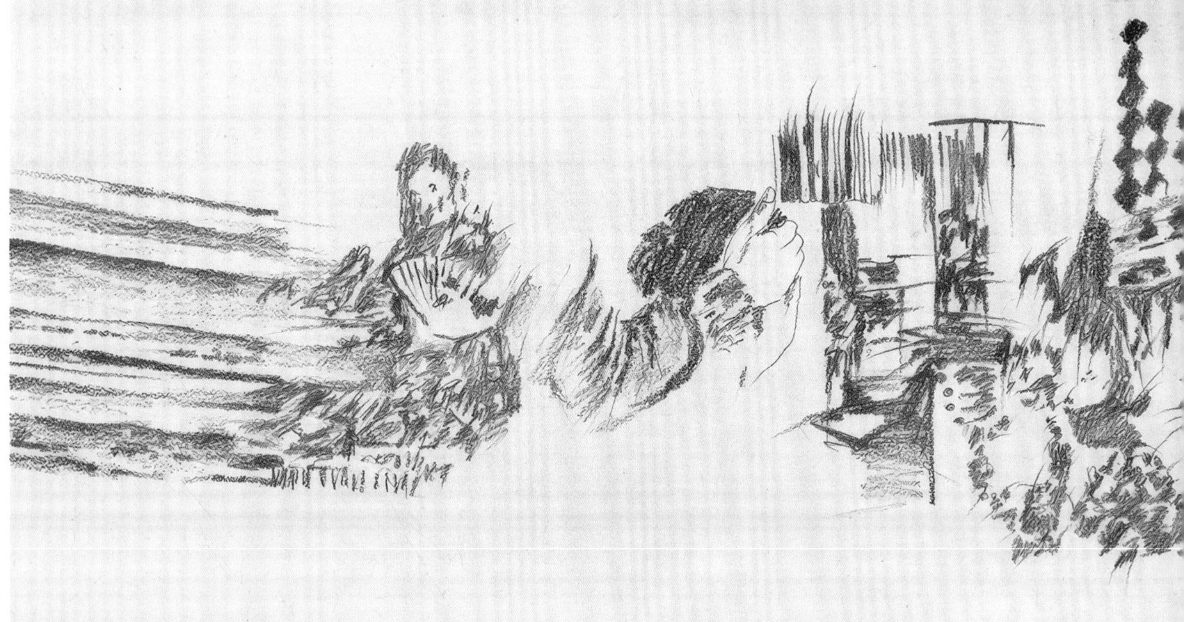

Die Zeichnung geht dieser Bewegung nach: von der Architektur zur Bestimmung des Sujets (der Geschichte, des Menschen, der Person in ihrer Einbettung innerhalb eines gesellschaftlichen Kontextes aus einem bestimmten Land) und weiter zur Abstraktion, in der Vorstellungen und Allianzen kollidieren und aktiv nach gemeinsamen moralischen Vorstellungen gesucht wird. Wie versetzen wir uns überhaupt erst einmal in die Lage, über Pazifismus nachzudenken?

(Womit ich nicht den unaufrichtigen Pazifismus meine, der letztlich nur der Steigerung des Bruttoinlandsprodukts oder einem Wahlsieg dient oder der sich in den Dienst einer ungerechten Politik stellt.)

Der bloße Gedanke an eine wirkliche Friedenspolitik setzt die Bereitschaft voraus, unsere heutige Lebensweise von Grund auf zu verändern und das

yardstick we are forced to live by. Changing this involves reorganization on every single level: the destruction of what is concrete (capital, untenable power structures, domination over entire peoples/lands, bad statecraft, etc.) and the creation of different systems, some of which will be self-organizing, some decentralized, and others that will need to be tested, tried out, and experimented with.

That is where the drawing comes from. There is an act of erasure taking place; it is an erasure of a concrete object, and it is transformative. These are the strokes of the colonial enterprise, the *janeu* lines, the lines that scrambled Africa, the many lines of people who mine cobalt in the Democratic Republic of Congo,

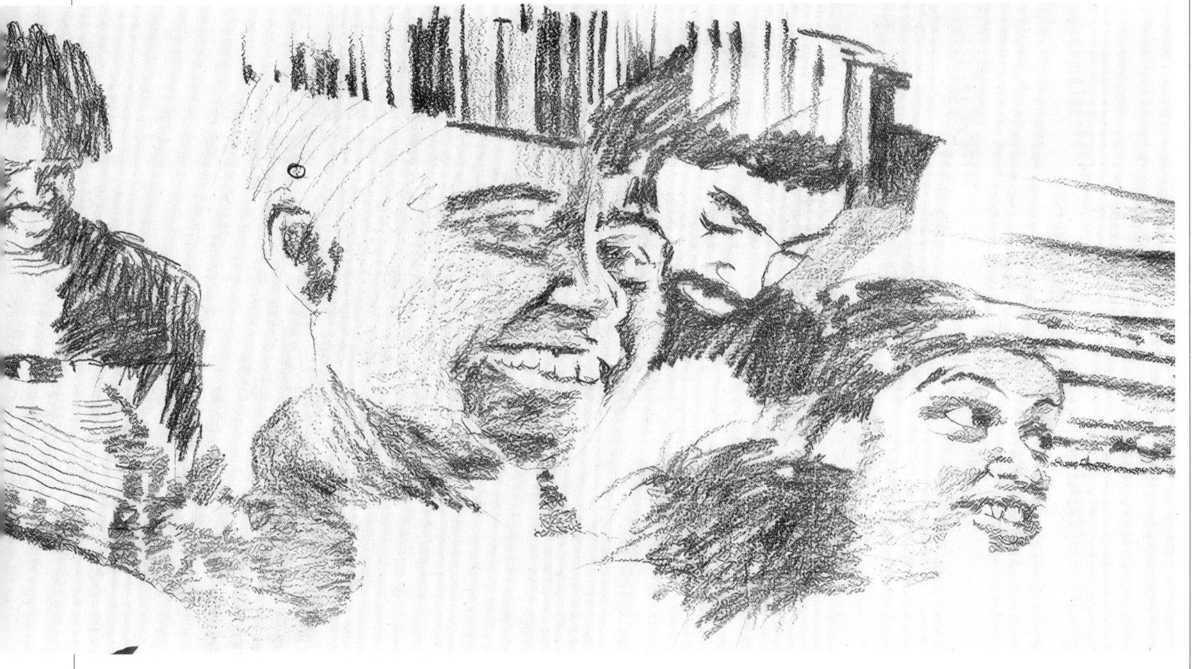

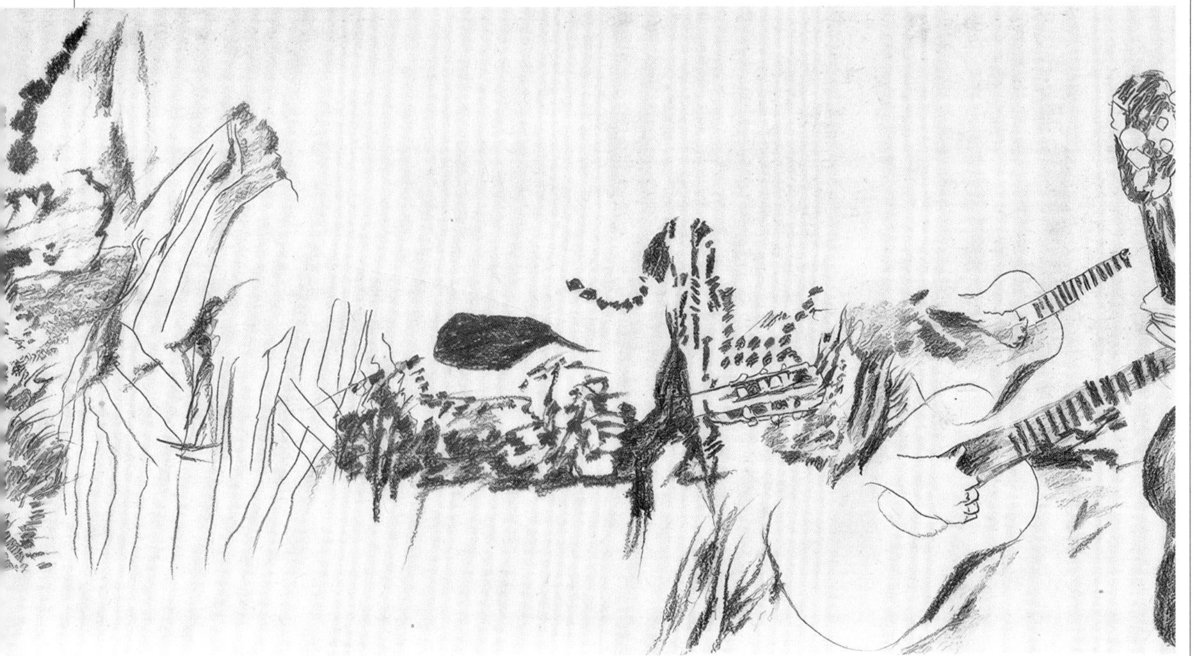

BIP als alleiniges Kriterium, an dem wir unser Leben auszurichten haben, hinter uns zu lassen. Davon wegzukommen heißt, eine Neuordnung auf allen Ebenen vorzunehmen: das Konkrete (das Kapital, unhaltbare Machtstrukturen, Unterjochung ganzer Völker und Länder, schlechte Regierungsführung und so weiter) aufzusprengen und ganz andere Systeme zu schaffen, von denen einige selbstorganisiert, andere dezentral sein werden und weitere ihre Probe erst noch bestehen müssen.

Alldem entspringt meine Zeichnung. Es findet darin ein Akt der Auslöschung statt, nämlich die Auslöschung eines konkreten Objekts, und das setzt Wandlungspotenzial frei. Da sind sie – die groben Striche des kolonialen Abenteuers, die heiligen Janeu-Schnüre, die Linien, die Afrika durcheinanderbrachten,

and the continuously shrinking borders of autonomy, the lines of debt that people and countries owe to predators. Those are the lines that disappear.

What is retained is everything else that lies in between. The drawing is long, you can walk along it, and something visibly changes in it as the viewer moves: objects disappear, and reappear as impressions of their former selves, their outlines vanishing to reveal what lies inside. It is meant to be malleable: self-organization, decentralization, and transformation are like a mass of moving graphite lines that exist only if you look for them, consider them, and will them into existence; they are not an inevitable fact. The objectives of the lines that remain are to construct

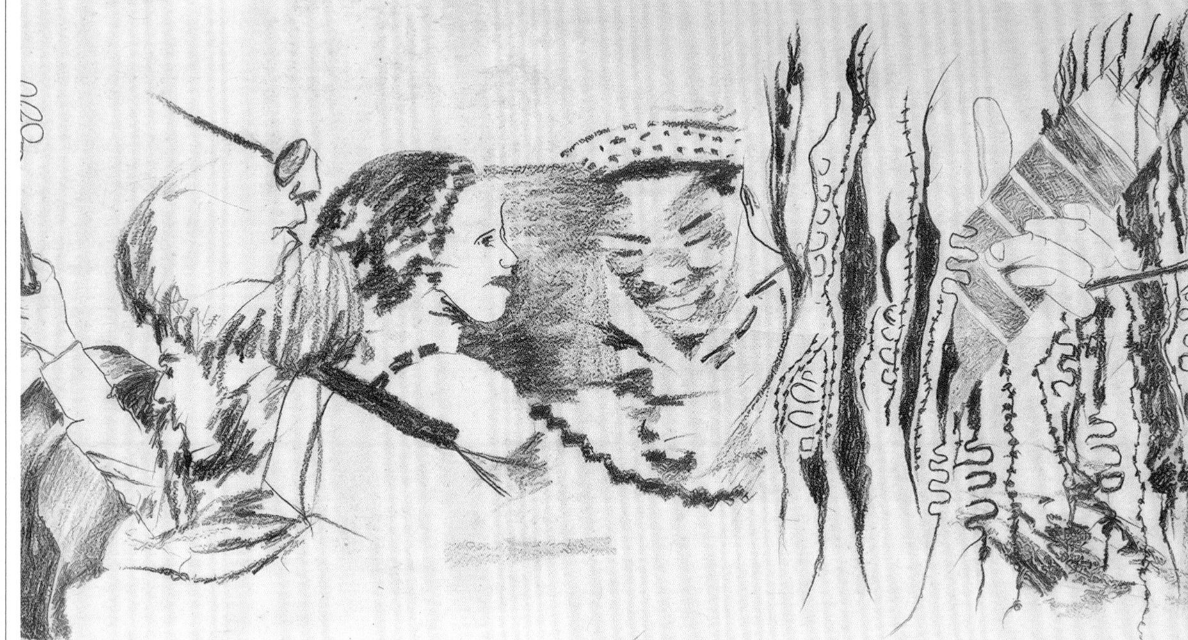

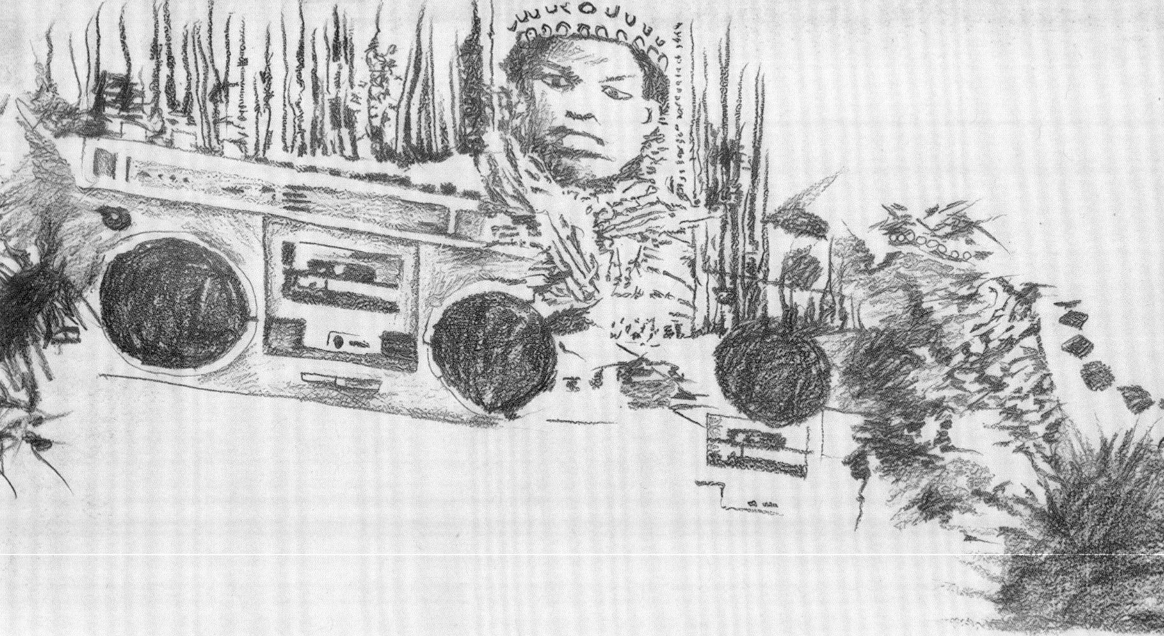

die endlosen Schlangen derjenigen, die in der Demokratischen Republik Kongo Kobalt abbauen, die immer enger gezogenen Grenzen der Autonomie, das Band der Verschuldung, das Menschen und Länder den Räubern ausliefert. Alle diese Linien verschwinden.

Was bleibt, ist all das, was dazwischen liegt. Die Zeichnung erstreckt sich in die Länge, man kann sie abwandern, und wenn man das tut, verändert sich sichtbar etwas: Objekte verschwinden und tauchen als Eindrücke ihrer früheren Gestalt wieder auf, ihre Konturen verschwinden und offenbaren, was davon umschlossen war. Die Zeichnung soll formbar bleiben: Selbstorganisation, Dezentralisierung und Wandel erscheinen darin als eine Masse von Graphitlinien, die es nur gibt, wenn man sie sucht, betrachtet und willentlich ins Leben ruft. Sie

perspective, to select a reality and ask how the experience of that might look. If the answer is not sufficiently favorable, we erase, draw again, and ask once more. These lines have in them that order and invention in motion.

What does it mean to see through freestanding windows? This may seem impossible and even pointless at the outset, since holding on to facts, amplifying trustworthy information, and offsetting dangerous fictions are of the utmost importance. Physiologically, vision is always mediated by gravity, and together they determine how we navigate and move. In some sense, we can only see and move to the extent that we are grounded. The suspended window cannot exist

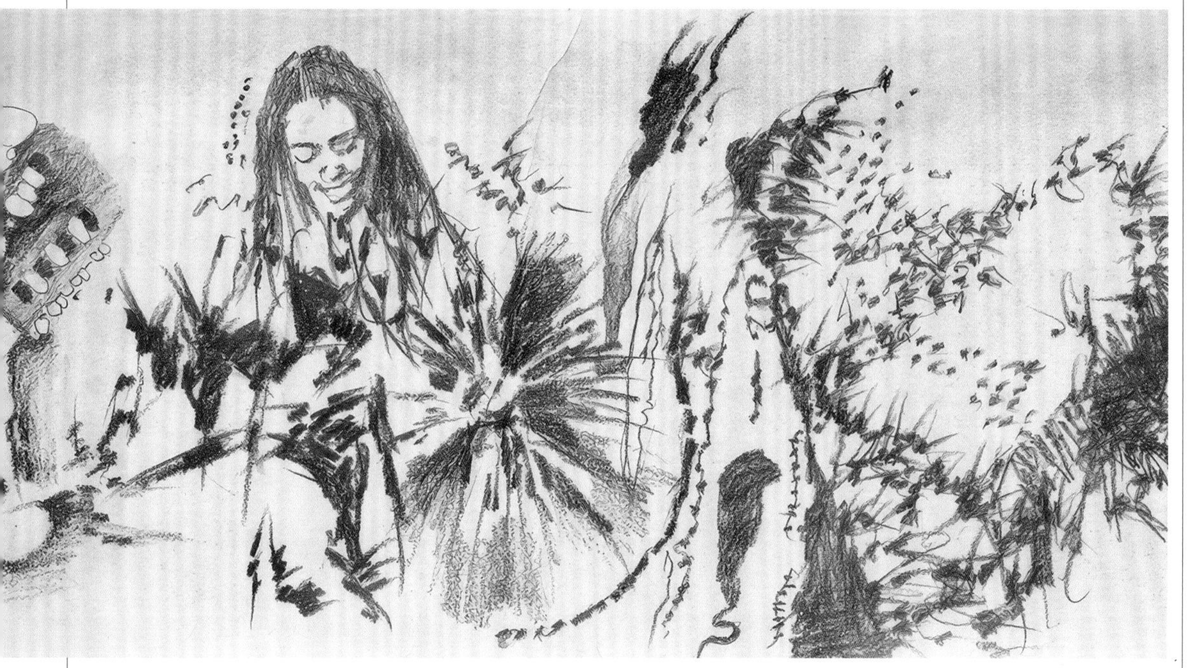

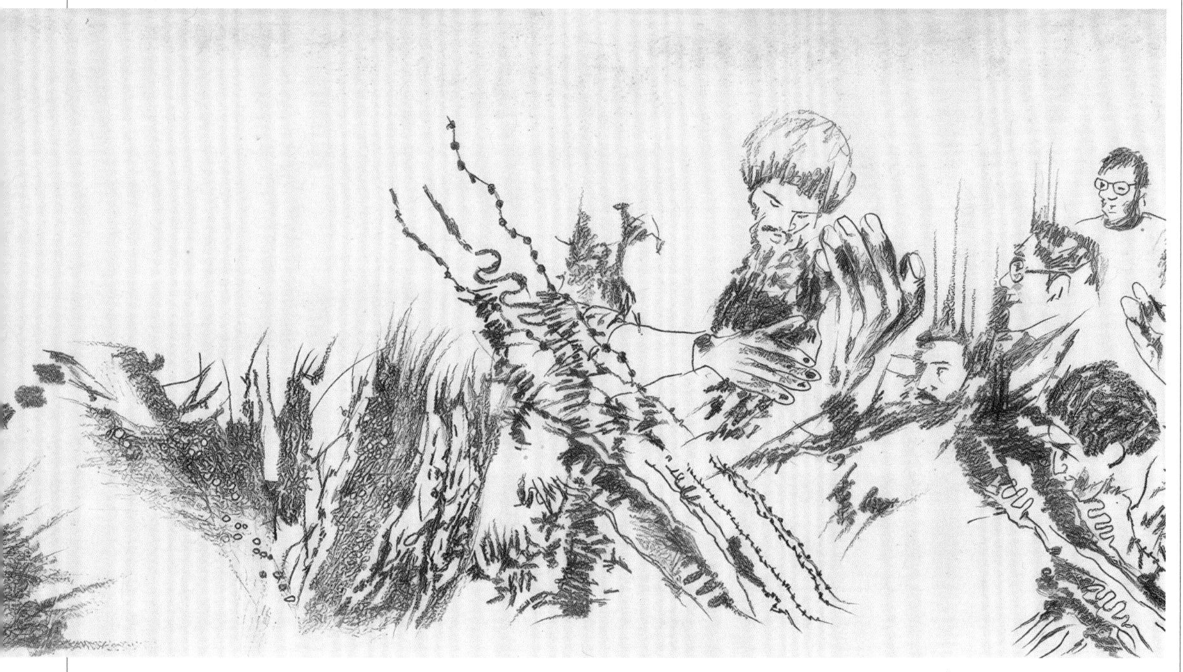

sind keine unausweichlichen Tatsachen. Zweck der übrigbleibenden Linien ist es, Perspektiven zu konstruieren, sich für eine Wirklichkeit zu entscheiden und zu fragen, wie sich ihr Erleben ausnehmen könnte. Fällt die Antwort nicht günstig aus, radieren wir, zeichnen erneut und stellen die Frage noch einmal. Diese Linien tragen die Ordnung und Schöpfung aus der Bewegung heraus in sich.

Was heißt es, durch freistehende Fenster zu schauen? Das mag zunächst unmöglich oder sogar widersinnig erscheinen, denn das Festhalten an Tatsachen, das Herausstellen vertrauenswürdiger Informationen, das Entlarven gefährlicher Einbildungen sind von größter Wichtigkeit. Physiologisch betrachtet unterliegt das Sehen immer der Schwerkraft. Beide zusammen bestimmen, wie wir uns in der Welt zurechtfinden und uns in ihr bewegen. In gewissem Sinn können wir

according to the laws of physics, since any structure needs another structure to support and hold it on the earth; structures, too, need grounding. But maybe the suspended viewing apparatus is useful as a means to consider an altered vision for a brief time. So that we can learn to navigate differently and experiment with different ways of organizing ourselves and what is left of the ground that we have to build on.

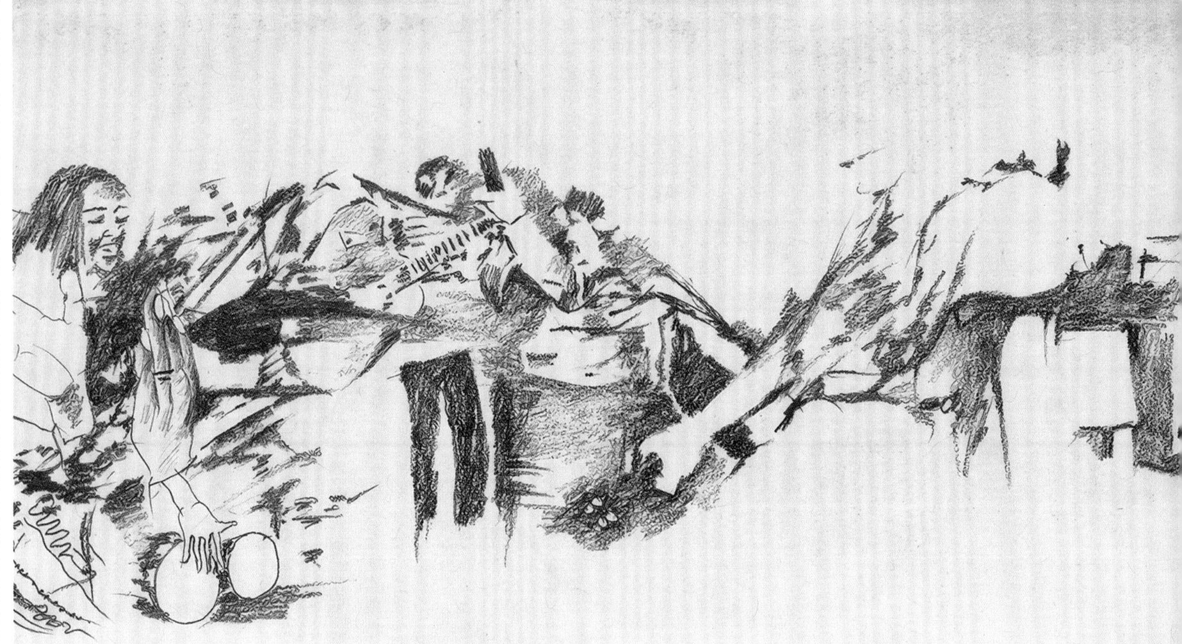

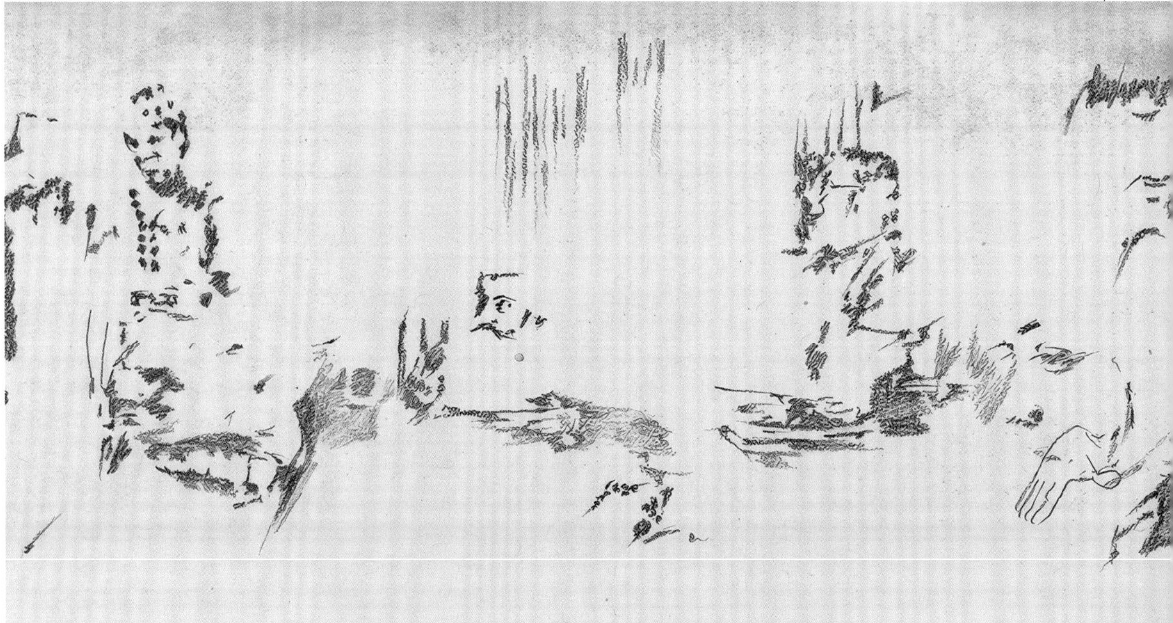

sehen und uns bewegen nur so weit, wie wir Boden unter den Füßen haben. Ein in der Luft hängendes Fenster kann es schon aus physikalischen Gründen nicht geben, denn alles Gebaute braucht ein anderes, das es im Boden verankert; auch Strukturen brauchen ein Fundament. Vielleicht ist aber der außer Kraft gesetzte Sehapparat nützlich, um für einen kurzen Moment die Möglichkeit eines anderen Sehens zu erwägen, so dass wir lernen können, uns auch anders zurechtzufinden und mit anderen Arten von Selbstorganisation zu experimentieren, lernen, wie viel Boden noch da ist, auf den wir bauen können.

Aarti Sunder, *Panorama of a Song*, 2024

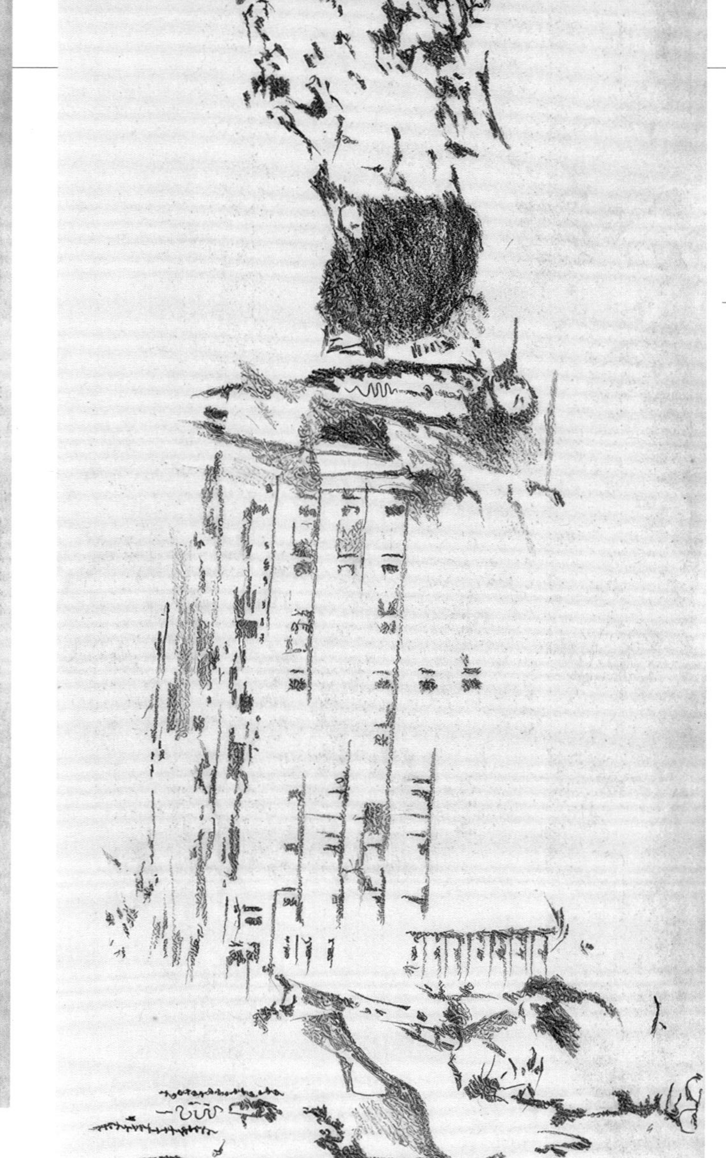

NOTES ON CHARTING OYOYO

Moses März

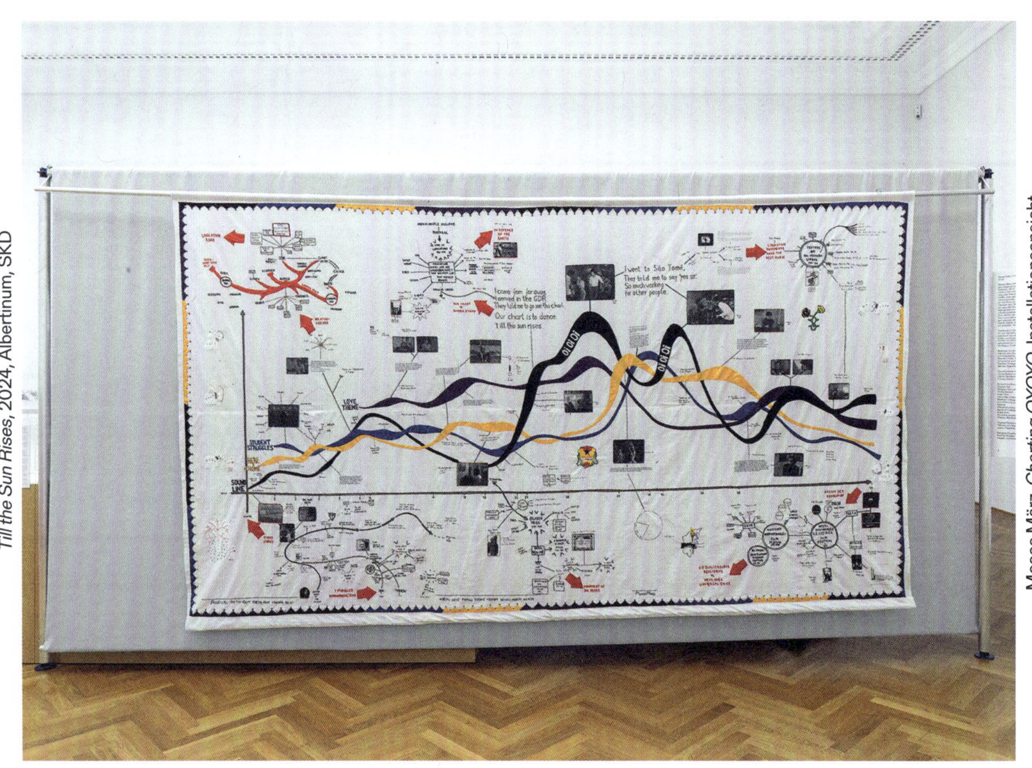

Moses März, *Charting OYOYO*, installation view, *Till the Sun Rises*, 2024, Albertinum, SKD

Moses März, *Charting OYOYO*, Installationsansicht, *Bis zum Sonnenaufgang*, 2024, Albertinum, SKD

Moses März

ANMERKUNGEN ZU CHARTING OYOYO

How could a map of Chetna Vora's *OYOYO* be drawn, a film that feels as if it had been composed like a song? How could its poetic quality be translated into a single image? In the course of our conversations in the context of the research project *Decolonizing Socialism: Entangled Internationalisms*, these were some of the questions to which I wanted to respond. By mapping, I refer, quite generally, to visualizations of information that are useful for travels, real and imagined, in that they offer a sense of direction or orientation in space and time. For me, this includes diagrams and charts that are mainly concerned with measuring flows of varying intensities. By poetic quality, I mean that the film requires a particular kind of attention, a close reading, as literary scholars would say. A kind of reading that pays attention to the relation between form and content, as well as to relations between major themes and small details playing out inside and around the film. Every sign matters. As with a poem or a song, its beauty and its ambiguity appeared to be some of the attractions that drew us to *OYOYO*. Just like the theme song "Forti trabadja p'alguém" (So Much Working for Other People), the film may be perceived as lamentation or jubilation. The kind of experimental mapping that I am engaged in is attuned to tracing the directions that are indicated by these—at times diverging—lines of association.

As a starting point in my attempt to translate *OYOYO* into a map, I identified what I perceived to be the main themes playing out in the film. The diagram shows these four themes as black, yellow, blue, and purple strands whose intensity (y-axis) is measured along the timeline of the film (x-axis). The width of the strands increases as the intensity of a theme grows stronger and thins out as it shifts into the background. These intensities are measured in a relatively structured, yet ultimately unscientific way, since they are based on feelings. The same goes for the timeline, where the length of a minute variably expands and contracts based on the density of the sequence in the film.

The black line refers to the role of sound and music in the film. It ranges from the noise of street traffic at the start of the film, to the group of students making music and singing together, which marks the climatic moment around the 25-minute mark toward the middle of the film. Titled "Here & At Home,"

Wie ließe sich eine Karte von *OYOYO* zeichnen – einem Film, der seinerseits wirkt, als hätte Chetna Vora ihn wie ein Lied komponiert? Wie könnte man seine poetische Qualität in ein einzelnes Bild übersetzen? Im Zuge unserer Gespräche im Rahmen des Forschungsprojektes *Decolonizing Socialism: Entangled Internationalisms* wollte ich unter anderem Antworten auf diese Fragen finden. Karten zeichnen bedeutet für mich recht allgemein, Informationen bildlich darzustellen, die auf Reisen, seien sie real oder imaginär, nützlich sind, da sie Orientierung in Raum und Zeit bieten. Dazu gehören für mich auch Diagramme und Schaubilder, in denen es hauptsächlich darum geht, Ströme verschiedener Intensität zu erfassen. Mit poetischer Qualität meine ich, dass der Film eine bestimmte Art von Aufmerksamkeit, genauem Hinsehen oder „Lesen" erfordert, wie Literaturwissenschaftler·innen sagen würden: eine Lektüre, die auf das Verhältnis zwischen Form und Inhalt achtet und darüber hinaus auf Bezüge zwischen Hauptmotiven und Details im und rund um den Film. Jeder Hinweis ist von Belang. Wie bei einem Gedicht oder Lied waren es unter anderem die Schönheit und Mehrdeutigkeit, die uns für den Film *OYOYO* einnahmen. Wie das Titellied *Forti trabadja p'alguém* („So viel arbeiten für andere Leute") kann man auch den gesamten Film als Klagelied oder Hymne verstehen. Das experimentelle Kartieren, wie ich es betreibe, eignet sich gut dazu, den verschiedenen Richtungen nachzugehen, in die bisweilen auseinanderstrebende Assoziationslinien führen.

Zu Beginn meines Versuchs, *OYOYO* in eine Landkarte zu übersetzen, bestimmte ich mehrere von mir als solche ausgemachte thematische Hauptlinien, die sich durch den Film ziehen. Das Diagramm veranschaulicht diese vier Themen in Form schwarzer, gelber, blauer und violetter Bänder, deren Intensität (y-Achse) entlang des Zeitstrahls des Films (x-Achse) dargestellt ist. Die Bänder werden umso breiter, je vordringlicher ein Thema zur jeweiligen Zeit ist, und wieder dünner, wenn dieses in den Hintergrund tritt. Diese Intensitäten sind in einer zwar relativ strukturierten, aber letztlich unwissenschaftlichen Weise erfasst, da meine Gewichtung allein auf Empfindungen beruht. Dasselbe gilt für den Zeitstrahl, auf dem die Länge einer Minute sich abhängig von der Dichte der betreffenden Sequenz im Film ausdehnt oder zusammenzieht.

Das schwarze Band bezeichnet den Stellenwert von Klang und Musik im Film. Das umfasst alles vom Verkehrslärm auf der Straße am Beginn bis zu

the yellow strand broadly deals with the theme of migration. It includes the protagonists sharing memories of their family and friends at home, and how they navigate cultural differences between the East German society in which they live and their respective home countries. The blue strand traces the issues relating to student life. Scenes of students doing homework, speaking about their political activism or their professional aspirations once they have completed their studies in the GDR all form part of this. The love theme, which the chart indicates in the color purple, appears at a relatively late point in time but features prominently from here on out. Running almost parallel to the black sound line, I understood love to not only refer to the presence of romantic couples ("Irene hat einen kubanischen Freund"), and the protagonists talking about what love means to them ("Hauptsache ein Mann, der dir richtig zuhören kann"). For me, the love theme in the film appeared to exercise an allegorical function that alludes to a utopian socialist world-community united in its diversity. I see the subtle eroticism associated with this kind of revolutionary romance play out in the dance scenes, as well as in smaller acts of caring and friendship among the group of students.

The red arrows indicate allusions in the film that made me want to find out more about the context in which it was produced and about the geopolitical canvas from which the film's protagonists emerge. The cluster named "Relation-Nations" at the top left takes a protagonist's quote about the possibilities of studying abroad for students from Guinea as a springboard to revisit the Afro-Asian movement from which this landscape emerged. The movement is drawn in red crayon, beginning with Indian independence in 1947, gaining momentum at the Bandung Conference in 1955, and eventually dissipating in Cuba in 1966. The cluster of institutions and organizations branching out of the GDR illustrates how East Germany was interwoven into the project of Afro-Asian solidarity via relations of exchange, solidarity, and material support. The cluster "Our Chart Is Guinea-Bissau" is named after a song line in the film to point out the violent history of Guinea-Bissau's war of liberation against Portugal and its neocolonial allies. The cluster points in two directions: one connects the war waged by the African Party for the Independence of Guinea and Cape Verde (PAIGC) with Sékou Touré's socialist project in

einer Gruppe von Studierenden, die gemeinsam musizieren und singen, was den Höhepunkt etwa bei Minute 25 darstellt, ziemlich in der Mitte des Films. Das gelbe Band ist beschriftet mit „here & at home" und behandelt im Wesentlichen das Thema Migration. Dazu gehört, dass die Protagonist·innen von ihren Erinnerungen an ihre Angehörigen und Freund·innen in der Heimat erzählen und wie sie mit kulturellen Unterschieden zwischen der ostdeutschen Gesellschaft, in der sie leben, und ihrem jeweiligen Heimatland umgehen. Das blaue Band verzeichnet Dinge, die im studentischen Leben eine Rolle spielen, etwa wenn die Betreffenden ihre Hausaufgaben machen, über ihr politisches Engagement sprechen oder Hoffnungen auf eine Berufslaufbahn nach dem Abschluss ihres Studiums in der DDR äußern. Das Thema Liebe, auf der Karte violett eingezeichnet, taucht erst relativ spät im Film auf, tritt von da an aber stark in den Vordergrund. Es verläuft beinahe parallel zum schwarzen Band der Tonspur, und ich habe Liebe hier nicht allein auf das Auftreten von Liebespaaren bezogen („Irene hat einen kubanischen Freund"), sondern auch auf Gespräche unter den Protagonist·innen über die Bedeutung der Liebe für sie („Hauptsache ein Mann, der dir richtig zuhören kann"). Das Liebesmotiv scheint mir im Film eine allegorische Funktion zu übernehmen, da darin auch Vorstellungen von einer utopischen sozialistischen, in Vielfalt geeinten Weltgemeinschaft anklingen. Die subtile Erotik, die von dieser Art Revolutionsromantik ausgeht, nehme ich in den Tanzszenen wahr, aber auch in beiläufigeren Akten der Fürsorge und Freundschaft unter den Studierenden.

Die roten Pfeile bezeichnen Bezugnahmen im Film, die in mir den Wunsch weckten, mehr über den Kontext seiner Entstehung zu erfahren und über den geopolitischen Hintergrund, aus dem die Protagonist·innen des Films hervortreten. Der Knoten mit der Bezeichnung „relation – nations" oben links nimmt jemandes Äußerung im Film wieder auf, wonach die Möglichkeit eines Auslandsstudiums für Studierende aus Guinea einem Sprungbrett für die Beschäftigung mit jener afro-asiatischen Bewegung gleichkam, aus der diese neue politische Landschaft hervorgegangen war. Diese Bewegung ist mit rotem Kreidestift gezeichnet und beginnt bei der Unabhängigkeit Indiens 1947, gewinnt an Fahrt mit der Bandung-Konferenz von 1955 und verläuft sich schließlich in Kuba 1966. Der von der DDR ausgehende Knoten von Institutionen und Organisationen veranschaulicht den Grad der Einbindung Ostdeutschlands in das Projekt

neighboring Guinea, which the PAIGC used as a military hinterland, and where a cultural revolution had been underway since the early 1960s. The other direction points out the progressive quality of the PAIGC with regard to its educational practice, its implementation of gender equality, and its elaborate engagement with ecological questions, as is apparent in Amílcar Cabral's agronomic writings.

The cluster "Liberation Movements Make the Best Music" branches off from the role of political songs as an alternative educational archive to revisit the role of music in the national liberation struggles more generally. A particularity of the GDR was that protest songs from the so-called Third World were in line with and actively supported by the government. This is particularly apparent with regards to the annual Festival des politischen Liedes (Festival of Political Song), which was organized by the Free German Youth (FDJ) movement from 1970 to 1990. "Archiv der Revolution" (Archive of the Revolution), the cluster at the bottom right, indicates that the Leipzig International Film Festival played a similar role in the realm of documentary filmmaking. In contrast to the Berlinale's early endorsement of fiction, short, and avant-garde films, the Leipzig festival celebrated films that were committed to the socialist project and created a forum for filmmakers that recorded or actively participated in the anti-colonial struggles in South America, Africa, and Asia.

The cluster to its left branches out of an anecdote about the Ethiopian-Djibouti railway line to provide a schematic overview of how the relations of trade, cooperation, and cultural exchange between the GDR and Ethiopia evolved following the coup d'état of the socialist Derg regime that overthrew Emperor Haile Selassie I in 1974. The red "*OYOYO* Studies" arrow to the far left provides a biographical background of Chetna Vora's trajectory in and out of the GDR and the Film and Television Academy of the GDR, where *OYOYO* was produced. Her personal black lifeline is complemented by information in gray that provides an overview of GDR–Indian relations leading up to the official diplomatic recognition of the GDR by India in 1972. The additional red arrows that point outside the borders of the map indicate thematic clusters that I have already drawn maps of and others that are still waiting to be mapped.

afro-asiatischer Solidarität über Tauschbeziehungen, Solidaritätsleistungen und materielle Unterstützung. Der Knoten „Our chart is Guinea-Bissau" ist nach einer Liedzeile im Film benannt und soll die Geschichte von Guinea-Bissaus blutigem Befreiungskampf gegen Portugal und seine neokolonialen Verbündeten veranschaulichen. Er weist in zwei Richtungen: Nach der einen verbindet sich der Krieg der Afrikanischen Unabhängigkeitspartei von Guinea und Kap Verde (PAIGC) mit dem sozialistischen Projekt im benachbarten Guinea unter Ahmed Sékou Touré, das die PAIGC als militärisches Hinterland nutzte und wo seit Anfang der 1960er Jahre eine Kulturrevolution im Gang war. Nach der anderen Richtung weist er auf die Fortschrittlichkeit der PAIGC hin, was Bildung und Erziehung anging, nämlich die Durchsetzung der Geschlechtergleichheit und die eingehende Auseinandersetzung mit ökologischen Fragen, die auch in Amilcar Cabrals Schriften zur Agronomie deutlich wird.

Der Knoten „Liberation Movements Make the Best Music" folgt der Spur des politischen Lieds als Archiv alternativer Bildung und betont allgemeiner den Stellenwert von Musik in nationalen Befreiungsbewegungen. Eine Besonderheit der DDR war, dass hier Protestlieder aus der sogenannten Dritten Welt der Parteilinie entsprachen und aktive staatliche Förderung erfuhren. Besonders augenfällig wurde das beim alljährlichen Festival des politischen Liedes, das die FDJ von 1970 bis 1990 veranstaltete. „Archiv der Revolution", der Knoten unten rechts, lässt erkennen, dass das Internationale Leipziger Festival für Dokumentar- und Animationsfilm eine vergleichbare Rolle auf dem Gebiet dieser beiden Filmgattungen spielte. In Abgrenzung zur Berlinale, die von Anfang an auf Spiel-, Kurz- und Experimentalfilme setzte, pries das Leipziger Festival ein Filmschaffen, das dem Sozialismus verpflichtet war, und diente als Forum für Filmemacher·innen, die antikoloniale Befreiungsbewegungen in Südamerika und Afrika dokumentierten oder selbst aktiv daran teilnahmen.

Der Knoten links davon zweigt ab bei einer Anekdote über die Eisenbahnverbindung von Äthiopien nach Dschibuti und bietet eine schematische Darstellung der Handels-, Kooperations- und Kulturbeziehungen zwischen der DDR und Äthiopien nach dem Staatsstreich des sozialistischen Derg-Regimes, das 1974 Kaiser Haile Selassie I. stürzte. Der rote „OYOYO Studies"-Pfeil ganz links bietet biografische Informationen zum Weg von Chetna Vora, der sie in die DDR

What does it mean to pick up on these specific associations in the context of a research project that seeks to apply a decolonial lens to the history of socialism? After all, the relevance of a map stands and falls with the kinds of relations or routes it renders visible. As part of my ongoing *Mapping Decolonial Berlin* series, I have been interested in revisiting practices of collaboration across the colonial North-South divide that are worth re-interrogating from a decolonial perspective. The GDR's active support of anti-colonial liberation movements—both at an international level and in the realm of cultural production—is worth revisiting, especially in contrast to West Germany's alliance with colonial and neocolonial regimes. Instead of prosaic political proclamations of Afro-Asian solidarity, *OYOYO* provides an intimate view of young people, mainly People of Color from socialist-leaning countries across the world, who live and work together. In part, the sense of a heterotopia that the film suggests is achieved by blocking out the immediate social context of East Germany, whose citizens remain invisible in the film. More importantly, however, this sense of harmony arises when the group makes music and dances in the narrow corridor of their student residence. As a structural equivalence to these free movements in a confined space, the film also balances the individual personalities of the protagonists with a shared sense of community, a nondogmatic kind of collaboration shaped by heterogeneity, provisionality, and

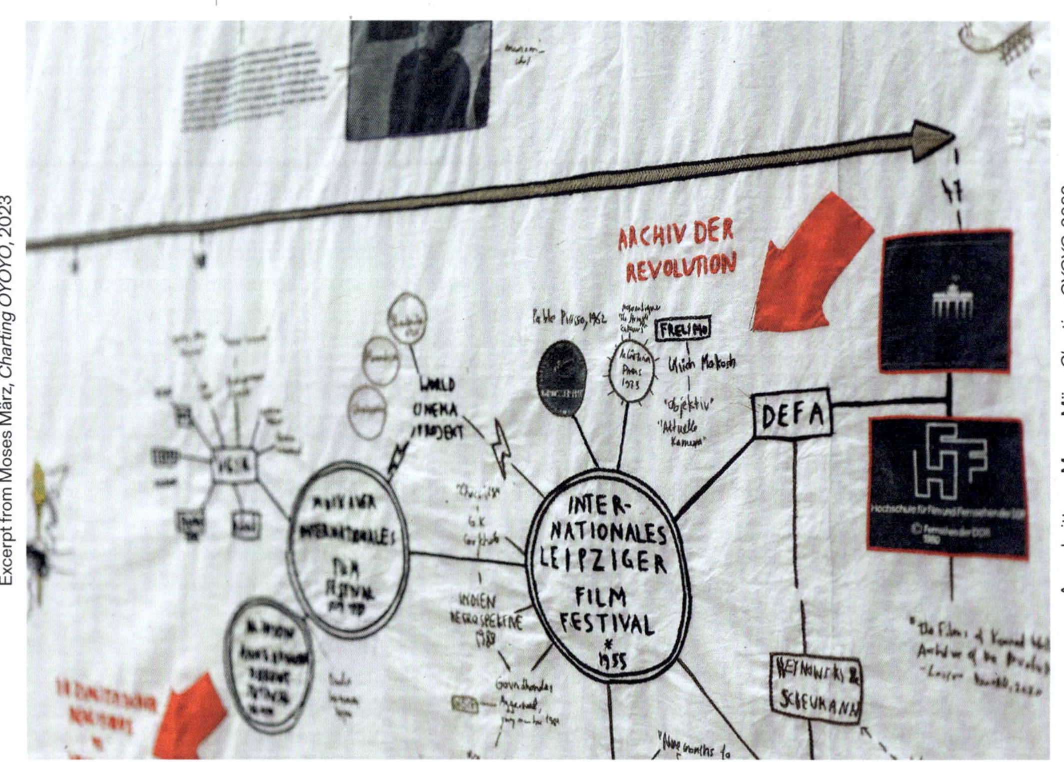

Excerpt from Moses März, *Charting OYOYO*, 2023

Ausschnitt aus: Moses März, *Charting OYOYO*, 2023

und an die Hochschule für Film und Fernsehen der DDR führte, wo auch *OYOYO* produziert wurde. Ihre persönliche schwarze Lebenslinie ist vervollständigt um grau unterlegte Informationen, die einen Einblick in die Beziehungen zwischen der DDR und Indien und dessen Anerkennung des ostdeutschen Staates im Jahr 1972 geben. Zusätzliche rote Pfeile, die über den Rand der Karte hinaus zeigen, verweisen auf Themenstränge, die ich bereits anderswo zu Karten verarbeitet habe, und weitere, die noch auf ihre Kartierung warten.

Was bedeutet es, solche spezifischen Assoziationen im Rahmen eines Forschungsprojekts aufzugreifen, das die Geschichte des Sozialismus in dekolonialer Optik betrachten will? Immerhin steht und fällt die Relevanz einer Karte mit jener der Beziehungen und Wegverläufe, die sie sichtbar macht. Als Teil meiner fortlaufenden Serie *Mapping Decolonial Berlin* widme ich mich Praktiken der Zusammenarbeit über die koloniale Nord-Süd-Kluft hinweg, die mir eine eingehendere Betrachtung und Befragung aus dekolonialer Sicht wert scheinen. Insbesondere im Kontrast zum Bündnis der BRD mit kolonialen und neokolonialen Regimes verdient die aktive Unterstützung antikolonialer Befreiungsbewegungen durch die DDR sowohl auf internationaler Ebene als auch in der Kulturproduktion eine Neubewertung. Anstatt prosaischer politischer Verkündungen afrikanisch-asiatischer Solidarität bietet *OYOYO* aus nächster Nähe einen Einblick in die Welt junger, hauptsächlich nicht weißer Menschen aus sozialistisch orientierten Ländern der ganzen Welt, die miteinander leben und arbeiten. Zum Teil verdankt

an indefinite, nondoctrinaire vision of a more egalitarian future. Just as the film accords space to the dimensions of the personal and the political, of individual and collective freedom, this is also a kind of balance to which the map aspires.

Embroidery and patchwork specific to western Rajasthan, India, made by women artisans from villages in the Barmer district close to the India-Pakistan border, previously known as the Sindh region. The following craftspeople were involved: Hakima Devi (master artisan and trainer), Khemi Devi, Rangu, Sugni, Poonam, Khaki, Miremi, and Mamta (women artisans supported by the field center of the Barefoot College in Dhanau village, Barmer, Rajasthan). Implementing craft organization: Tilonia Bazaar, a craft initiative of Hatheli Sansthan located at Barefoot College, Tilonia, Ajmer district, Rajasthan, India. Design and coordination: Shweta Rao (member of governing body, Tilonia Bazaar), Hothi Ram (facilitator, Dhanau field center, Barefoot College, Tilonia). Execution and implementation: Badrilal (field center coordinator, Dhanau, Barefoot College, Tilonia), Kheta Ram (master artisan & trainer, Dhanau, Barefoot College, Tilonia). Digital textile print: Textures by Shaifali Gupta and Kunal Gupta, Jaipur, Rajasthan, India. *Karigars* (artisans) for Kantha work on the proto map: Haseen and Sohail. Realized between October 2023 and January 2024.

sich der Eindruck einer Heterotopie im Film der Tatsache, dass der unmittelbare gesellschaftliche Kontext der DDR ausgeblendet wird. Deren Bürger·innen bleiben im Film unsichtbar. Wichtiger noch ist, dass sich ein Gefühl der Harmonie immer dann einstellt, wenn die Gruppe auf dem schmalen Flur des Wohnheims musiziert und tanzt. Als strukturelle Entsprechung zu diesen freien Regungen in einem geschlossenen Raum schafft der Film auch ein Gleichgewicht zwischen den Persönlichkeiten der Protagonist·innen und einem Sinn für Gemeinschaft, für eine undogmatische Zusammenarbeit im Zeichen von Verschiedenheit, Vorläufigkeit und theorieoffenen Erwartungen einer Zukunft mit mehr Gleichheit in der Welt. Ebenso wie der Film den Dimensionen des Persönlichen und Politischen, der Freiheit des Einzelnen und der Freiheit aller Raum lässt, strebt auch diese Karte nach einer solchen Ausgewogenheit.

Solche Stickereien und Patchworkarbeiten sind typisch für das westliche Rajasthan (Indien). Sie wurden angefertigt von Kunsthandwerkerinnen in Dörfern des Distrikts Barmer unweit der Grenze zu Pakistan (ehemals als Sindh-Region bekannt). Folgende Handwerkerinnen waren an der Realisierung beteiligt: Hakima Devi (Meisterin und Ausbilderin), Khemi Devi, Rangu, Sugni, Poonam, Khaki, Miremi und Mamta (Kunsthandwerkerinnen, die im regionalen Zentrum des Barefoot College in Dhanau, Barmer, Rajasthan, unterstützt werden). Umsetzung der handwerklichen Arbeiten: Tilonia Bazaar, eine handwerkliche Initiative der Firma Hatheli Sansthan am Barefoot College, Tilonia, Distrikt Ajmer, Rajasthan, India. Design und Koordination: Shweta Rao (Leitung Tilonia Bazaar), Hothi Ram (Mitarbeiter des regionalen Zentrums Dhanau, Barefoot College, Tilonia). Ausführung und Umsetzung: Badrilal (Koordinator am regionalen Zentrum Dhanau, Barefoot College, Tilonia), Kheta Ram (Handwerksmeister und Ausbilder, Dhanau, Barefoot College, Tilonia). Digitale Textildrucke: Texturen von Shaifali Gupta und Kunal Gupta, Jaipur, Rajasthan. *Karigars* (Handwerker·innen) für die Kantha-Arbeiten der Proto-Karte: Haseen und Sohail. Realisiert zwischen Oktober 2023 und Januar 2024.

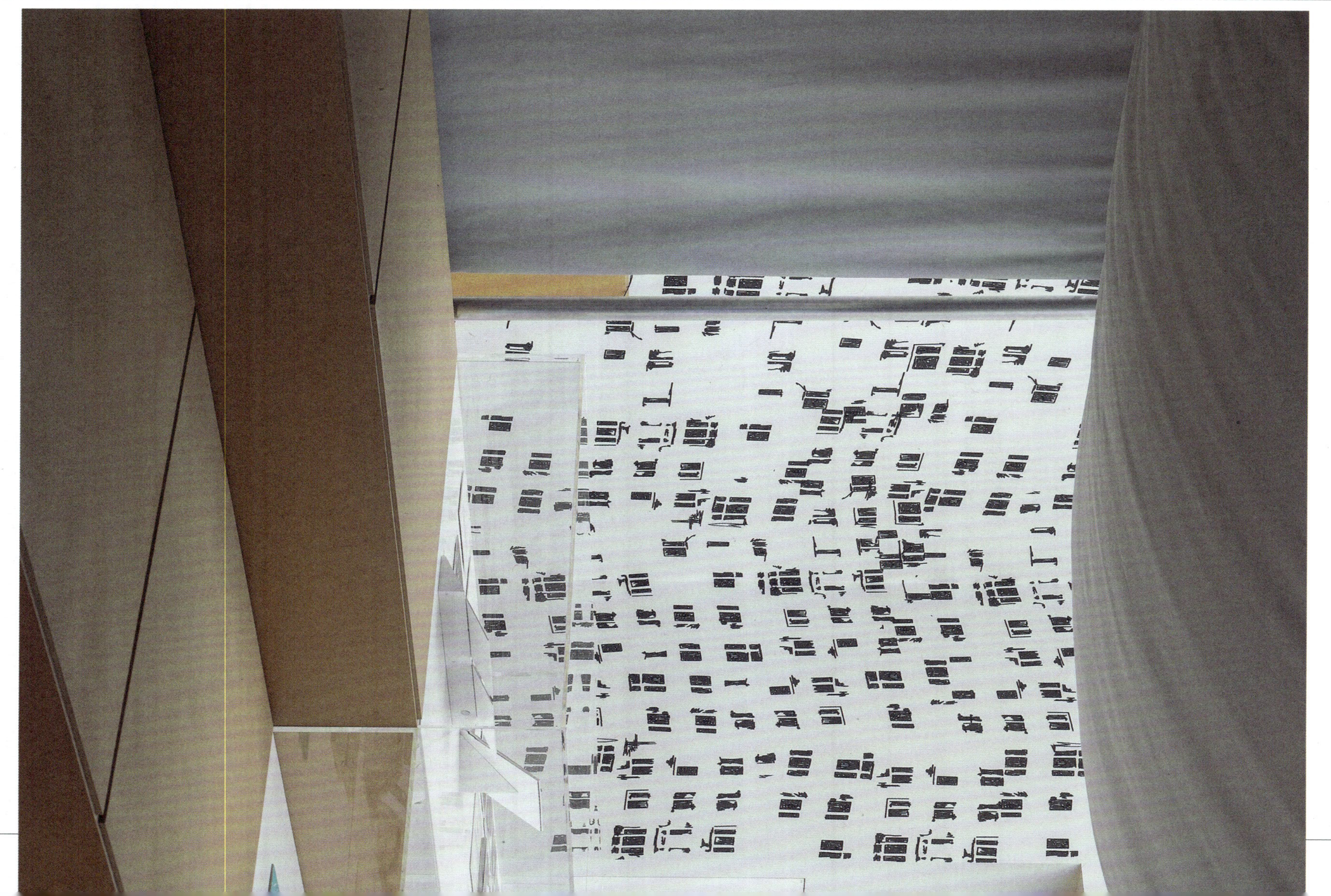

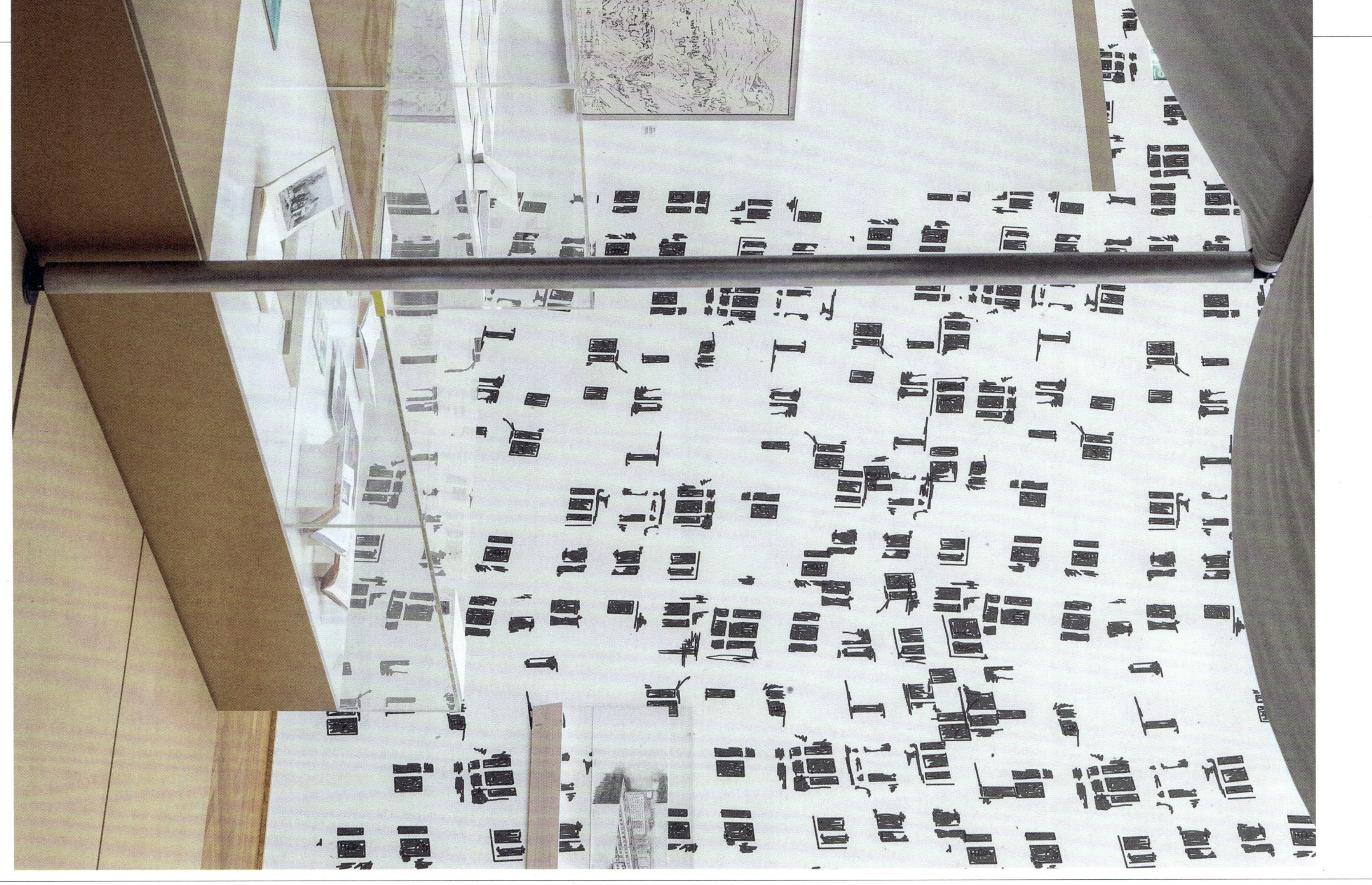

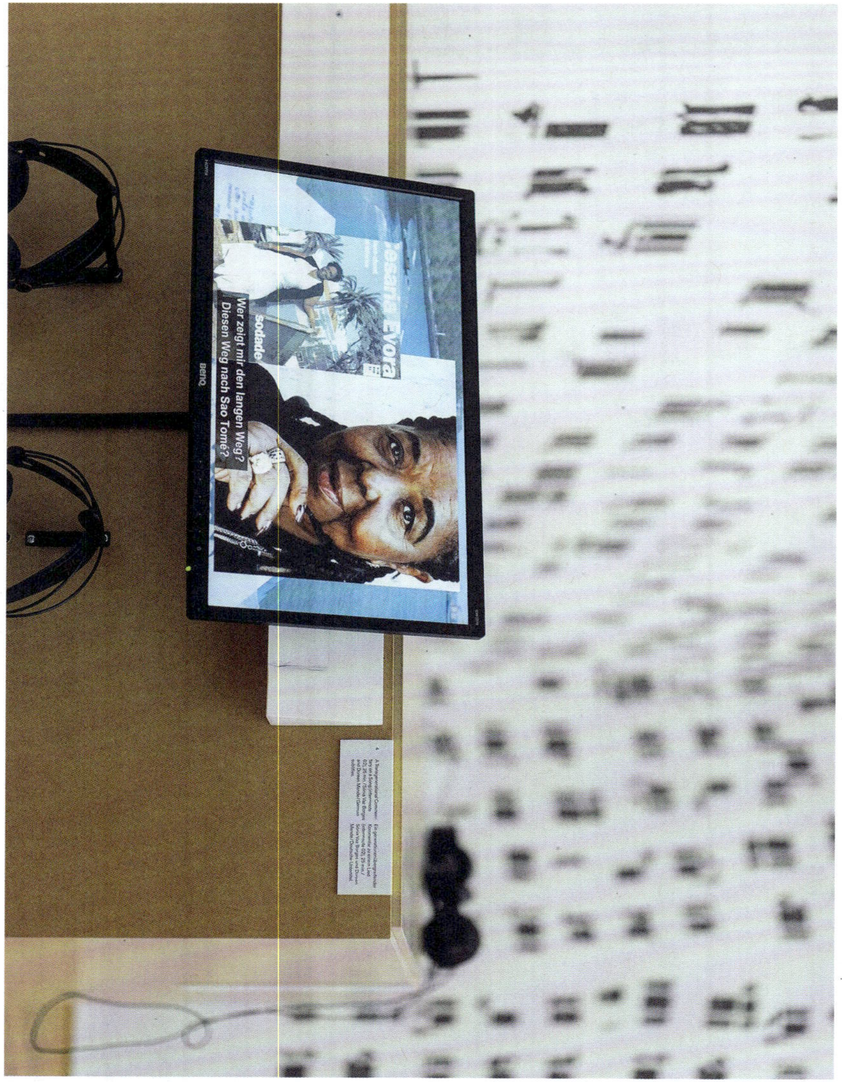

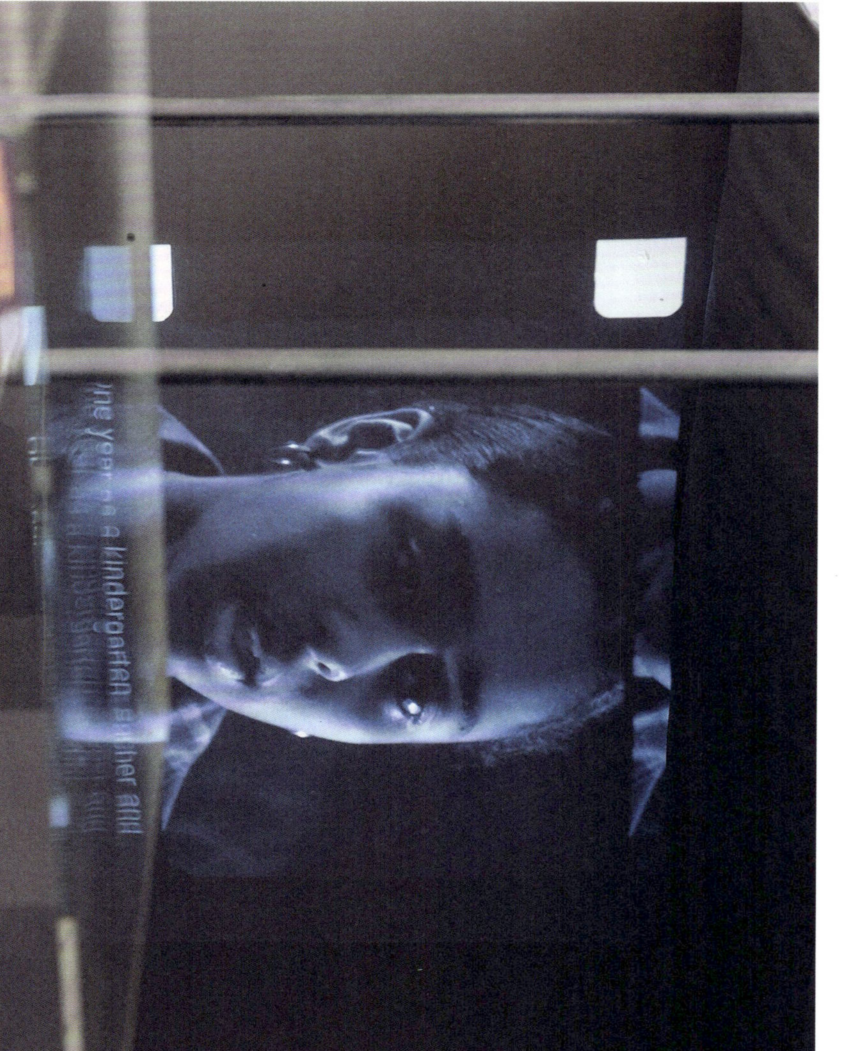

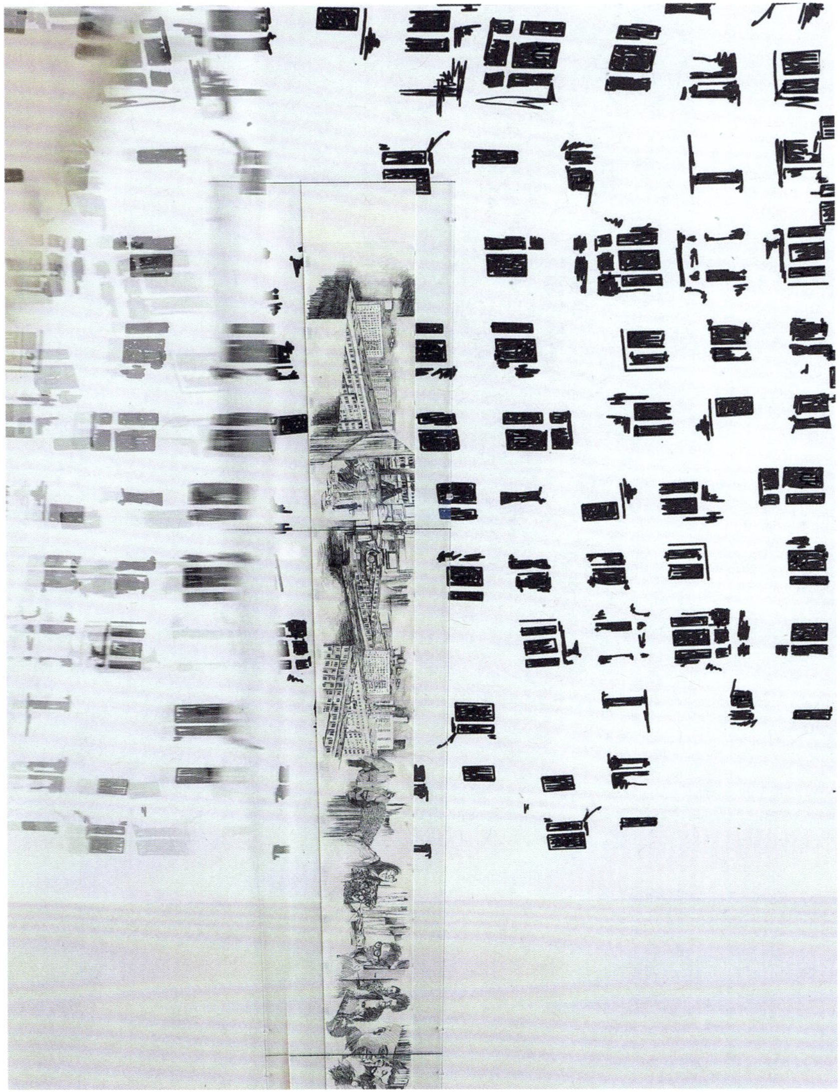

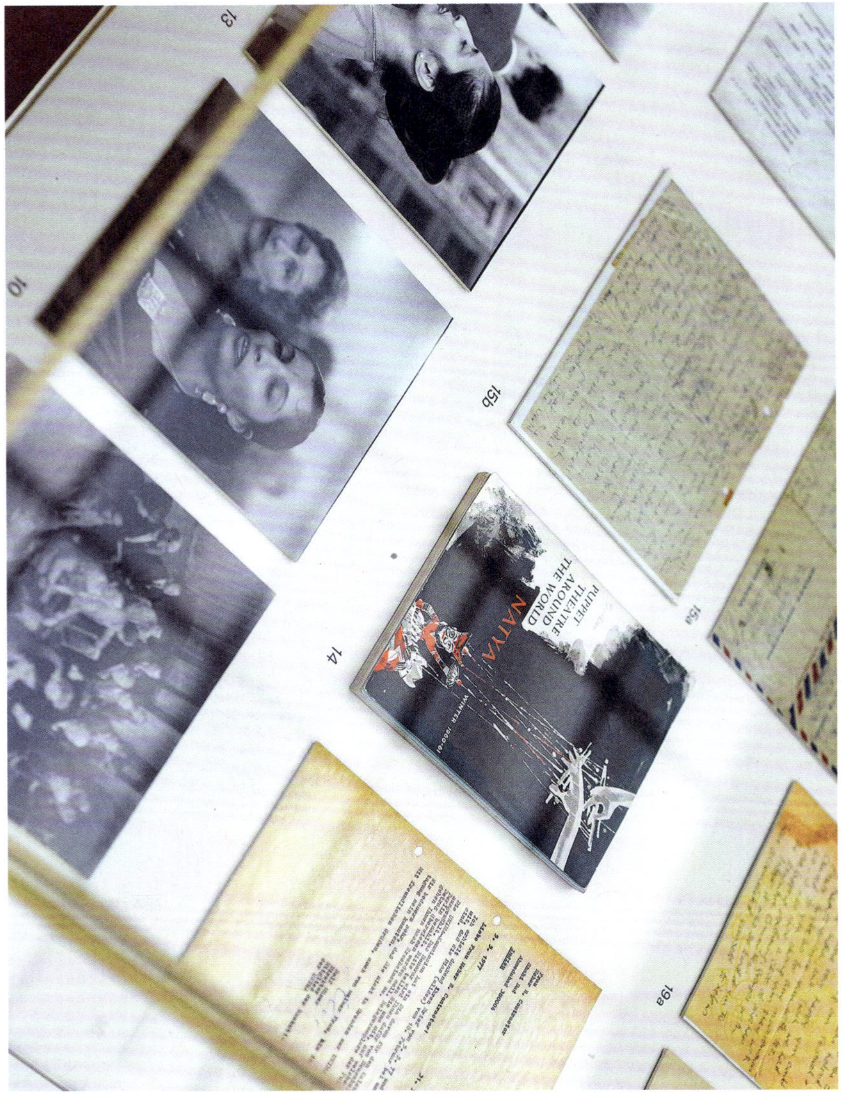
PUPPET
THEATRE
AROUND
THE WORLD
NATYA

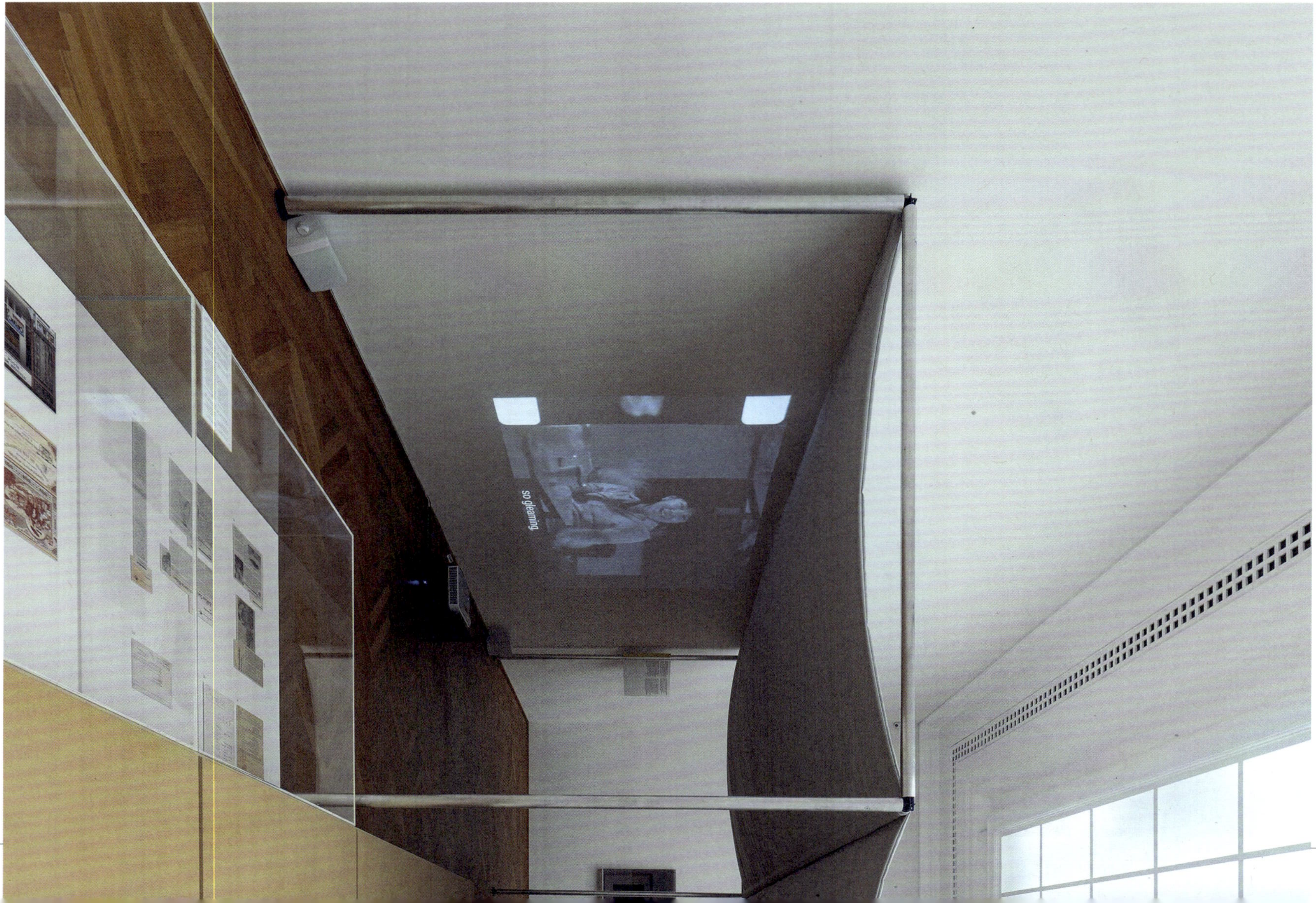

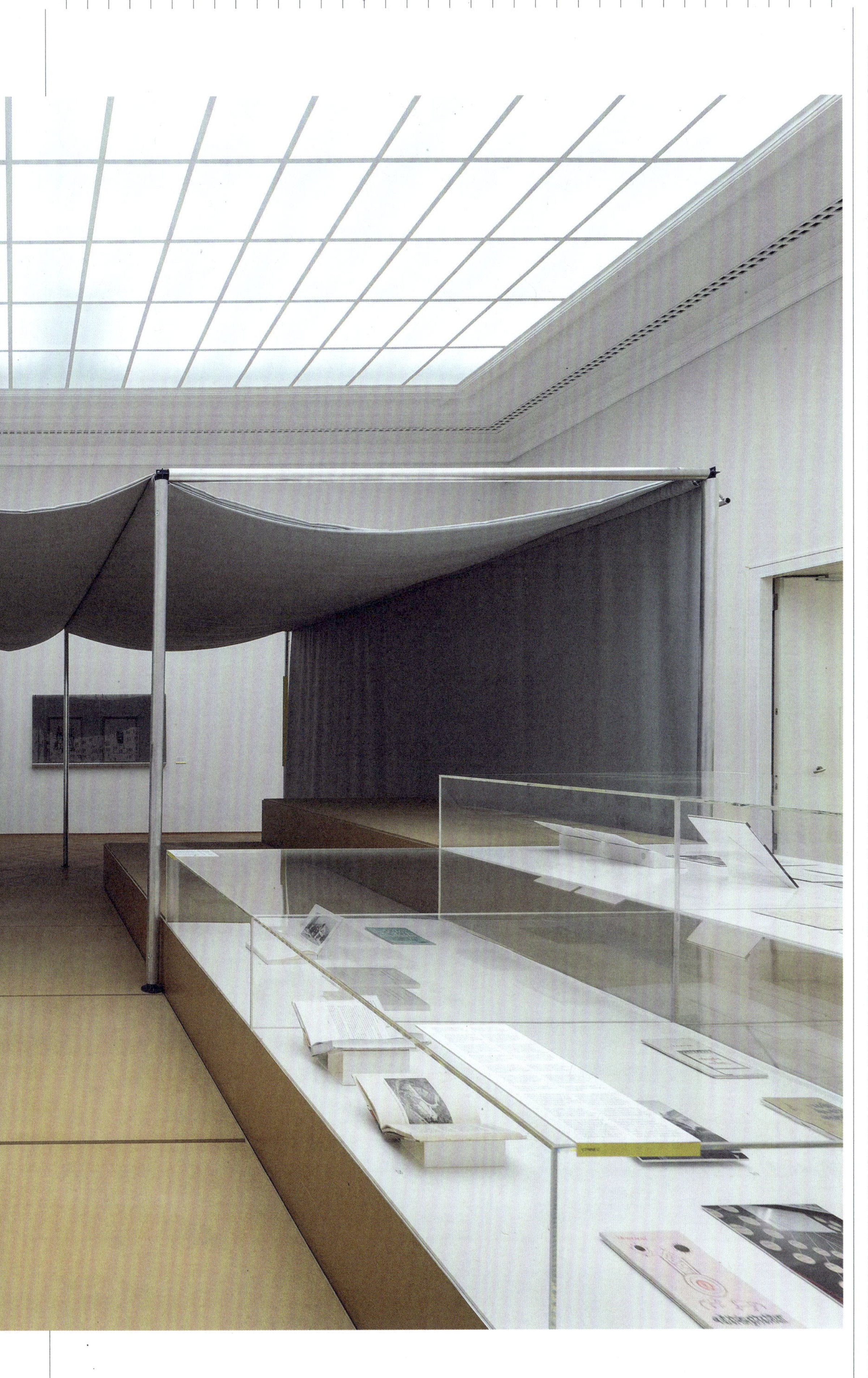

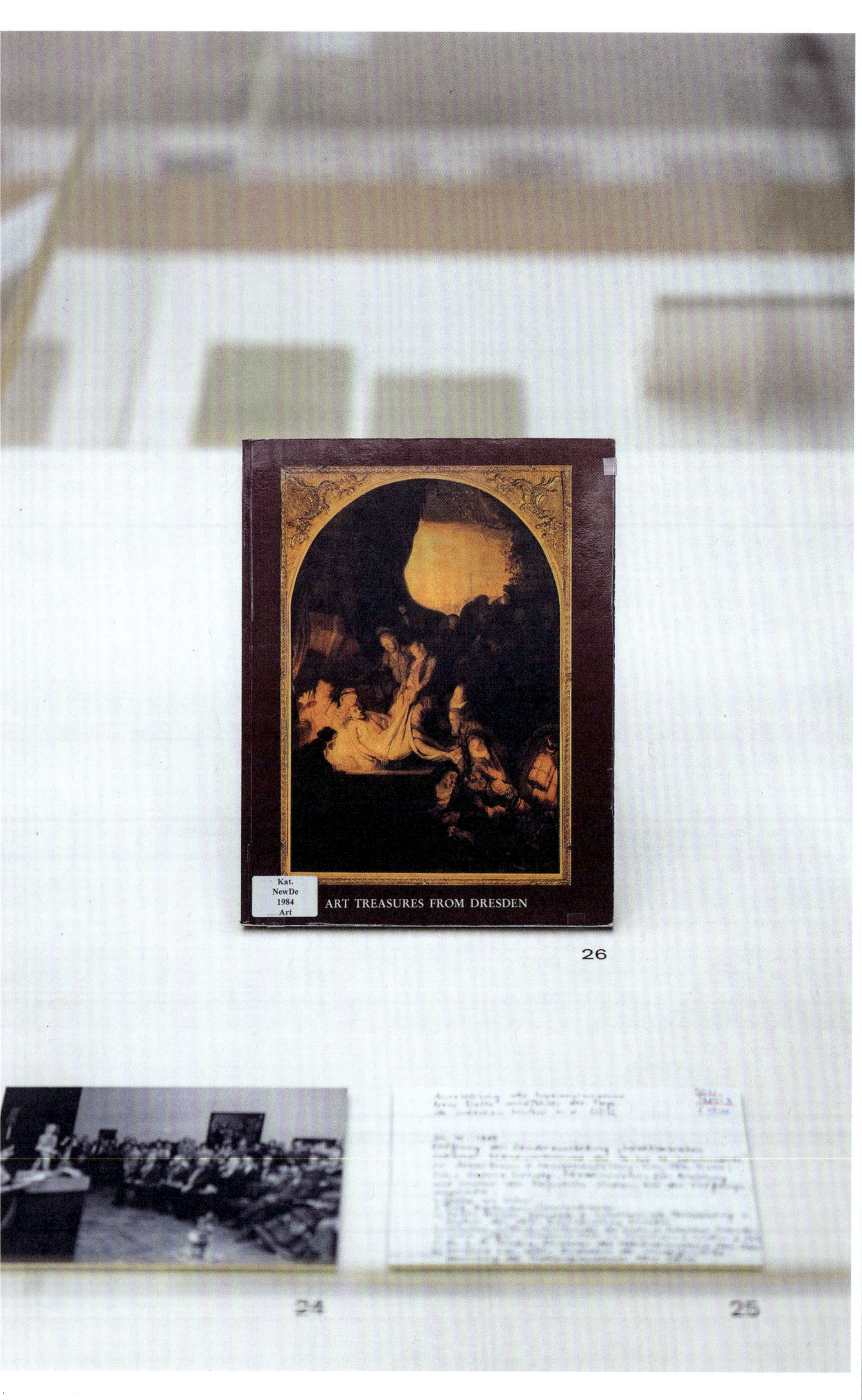
Kat.
NewDe
1984
Art
ART TREASURES FROM DRESDEN
26
24
25

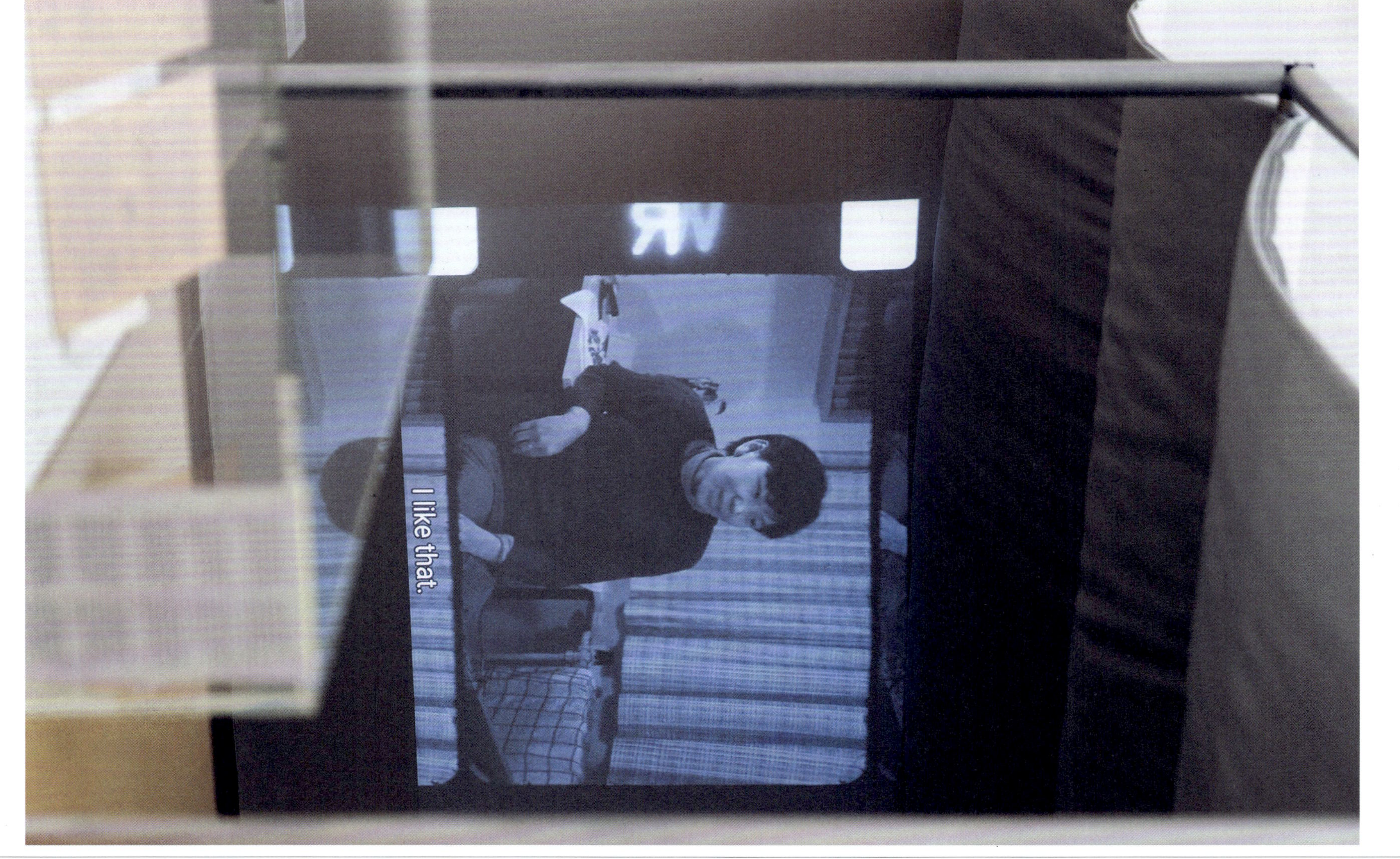
I like that.

THINKING WITH …

vinit agarwal

DENKEN MIT …

CARMEN MARIA BARBOSA É SA: A SEMANTIC CORRESPONDENCE

OYOYO portrays anti-colonial internationalism as a quasi-diplomatic encounter between students. *OYOYO* is filmed with various students, the majority of whom come from former Portuguese colonies like Guinea-Bissau. Apart from Bissau creole, South Korean, Spanish, and German, there are many visual and acoustic languages in the film that develop a multilayered semantics of this diplomatic encounter between them, sidelining the formal setting (or rather creating a new, cinematic setting). These semantics host Carmen. Carmen Maria Barbosa é Sa tells Chetna (and the viewers) about herself. Her initial period of study was in Portugal; she returned to Guinea-Bissau for three years and then came to the GDR to study medicine. She will eventually return, she says, to Guinea-Bissau. Chetna Vora returned to India in 1983 and died in 1987. In this encounter between Chetna and Carmen, the translation and diplomacy transcend the question of nation-states. This interview opens a fourth space beyond the bipolarity of the Cold

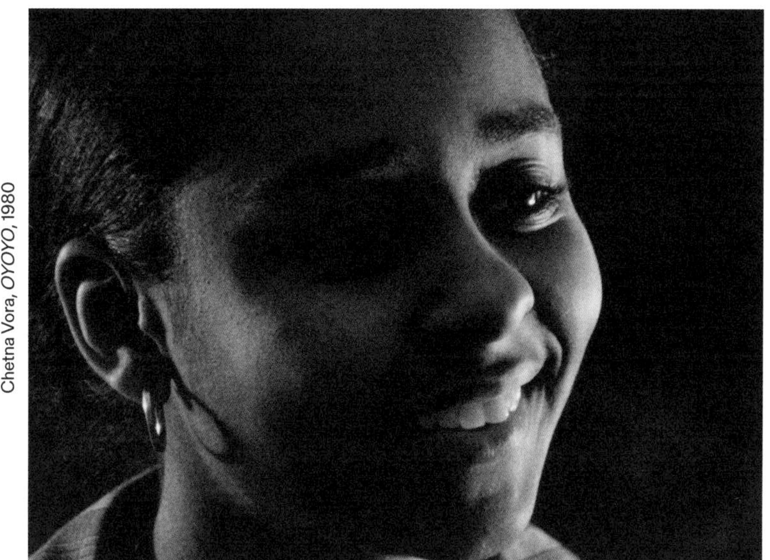

Chetna Vora, *OYOYO*, 1980

Chetna Vora, *OYOYO*, 1980

CARMEN MARIA BARBOSA É SA: EINE SEMANTISCHE ÜBEREINSTIMMUNG

Der Film *OYOYO* inszeniert den antikolonialen Internationalismus als gleichsam diplomatische Begegnung von Studierenden, die größtenteils aus ehemaligen portugiesischen Kolonien wie Guinea-Bissau stammten. Neben kreolisiertem Portugiesisch aus Bissau, Koreanisch, Spanisch und Deutsch sind in *OYOYO* noch zahlreiche Bild- und Klangsprachen eingegangen, die eine vielschichtige Semantik dieser anderen Art von Diplomatie unter den Beteiligten erschließen und den nominellen Ort des Geschehens um einen zweiten, filmischen Schauplatz ergänzen. Ebendiese Semantik bietet auch Carmen eine Bühne. Carmen Maria Barbosa é Sa erzählt Chetna (und uns Zuschauer·innen) von sich: Ihr Grundstudium absolvierte sie in Portugal. Danach kehrte sie zurück nach Guinea-Bissau und blieb dort drei Jahre, bevor sie in die DDR kam, um Medizin zu studieren. Danach, sagt sie, werde sie wieder nach Guinea-Bissau gehen. Chetna Vora kehrte 1983 zurück nach Indien und verließ unseren Planeten 1987. In diesem Gespräch zwischen Chetna und Carmen überwinden Übersetzung und Diplomatie das nationalstaatliche Denken. Das Interview öffnet einen vierten Raum jenseits der Bipolarität des

War and the postcolonial "Third World" shaped by developmental and trade/extraction politics. The interlocutors' everyday cohabitation in the GDR has opened up a possibility of radical politics.

What happened to Carmen on her return? Where is Carmen now? What became of her life and her desires within and outside of the "translation zone"? This search leads us to the question of the aftermath of translation as a diplomatic encounter. Various archival documents found during the period of research in Portugal and Bissau provide us with a utopian imagination of post-translation.

Kalten Krieges und der postkolonialen, von Entwicklungs- und Handels- bzw. Extraktionspolitik gezeichneten „Dritten Welt". Das Miteinander der beiden Dialogpartnerinnen im Alltag der DDR hat eine Möglichkeit radikaler Politik aufgetan.

Wie erging es Carmen nach ihrer Rückkehr in die Heimat? Wo ist Carmen jetzt? Was wurde aus ihrem Leben und ihren Sehnsüchten innerhalb und außerhalb der Sphäre der Übersetzung? Die Suche danach führt uns zur Frage nach dem, was von der Übersetzung als diplomatischer Begegnung bleibt. Archivdokumente, die uns während der Recherchephase des Projekts in Portugal und Bissau untergekommen sind, lassen vor unserem inneren Auge ein utopisches Jenseits der Übersetzung entstehen.

KARL ERICH MÜLLER: DRAWINGS IN INDIA

When we first visited the Museum of Prints, Drawings, and Photographs (Kupferstich-Kabinett) in the Dresden State Art Collections (Staatliche Kunstsammlungen Dresden, SKD), we were unaware of Karl Erich Müller's material presence in relation to India within the collection (as was the museum itself). However, as soon as we learned about these artworks, their presence became telling. In all, there were six of these works in the collection—five of them acquired after Müller's return from his visit to India and Sri Lanka in 1972. In the context of this research, it is important to recount that it is around this year that Chetna Vora might have first thought about studying in the GDR, a notion she got from the visits made by her father, Batuk Lal Vora. Each of these drawings and watercolor portraits is marked with titles and dates along with Müller's signatures—*Textilhändler* (Delhi, November 26, 1972), *Sauleler* (November 29, 1972) *Santhalfrau* (November 12, 1972), *Mahathera N. Jinaratana* (Kolkata, November 13, 1972), and a portrait of Indrani (Bombay, November 5, 1972). From the dates marked on the drawings, we can deduce that his itinerary in India must have taken him from the east coast (Kolkata) to the west coast (Mumbai), passing through Delhi.

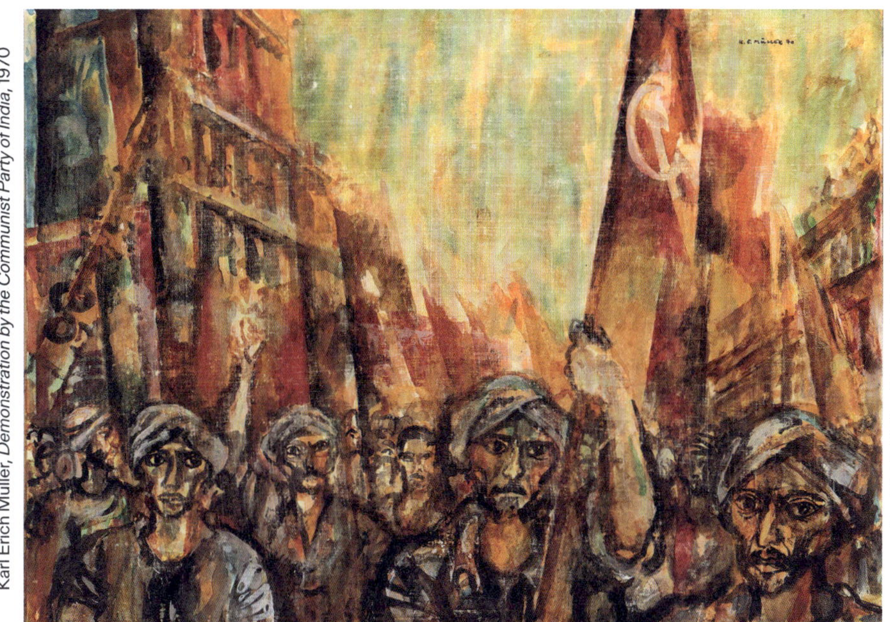

Karl Erich Müller, *Demonstration by the Communist Party of India*, 1970

Karl Erich Müller, *Demonstration der KP Indiens*, 1970

KARL ERICH MÜLLER: ZEICHNUNGEN AUS INDIEN

Als wir das Kupferstich-Kabinett der Staatlichen Kunstsammlungen Dresden zum ersten Mal besuchten, ahnten wir nicht, dass wir dort in den Hinterlassenschaften von Karl Erich Müller Indien begegnen würden (das Museum wusste es ebenso wenig). Kaum hatten wir aber seine Werke dort kennengelernt, sprachen sie für sich. Insgesamt gibt es sechs Arbeiten von Müller im Kupferstich-Kabinett – fünf davon angekauft nach seiner Rückkehr von einer Reise durch Indien und Sri Lanka 1972. Im Rahmen dieses Forschungsprojekts und im historischen Kontext ist der Hinweis wichtig, dass Chetna Vora im selben Jahr womöglich erstmals in Erwägung zog, in der DDR zu studieren, nachdem ihr Vater Batuk Lal Vora bereits mehrfach dorthin gereist war. Auf jeder Zeichnung und jedem Aquarell finden sich neben Karl Erich Müllers Signatur auch Titel und Datum: *Textilhändler* (Delhi, 26. November 1972), *Sauleler* (29. November 1972), *Santhal-Frau* (12. November 1972), *Mahathera N. Jinaratana* (Kolkata, 13. November 1972) und ein Porträt von Indrani (Bombay, 5. November 1972).

Aus den Daten auf den Zeichnungen ergibt sich, dass Müllers Reiseroute durch Indien von der Ostküste (Kolkata) über Delhi zur Westküste (Mumbai) führte.

The most impressive of them, a watercolor portrait depicting a scene of protest organized by Communist Party workers, is marked 1970 (it is not known when exactly this artwork was created). It thus predates the famous painting *Funerali di Togliatti* (1972) by Renato Guttuso which is currently on permanent display in the Museum of Modern Art (MAMBo) in Bologna, to which it has obvious visual links. There is a press clipping that identifies another very similar work as "'Die große Demonstration in New-Delhi,' 1976" (Great Demonstration in New Delhi), made during his fifth study trip to India. This oil painting by Karl Erich Müller was acquired for the 8th Dresden Art Fair, where it was exhibited (*Die große Demonstration in New-Delhi*, 1976, oil, 110 × 140 cm, in the collection of the District Council of Halle). It is distinguished from the first work by an ominous allegorical cloud hovering over the crowd.

The winner of various Indian prizes in exhibitions and competitions in the top art institutions of Delhi, Müller had a long involvement with the Indian subcontinent. Between 1966 and 1983, he made several trips to India, Sri Lanka,

Liberal-Demokratische Zeitung
Halle

22. Juni 1977

VIII. Kunstausstellung der DDR Dresden

Blickpunkt VIII. Kunstausstellung der DDR:

Engagement und Leistung

Ein Atelierbesuch bei dem halleschen Maler und Grafiker Nationalpreisträger Karl-Erich Müller / Erlebnis Indien

Neben reizvollen Originalen u. a. von Otto Müller und Albert Ebert sowie einer beachtlichen Menge eigener Werke des „Hausherrn" entdeckt der Besucher in den zwischen Nord-Süd-Magistrale und Naherholungsgebiet „Saaleaue" gelegenen Wohn- und Arbeitsräumen des im In- wie im Ausland geschätzten halleschen Malers und Grafikers NPT Karl-Erich Müller viele indische Reminiszenzen: wertvolle Holzschnitzereien zum Beispiel, das 1966 entstandene große Oelbild einer Inderin und in den langen Bücherreihen manche Publikation über den Subkontinent.

Schon vor elf Jahren vertrat der 1917 in Halle geborene Künstler zusammen mit Bert Heller und Willi Sitte die DDR anläßlich einer internationalen Ausstellung in Kalkutta, und seitdem ist der mittlerweile intim gewordene Kontakt zu dem einstigen Traumland nicht mehr abgerissen. Der anfängliche Touristenblick jedoch wich dem realen Verständnis für die sozialen Probleme und nationalen Eigenheiten Indiens. Davon zeugen u. a. 55 aus der unmittelbaren Impression heraus entstandene Steindrucke, die soeben erst fertiggestellt wurden und aus einer Serie von 200 Lithokreide-Skizzen stammen. Eine Reihe von kleinen Oelbildern setzt jetzt die Auswertung der jüngsten Reise von 1975 fort; Ausstellungen auch in den ebenfalls besuchten Ländern Nepal und Sri Lanka stehen bevor. Die Menschen und die Landschaften Indiens ziehen sich seit über zehn Jahren quasi wie ein roter Faden durch das reichhaltige malerische und grafische Werk Karl-Erich Müllers, der als Mitglied der Akademie der Künste der DDR inzwischen auch Mentor mehrerer Meisterschüler ist.

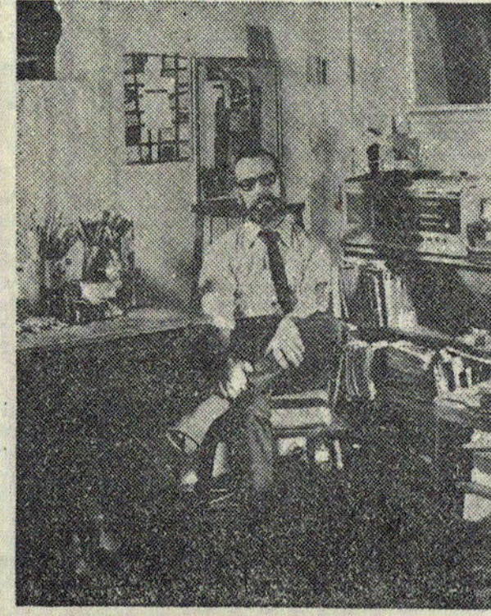

Der Künstler in seinem Atelier

Unter den fünf für die bevorstehende VIII. Dresdner Kunstausstellung eingereichten Arbeiten aus den letzten Schaffensjahren befindet sich – ebenfalls als Ergebnis der bereits fünften Studienreise nach Indien – die in hellen Farben gehaltene „Große Demonstration in New-Delhi" (1976). Das anerkannte bildkünstlerische Leistungsvermögen und zugleich das produktive gesellschaftliche Engagement Karl-Erich Müllers belegen auch die anderen vier Oelmalereien: Das „Porträt Otto Müller" ist ein neues, liebenswürdiges Dokument der jahrzehntelangen Freundschaft mit dem Senior der halleschen Maler und gleichzeitig der Verbundenheit des Künstlers mit der lebendigen, von ihm selbst wesentlich mitgeprägten Kunstszene in der Saalestadt. Hier studierte Müller von 1946 bis 1948 an der heutigen Hochschule für industrielle Formgestaltung Burg Giebichenstein, und der meist konstruktive, tektonisch strenge Bildaufbau verweist auf seinen namhaften Lehrer Prof. Erwin Hahs. Das wird vor allem an der – neben „Angola 1975" und „Venedig 1976" – ebenso für die „VIII." gedachten Arbeit „Im Förderkorb" deutlich. Es handelt sich dabei um die farblich besonders interessante Wiedergabe von Eindrücken während der Einfahrt in einen Schacht des Erzbergbaus von Kriwoi Rog. Die Studienreise in die UdSSR hatte 1974 das Mansfeld-Kombinat arrangiert.

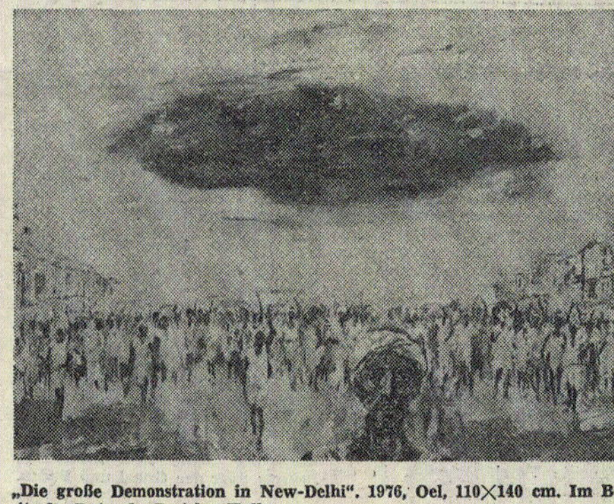

„Die große Demonstration in New-Delhi". 1976, Oel, 110×140 cm. Im Besitz des Rates des Bezirkes Halle.

Fotos (2): Danz

Karl-Erich Müller, der in seinem kleinen Atelier mit Freude, großer Gewissenhaftigkeit und zielgerichteter Kontinuität wirksam wird, sich sehr viel mit Literatur beschäftigt und auch schon mehrfach als Illustrator hervorgetreten ist, bezeichnet die sichtbar gewachsene individuelle Vielfalt unserer bildenden Kunst als eine wichtige Bereicherung. Er betont, daß „Engagement zum Kunstwerk führen, gültig werden und wiederum Engagement beim Betrachter auslösen" muß – er hat in entscheidendem Maße dazu beigetragen.

Dr. M. Frede

Press clipping about Karl Erich Müller with his work *The Great Demonstration in New Delhi*, 1979

Zeitungsartikel über Karl Erich Müller mit seinem Werk *Die große Demonstration in New-Delhi*, 1979

Besonders beeindruckend ist ein Aquarell, das eine Demonstration kommunistischer Arbeiter darstellt und auf das Jahr 1970 datiert ist (wann genau es entstanden ist, wissen wir nicht). Somit ist dieses Bild älter als Renato Guttusos berühmtes Gemälde *Funerali di Togliatti* aus dem Jahr 1972, das gegenwärtig in der Dauerausstellung des Museums für moderne Kunst in Bologna (MAMBo) zu sehen ist und unübersehbare Ähnlichkeiten mit Müllers Werk aufweist. Erhalten ist ein Zeitungsausschnitt, der eine weitere, sehr ähnliche Arbeit mit dem Titel *Die große Demonstration in New-Delhi* (1976) erwähnt. Diese entstand während Karl Erich Müllers fünfter Studienreise nach Indien. Das Ölgemälde wurde für die VIII. Kunstausstellung der DDR in Dresden angekauft und dort unter demselben Titel gezeigt (1976, Öl, 110 x 140 cm, Sammlung des Bezirksrats Halle). Es unterscheidet sich von der älteren Arbeit durch eine unheilvolle allegorische Wolke, die tief über der Menge hängt.

In Indien wurde Karl Erich Müller bei einer Reihe von Ausstellungen und Wettbewerben der wichtigsten Kunstinstitutionen in Delhi mit Preisen geehrt. Er pflegte über viele Jahre Beziehungen zum indischen Subkontinent. Zwischen 1966 und 1983 unternahm er mehrere Reisen nach Indien, Sri Lanka, Nepal und Pakistan,

Nepal, and Pakistan. Numerous pictures of the people and landscapes of South Asia were created there. In 1960, he was the first recipient of the Käthe Kollwitz Prize and later a member of the East German Academy of Arts. He died on January 10, 1998, in Halle.

Working through the archives of the SKD, we were able to find many documents that relate to his drawings from or about India, including acquisition papers, copies of press clippings, and letters from museum officials to Müller, along with his responses. Today, Müller's drawings are generally not exhibited because they are considered propaganda or "state art." Seen through the lens of transactions and personal relations, we can identify aspects of the "internationalisms" proposed by this research edition. These internationalisms are further highlighted by works like *Angola 1975* and *Algerische Mutter*, which were in the SKD's New Masters Gallery.

What is also notable here is a keen interest in workers' politics and the absence of an ethnographic gaze in Müller's drawings, which he produced long before the publication of Edward Said's *Orientalism*. This seminal work first ushered in a sensitization to the phenomenon of orientalism as a negative value in art and literature that was slow to take effect in the West. Müller's drawings are also free of romanticized workers' politics. Rather, Müller approaches his subjects as if they were members of his family. This acute kinship is visible in his close studies of faces, such as in the *Textilhändler* or even in *Santhalfrau*. This is a major reversal of a solidarity politics that is often called "brotherhood" by various authors on the subject (and referred to in these terms in the official speeches and documents themselves).[1] Müller's drawings are familiar and familial without any hierarchy. Their uncanniness withdraws from power politics to enter into an everyday encounter through an understanding of the "slow passage of time." There are no big scene setups here or any tragic or heroic grandeur. There is no seeking of the bizarre or an ulterior meaning. What can be seen instead is the slow routine of the everyday on its own terms, as if Bertolt Brecht were drawing (instead of doing theater), through his technique of alienation to combat immersion. What we are transferred to is not a feeling of "as if we were there"

1. In my opinion, Karl Erich Müller's work steers clear of the widespread criticism identifying the GDR's solidarity with the Afro-Asian liberation struggle as a form of Big Brother politics. There are many examples of this kind of writing, such as Bidyut Sagar Boruah's "Memorialising the GDR," which is important in its recounting of Indian musician Bhupen Hazarika's visit to the GDR. As Boruah writes, "However, while he or she can experience the constrained life of an individual in the GDR times, the visitor can also slip into the figure of the secret police agent. Thus, the terror-stricken experience[s] of the past are now transformed into the voyeuristic indulgence afforded by the late capitalist society's fluidity. In the make-believe world of the museum, Capital—instead of the totalitarian big brother—becomes the master figure."

wo zahlreiche Darstellungen der Menschen und Landschaften Südasiens entstanden. 1960 war er der erste Träger des Käthe-Kollwitz-Preises, später gehörte er der Akademie der Künste der DDR an. Karl Erich Müller starb am 10. Januar 1998 in Halle.

Bei der Suche im Archiv der SKD fanden wir mehrere Dokumente mit Bezug zu seinen Zeichnungen aus oder über Indien, darunter Kaufverträge, Kopien von Zeitungsausschnitten, Briefe von Museumsangestellten an Karl Erich Müller und dessen Antworten. Heute werden Müllers Zeichnungen kaum noch gezeigt, weil sie als Propaganda- oder „Staatskunst" gelten. Anhand dieser Geschäftsvorgänge und persönlichen Beziehungen zeigen sich jedoch Aspekte gerade jener „Internationalismen", denen diese Forschungsedition nachgeht. Sie kommen auch in anderen Werken von ihm wie *Angola 1975* oder *Algerische Mutter* zur Geltung, die in die Sammlung Neuer Meister der SKD eingegangen sind.

Auffällig ist Müllers großes Interesse an der Arbeiterbewegung und die Tatsache, dass in seinen Zeichnungen – lange vor dem Erscheinen von Edward Saids Buch *Orientalismus* – kein ethnografischer Blick zum Tragen kommt. Saids wegweisende Untersuchung hat für das Phänomen des Orientalismus als Abwertung in Kunst und Literatur sensibilisiert, doch es dauerte im Westen noch eine ganze Weile, bis diese Verschiebung des Blicks Wirkung zeigte. Müllers Zeichnungen sind ebenso frei von romantisierter Arbeiterpolitik. Stattdessen begegnet der Künstler den von ihm porträtierten Menschen, als handelte es sich um Familienmitglieder. Seine scharfsichtige Wahlverwandtschaft erweist sich in der genauen Beobachtung der Gesichter, etwa beim *Textilhändler* oder bei der *Santhal-Frau*. Spürbar wird eine grundsätzliche Abkehr von jener Politik der Solidarität, die sich von verschiedener Seite immer wieder als „Brüderlichkeit"[1] verklärt sah und so auch in offiziellen Reden und Unterlagen genannt wurde. Karl Erich Müllers Zeichnungen vermitteln Vertrautheit und Nähe ohne jedes hierarchische Gefälle. Ihre Unheimlichkeit hält sich von Machtpolitik fern und begibt sich auf das Terrain der Alltagsbegegnungen, ausgehend von der Wahrnehmung eines „langsamen Vergehens der Zeit". Es gibt hier weder bombastische Kulissen noch irgendeine tragische oder heroische Pracht, ebenso keinerlei Suche nach dem Grotesken oder einer eigentlichen Bedeutung. Was wir stattdessen zu sehen bekommen, ist die träge Routine des Alltags zu dessen eigenen Bedingungen, als würde Bertolt Brecht zeichnen (anstatt Theater zu machen) und seine Technik

1. Meiner Ansicht nach läuft die Kritik an der Solidarität der DDR mit den afrikanischen und asiatischen Befreiungskämpfen als ein Abgleiten in Big-Brother-Politik bei Müller ins Leere. Für diese Argumentationslinie gibt es viele Beispiele, selbst Bidyut Sagar Barouha (*Memorializing the GDR*), dem wir eine bemerkenswerte Darstellung einer Reise des indischen Musikers Bhupen Hazarika in die DDR verdanken, tappt genau in diese Falle, wenn er über das Berliner DDR-Museum schreibt: „Während man als Besucher oder Besucherin das beengte Leben des Einzelnen in DDR-Zeiten erleben kann, darf man auch in die Rolle eines Spitzels der Staatspolizei schlüpfen. Und so werden die Schreckenserlebnisse der Vergangenheit nunmehr in den voyeuristischen Genuss einer Fluidität verwandelt, wie sie die spätkapitalistische Gesellschaft bereithält. In der Scheinwelt des Museums schwingt sich das Kapital – anstelle des totalitären Großen Bruders – zum Herren auf."

but rather a functional understanding of "what has been happening there" and a long, delayed, unhurried, and broken encounter with "where will this person that you see in this portrait move next." One of the later news articles that includes Müller's photograph describes him as an artist who gets to the bottom of things with his keen eye (*Der Blick*, March 10/11, 1989). We can imagine this keen eye at work in his studio in Halle, in a low-rise building between Albert-Schweitzer-Straße and Fischer-von-Erlach-Straße. It was known as an artists' colony. The administration in the district capital, Halle, had created the studios and living space for progressive artists including Richard Horn, Herbert Lange, Helmut Schröder, and Meinoff Splett.

Then I also think of what Lars Barthel, partner of Chetna Vora, who directed the film *OYOYO*, told me in an interview, that he and Chetna "lived initially in artists' accommodation in East Berlin." These two artist's apartments in Halle and Berlin, though geographically distant, yet again allow us to think of affective relationships. The affective relationships with *OYOYO* are further highlighted in Müller's work, in *Sagarika Lacht* (1973), for example.

In the SKD archives, we find a letter addressed to Prof. Karl Erich Müller at his address in Halle, Mühlweg 24. The letter is dated June 14, 1972—two years after his return from India. Signed by Director Werner Schmidt's secretariat, it lists various items and mentions their prices. The second item on the list is a watercolor painting titled *Demonstration der Kommunistischen Partei Indiens*

Karl Erich Müller, *Inderin* (Indian Woman), Bombay, 1972
Karl Erich Müller, *Santhal-Frau* (Santhal Woman), 1972

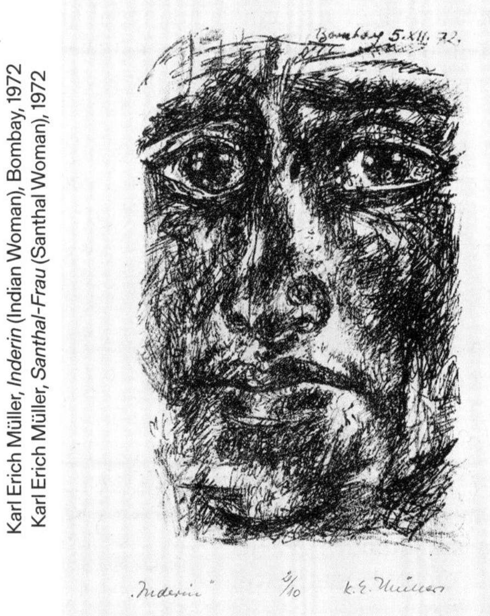

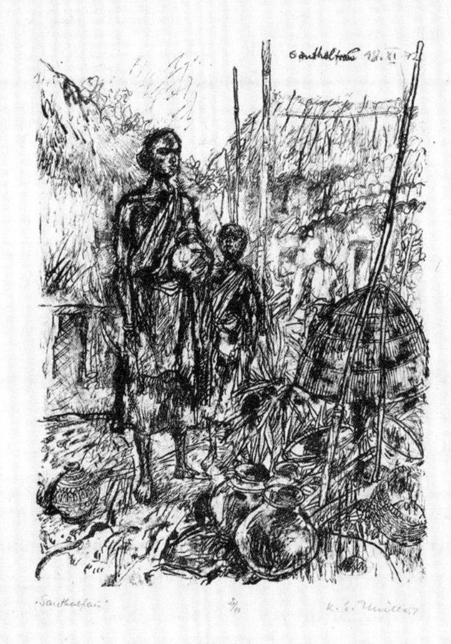

Karl Erich Müller, *Inderin*, Bombay, 1972
Karl Erich Müller, *Santhal-Frau*, 1972

der Verfremdung wider die Illusion anwenden. Uns wird nicht vermittelt, wir wären selbst dort; eher erleben wir ein funktionales Verständnis dessen, was dort geschieht, und eine lange, hinausgezögerte, von keiner Eile getriebene und gebrochene Begegnung mit der Vorstellung, wohin diesen Menschen, den man im Bild sieht, wohl als nächstes seine Schritte tragen. Ein Zeitungsartikel aus späterer Zeit beschreibt den auch im Foto abgebildeten Karl Erich Müller als Künstler, der den Dingen mit Scharfblick auf den Grund gehe (*Der Blick*, 10./11. März 1989). Wir können uns diesen Scharfblick gut bei der Arbeit in seinem Atelier in Halle vorstellen – in einem niedrigen Bau zwischen der Albert-Schweitzer-Straße und der Fischer-von-Erlach-Straße. Diese Gegend war als Künstlerkolonie bekannt. Die Verwaltung der Bezirkshauptstadt Halle hatte hier Ateliers und Wohnraum für fortschrittliche Künstler wie Richard Horn, Herbert Lange, Helmut Schröder und Meinolf Splett gebaut.

Dabei muss ich an etwas denken, das mir Lars Barthel, Lebensgefährte der *OYOYO*-Regisseurin Chetna Vora, in einem Gespräch erzählte: Chetna und er haben anfangs in Künstlerresidenzen in Ost-Berlin gewohnt. Die Künstlerwohnungen in Halle und Berlin waren räumlich weit voneinander entfernt, sie erlauben uns aber, eine affektive Nähe herzustellen. Werke von Karl Erich Müller wie *Sagarika lacht* (1973) verstärken diese Verbindung.

Im Archiv der SKD stießen wir auf ein Schreiben an Prof. Karl Erich Müller, Mühlweg 24, Halle 402, datierend vom 14. Juni 1972, zwei Jahre nach Müllers Rückkehr aus Indien. Der Brief trägt die Unterschrift des Sekretariats von Direktor Werner Schmidt und führt verschiedene Werke mit ihren jeweiligen Preisen an,

(Demonstration by the Communist Party of India), priced at 400 East German marks, and item number eight consists of six impressions with Indian depictions priced at 40 marks each—240 marks in total. Of the four drawings that were returned to Müller, *Indian Driver* stands out. The letter also mentions that while acquisition of these drawings will help them add to the existing collection of his work, they will not be able to "significantly expand" this collection. Director Werner Schmidt, who played a significant role in the Dresden art scene during the GDR era, organized a series of auctions at the Kupferstich-Kabinett from 1964 to 1979. These auctions were dedicated to contemporary fine art, not only from the GDR but also from abroad, with drawings, colored originals, prints of all kinds, paintings, and sculptures. In contrast to other auctioneers in the GDR, Schmidt also selected works by artists who had not submitted to the style of socialist realism, such as A. R. Penck. In this context, the acquisition of these works by Müller on the India–GDR axis take on a special significance. On June 20, 1974, Müller replied to this letter by expressing his agreement to the acquisition and requesting the return of his portfolio.

Müller's two most famous paintings are of the Indian poet Rabindranath Tagore (Müller's 1981 painting of Tagore in a pensive mood was famous) and Indira Gandhi (he painted her portrait in oil in 1985 as a tribute after her killing the previous year). Yet, we have accounts of various exhibitions in the galleries of Halle that displayed a great number of works from the subcontinent (in 1983,

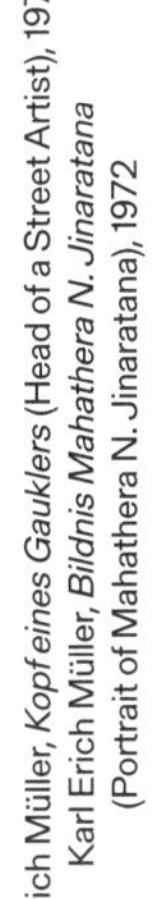
Karl Erich Müller, *Kopf eines Gauklers* (Head of a Street Artist), 1972
Karl Erich Müller, *Bildnis Mahathera N. Jinaratana* (Portrait of Mahathera N. Jinaratana), 1972

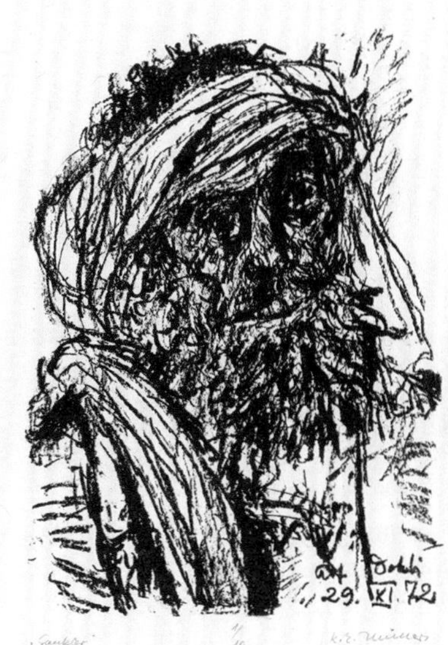

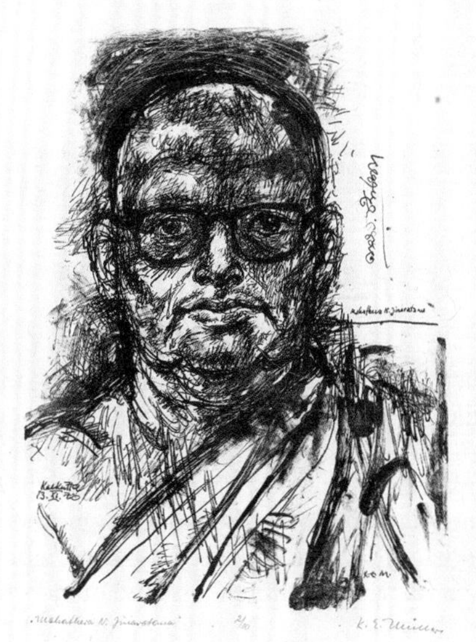

Karl Erich Müller, *Kopf eines Gauklers*, 1972
Karl Erich Müller, *Bildnis Mahathera N. Jinaratana*, 1972

darunter an zweiter Stelle ein Aquarell mit dem Titel *Demonstration der Kommunistischen Partei Indiens* für 400 DDR-Mark und an achter Stelle sechs Impressionen mit indischen Motiven zu je 40 Mark beziehungsweise 240 Mark insgesamt. Bemerkenswert unter vier weiteren Zeichnungen, die Karl Erich Müller zurückgegeben wurden, ist *Indischer Fahrer*. Der Brief erwähnt auch, dass der Ankauf der Zeichnungen den SKD zwar helfen werde, die bestehende Sammlung seiner Arbeiten zu ergänzen, eine „wesentliche Erweiterung" dieses Bestandes sei aber nicht möglich. Werner Schmidt, der im Dresdner Kunstgeschehen zuzeiten der DDR eine bedeutende Rolle spielte, organisierte von 1964 bis 1979 im Kupferstich-Kabinett mehrere Auktionen von Werken zeitgenössischer bildender Kunst insbesondere aus der DDR, aber auch aus anderen Ländern. Zeichnungen, farbige Originale, alle Arten von Drucken, Gemälde und Plastiken wurden angeboten. Im Gegensatz zu anderen Versteigerern in der DDR wählte Schmidt dafür auch Werke von Künstlern wie A. R. Penck aus, die sich nicht dem Stildiktat des Sozialistischen Realismus unterwarfen. In diesem Kontext wie auch in jenem der Achse Indien – DDR nehmen die Ankäufe dieser Arbeiten von Karl Erich Müller eine besondere Bedeutung an. Am 20. Juni 1974 antwortete dieser auf den Brief, stimmte dem Ankauf zu und bat um die Rückgabe seiner Mappe.

Die beiden bekanntesten Gemälde von Karl Erich Müller sind Porträts von Rabindranath Tagore (seine Darstellung des in Gedanken versunkenen indischen Dichters aus dem Jahr 1981 erlangte einige Berühmtheit) und Indira Gandhi (ein Ölbild von 1985, entstanden als Huldigung ein Jahr nach ihrer Ermordung). Wir wissen darüber hinaus von mehreren Ausstellungen in Hallenser Galerien mit

two galleries in Halle exhibited eighty of Müller's works from South Asia). His subjects included rice farmers and workers, eschewing the exotic in favor of a complex social and humanistic image. It is also important to highlight here that Müller was sensitive to the differences and continuities as he traveled between Nepal, Pakistan, India, and Sri Lanka. It is hard to find generalities in his distinct impressions of Nepal and India, for example. Averse to romanticism, he emphasized signs of social rebellion against the caste system in his works—for example, in his depictions of themes like monsoon rain or funeral processions.

einer großen Zahl von Werken aus dem Subkontinent (1983 zeigten zwei Galerien in Halle 80 Arbeiten von Müller aus Südasien). Unter den Porträtierten waren Reisbauern und -bäuerinnen und Arbeiter·innen, wobei Müller auch hier auf alles Exotische verzichtete und zu gesellschaftlich komplexen und humanistischen Darstellungen gelangte. Insbesondere zeigte er sich auf seinen Reisen durch Nepal, Pakistan, Indien und Sri Lanka gleichermaßen empfindsam für Unterschiede wie für Kontinuitäten. Es finden sich kaum Allgemeinplätze in seinen markanten Eindrücken aus Nepal und Indien. Er war jeder Romantik abhold und betonte auch bei Motiven wie dem Monsun oder den Bestattungsritualen Spuren eines Aufbegehrens gegen das Kastensystem.

MEHER RUSTOM CONTRACTOR AND ROLF MÄSER: LETTERS AND PHOTOGRAPHS

The online database of the International Puppetry Association (UNIMA) provides the following introduction to the life and work of Meher Rustom Contractor written by one of her students, Dadi D. Pudumjee: "Meher Contractor (known as Meherbehn [or Meher Behn]) was a major figure in Indian puppetry arts, recognized as much for her creative work (an abstract style as opposed to the epic realism influenced by Sergei Obraztsov then adopted in India) as for her contribution to the development of puppetry in education. Trained in London, Meher Contractor was a painter, book illustrator, and fashion designer before turning her hand to puppetry in 1952. In 1958, she undertook a study tour to various schools in Czechoslovakia, where puppetry was used in education. In the same year, she participated in and represented India at the 6th UNIMA Congress and 1st International Festival of Puppet Theaters held in Bucharest, where Marjorie Batchelder McPharlin (United States) encouraged her to continue in her chosen field."[1]

It is telling that the senior conservator of the collection, Lars Rebehn, found a photograph of her in the Puppet Theatre Collection at the Dresden State Art Collections (Staatliche Kunstsammlungen Dresden, SKD) that shows her sitting next to Batchelder and Max Jacob. This photograph, like others we found in the SKD collection, was taken by Carl Schröder, who was himself a puppeteer.[2]

"Meher Contractor became a teacher of the plastic arts at the Shreyas Foundation School in Ahmedabad, Gujarat, where she began using the puppet

1. Dadi Pudumjee, "Meher Rustom Contractor," World Encyclopedia of Puppetry Arts, UNIMA, https://wepa.unima.org/en/meher-rustom-contractor/, accessed February 17, 2025. Pudumjee is one of Meher Contractor's master students and her long-time associate. He was a guest student under Michael Meschke at the Marionette Theatre Institute in Stockholm, where he also participated in workshops run by Minosuke Yoshida of the National Bunraku Theatre in Osaka, Japan. Pudumjee is founder of the cross-cultural company, the Ishara Puppet Theatre Trust (New Delhi), where he works as director, designer, and puppeteer, collaborating with puppeteers, actors, and dancers, both traditional and modern.

2. It is important to thank Lars Rebehn here, whose collaboration and meticulous archiving efforts gave us access to these documents—Rebehn made the following note on this photograph: "Von Puppen und Menschen: Porträtfotos von Carl Schröder," *Dresdener Kunstblätter* 66, no. 4 (2022): 26–35.

MEHER RUSTOM CONTRACTOR UND ROLF MÄSER: BRIEFE UND FOTOGRAFIEN

In der Online-Datenbank der Union Internationale de la Marionette (UNIMA)[1] wird Meher Rustom Contractor von Dadi D. Pudumjee, einem ihrer Schüler, wie folgt vorgestellt: „Meher Rustom Contractor (genannt Meher Behn) war eine bedeutende Vertreterin des indischen Puppentheaters. Ihr Renommee verdankte sie sowohl ihrer künstlerischen Arbeit (deren abstrakter Stil in klarem Kontrast stand zu dem von Sergei Obraszow geprägten, in Indien damals tonangebenden epischen Realismus) als auch ihrem Beitrag zum Einsatz des Puppentheaters in Schulen. Meher Contractor studierte in London Malerei, Buchillustration und Modedesign, bevor sie sich 1952 dem Puppentheater zuwandte. 1958 unternahm sie eine Studienreise zu verschiedenen Schulen in der Tschechoslowakei, an denen Puppentheater im Unterricht genutzt wurde. Im selben Jahr vertrat sie Indien beim 6. UNIMA-Kongress und 1. Internationalen Festival des Puppentheaters in Bukarest, wo die US-Amerikanerin Marjorie Batchelder McPharlin sie ermutigte, den eingeschlagenen Weg weiterzugehen."

Dass wir ein Foto von Meher Contractor in der Puppentheatersammlung der SKD gefunden haben, spricht für sich. Es zeigt sie in Gesellschaft von Marjorie Batchelder und Max Jacob. Ein großer Dank gebührt an dieser Stelle Lars Rebehn für seine gewissenhafte Sammlung und Archivierung solcher Dokumente, ohne die sie uns heute nicht mehr zugänglich wären. Wie andere Fotos in der Sammlung der SKD stammten auch diese von Carl Schröder, der selbst Puppenspieler war.[2]

„Meher Contractor wurde Dozentin für Bildhauerei an der Shreyas Foundation School in Ahmedabad, Gujarat, Indien, wo sie Puppen zu Lehrzwecken einsetzte. Sie brachte Kindern bei, Puppen aus allen möglichen Materialien zu

1. Vgl. https://wepa.unima.org/en/meher-rustom-contractor; Pudumjee war Meisterschüler von Meher Contractor und hat lange mit ihr zusammengearbeitet. Er war auch Gaststudent am Marionettentheater in Stockholm bei Michael Meschke und hat dort an Workshops von Minosuke Yoshida (National Bunraku Theatre, Osaka) teilgenommen. Pudumjee ist Gründer des interkulturellen Ishara Puppet Theatre Trust in Neu-Delhi, das er leitet und in dem er als Gestalter und Puppenspieler tätig ist – in Zusammenarbeit mit traditionellen wie modernen Puppenspieler·innen, Schauspieler·innen, Tänzer·innen.

2. Zu diesem Foto gibt es eine Anmerkung von Lars Rebehn in „Von Puppen und Menschen. Porträtfotos von Carl Schröder", in: *Dresdner Kunstblätter*, 66, 2022, Nr. 4, S. 26–35.

3. Pudumjee, "Meher Rustom Contractor."

figure for educational purposes. She taught children how to make puppets from all kinds of materials (shoes, boxes, paper bags, and other waste materials) that could easily be manipulated and worked with by the children. She headed the puppetry section at the Darpana Academy of Performing Arts in Ahmedabad, where she trained several contemporary Indian puppeteers, including Shri Mahipat Kavi, Bela Shodhan, and Mansingh Zala, from Ahmedabad, Dadi Pudumjee, from Delhi, and Ratnamala Nori, from Hyderabad. In addition to her contribution as a pedagogue, she made her mark with her work with shadow theater in the Andhra Pradesh style (*tolu bommalata* [dance of leather puppets]), in her productions *Ramayana* and *Shah-Nama* (The Book of Kings), as well as with her rod puppet creations."[3]

Her *tolu bommalata* gained internationalist popularity in the Eastern Bloc, at the same time as Rolf Mäser's collection became famous in India. As a testimony to this, we find a note from May 21, 1979, in the Puppet Theatre Collection of the SKD, in which the famous M. V. Ramana Murty requests an invitation and a collection of *Tholu bommalata*, sending a catalog of his troupe and the puppets they make (the note is typed over the catalog):

"Our Troupe of Three Puppeteers was invited to the International Puppet Festival at Charleville-Mezieres (France) which was held from 28.9. till 4.10.1979. We started here on 26.9.1979. Kindly explore the possibilities of

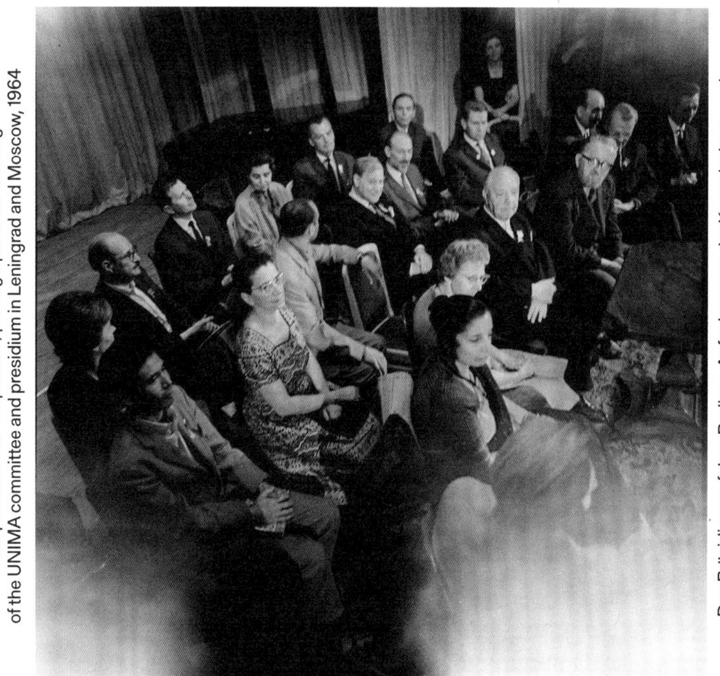

The presidium on the podium, photograph of the meeting of the UNIMA committee and presidium in Leningrad and Moscow, 1964

Das Präsidium auf dem Podium, Aufnahme von der Kommissions- und Präsidiumssitzung der UNIMA in Leningrad und Moskau, 1964

basteln (Schuhen, Schachteln, Papiertüten und anderen Abfallprodukten), die sich leicht umgestalten und von den Kindern verwenden ließen. Sie leitete die Abteilung Puppenspiel an der Darpana Academy of Performing Arts in Ahmedabad, wo sie mehrere zeitgenössische indische Puppenspieler ausbildete, darunter Shri Mahipat Kavi, Bela Shodhan und Mansingh Zala aus Ahmedabad, Dadi Pudumjee aus Delhi und Ratnamala Nori aus Hyderabad. Neben ihrer pädagogischen Tätigkeit machte Contractor auch durch ihre künstlerische Arbeit mit dem Schattentheater im Stil von Andhra Pradesh (Tholu bommalata, „Tanz der Lederpuppen") von sich reden, ebenso mit den Produktionen *Ramayana* und *Shah-Nama* (Buch der Könige) und mit ihren selbst gestalteten Stabpuppen."[3]

Ihr Schattentheater erlangte einige Berühmtheit in der internationalistischen Welt des Ostblocks. In dieser Zeit drang auch der Ruf von Rolf Mäsers Sammeltätigkeit bis nach Indien. Das bezeugt eine Notiz vom 21. Mai 1979, auf die wir im hauseigenen Archiv der Puppentheatersammlung der SKD gestoßen sind. Darin bittet der berühmte M. V. Ramana Murty um eine Einladung und um die Aufnahme von Tholu bommalata in das Museumsarchiv, indem er eine Publikation zu seiner Truppe und ihrem Puppenspiel übersandte (seine Mitteilung ist direkt auf die Publikation getippt): „Unsere Truppe von drei Puppenspielern wurde zum Internationalen Puppentheaterfestival in Charleville-Mézières (Frankreich) eingeladen, das vom 28.9. bis zum 4.10.1979 stattfindet. Wir reisen hier am 26.9.1979 ab. Bitte prüfen Sie die Möglichkeit, unsere Truppe nach dem Ende des französischen Festivals in Ihr Museum einzuladen. Mit Dank und der Hoffnung, bald

3. https://wepa.unima.org/en/meher-rustom-contractor

inviting our troupe to your museum after the French festival is over. Thanking you and hoping to read you soon."

This comes with a footnote (handwritten): "I understand that you are holding a great collection of puppets."[4] I introduce this note here because it is probably important to understand that the collection politics in the GDR were quite different from those in the West. The focus was not on the object as a fetish or the object's age but rather on its function. On September 20, 2023, during my research trip to Dresden, Lars Rebehn recounted an important story relating to this, which should form part of this oral history. He said, "There was once a delegation during the GDR era who were to be given a gift in return, and an important puppet was given to them without ascertaining that there was a copy."

"In her book, *Various Types of Traditional Puppets of India* (1968), Meher Contractor brought together important documents on the various traditions of Indian rod, string, and glove puppets and shadow theaters of India. She is also the author of works on puppetry and education (*Creative Drama in Education*, 1984)."[5]

In her important research paper, "Trends in World Puppetry," Meher Contractor adds an important note that should prompt us, in this context, to sense the internationalism in her work. She writes: "Recollections from the 1976 festivals in Bielsko-Biała in Poland and in Moscow at the 12th UNIMA Congress and festival reveal that the general trend in Puppetry is that the manipulators remain in full view with sometimes masked actors. Often this worked out wonderfully but more often it robbed much from the puppet characters, who merely appeared like props. Another trend was the huge size of puppets used by some troupes."[6] Further on, she comments on the performances from each of the countries, such as Uzbekistan or Sweden, and their internationalist reading.

"Very active in UNIMA, in which she set up the Indian chapter, UNIMA India, in 1985, and the Asia-Pacific Commission, Meher Contractor played a key role in the cultural exposure of the puppetry arts both in her own country and abroad. In 1983, Meher Rustom Contractor was given the prestigious Sangeet Natak Akademi Award for her contribution to Puppetry. She was nominated UNIMA Member of Honour in 1992 at the UNIMA Congress in Ljubljana, Slovenia."[7]

4. Document from the archives of the Puppet Theatre Collection, Staatliche Kunstsammlungen Dresden.

5. Pudumjee, "Meher Rustom Contractor."

von Ihnen zu lesen." Darunter eine (handgeschriebene) Fußnote: „Wenn ich richtig informiert bin, besitzen Sie eine hervorragende Sammlung von Puppen."[4]

Ich erwähne diese Notiz hier, weil sie verdeutlicht, dass sich die Sammlungspraxis der DDR sehr von jener im Westen unterschied. In ihrem Mittelpunkt stand nicht das Objekt als Fetisch oder die Zeit des Objekts, sondern dessen Funktion. Lars Rebehn erzählte mir am 20. September 2023 während meines Forschungsaufenthalts in Dresden diesbezüglich eine vielsagende Anekdote, die es verdient, in die Überlieferung einzugehen: „In DDR-Zeiten kam einmal eine wichtige Delegation auf Besuch", sagte er, „die eine Gegengabe erhalten sollte. Und so überreichte man ihr eine bedeutende Puppe, ohne überhaupt zu prüfen, ob es eine Kopie davon gab."

„In ihrem Buch *Various Types of Traditional Puppets of India* (1968) hat Meher Contractor Schlüsseldokumente zu den verschiedenen indischen Traditionen von Stab-, Faden- und Handschuhpuppen sowie Schattentheater mit Puppen zusammengetragen. Sie hat außerdem Texte zum Puppenspiel in der Bildungsarbeit veröffentlicht (*Creative Drama in Education*, 1984)."[5]

In ihrem grundlegenden Aufsatz *Trends in World Puppetry* aus dem Jahr 1977, veröffentlicht von der Sangeet Natak Akademi in Neu-Delhi, findet sich eine Bemerkung, die einen Eindruck vermittelt, welche Bedeutung der Internationalismus für ihre Arbeit hatte: „In der Rückschau auf die Festivals von Bielsko-Biała in Polen sowie anlässlich des 12. UNIMA-Kongresses auch in Moskau wird die allgemeine Tendenz im Puppenspiel deutlich, dass die Spieler sichtbar auftreten, wobei sie gelegentlich Masken tragen", schreibt sie. „Oft funktionierte das wunderbar, aber noch öfter nahm es den Puppencharakteren viel von ihrer Wirkung, da sie nur mehr wie Requisiten erschienen. Eine weitere Tendenz war die enorme Größe der Puppen bei einigen Theatern."[6] In der Folge kommentiert sie die Aufführungen jedes teilnehmenden Landes, darunter Usbekistan oder auch Schweden, und bietet eine internationalistische Deutung dazu an.

„Meher Contractor war in der UNIMA sehr aktiv. Sie gründete 1985 die indische Sektion UNIMA India und die Asia-Pacific Commission, außerdem setzte sie sich an vorderster Stelle für die kulturelle Präsenz des Puppenspiels in ihrem eigenen Land und andernorts ein. 1983 erhielt sie für ihre Beiträge zum Puppentheater den renommierten Sangeet Natak Adademi Award. Auf dem 16. Kongress der UNIMA im slowenischen Ljubljana wurde sie zum Ehrenmitglied ernannt."[7]

4. Dokument aus dem Archiv der Puppentheatersammlung, Staatliche Kunstsammlungen Dresden

5. https://wepa.unima.org/en/meher-rustom-contractor

There are traces of in-depth communication over an extended period between Rolf Mäser, the director of the Department of Puppet Theatre Arts at the SKD, and Meher Contractor during the GDR period (at that time, she lived mostly in Ahmedabad, the same state where Chetna and her parents lived and where they had friendships and collaborations through the Darpana Academy of Performing Arts). We found a rare extant copy of the Winter 1960–61 issue of the journal *NATYA,* published by Bhartiya Natya Sangh (Indian People's Theatre Association) under the editorship of Devraj Vadera, that was signed and sent to the collection by Meher Contractor.[8] This issue was important in the sense that it showed the struggles involved (the issue was delayed) and the commitment to publishing such a journal, which was made possible through ongoing collaborations with puppet theaters in the Eastern Bloc. Meher Contractor herself signed this journal, "To [my] dear friend Max Jacob with every good wish from Meher Contractor."[9] We can immediately sense a "politics of friendship" that adds on a layer of internationalism, as we intend to highlight in this research edition. This contribution of Meher Contractor to establishing an internationalism of puppet theater practices and their modern adaptation in the Eastern Bloc was not momentary but one of numerous such instances over the course of almost three decades. Around twenty-seven years after that edition of *NATYA*, she sent another letter on June 24, 1987, this time from UNIMA-India in Ahmedabad.[10] She writes:

6. Meher R. Contractor, "Trends in World Puppetry," *Sangeet Natak* 43 (1977): 60.

7. Pudumjee, "Meher Rustom Contractor."

8. "Puppet Theatre Around the World," *NATYA: Theatre Arts Journal* 4, no. 4 (Winter 1960/61), Puppet Theatre Collection, Staatliche Kunstsammlungen Dresden, inv. no. 17118.

9. For more on Max Jacob, see p. 64.

10. Meher Rustom Contractor to Rolf Mäser, June 24, 1987, Puppet Theatre Collection, Staatliche Kunstsammlungen Dresden, C14191,8_1 / C14191,8_2.

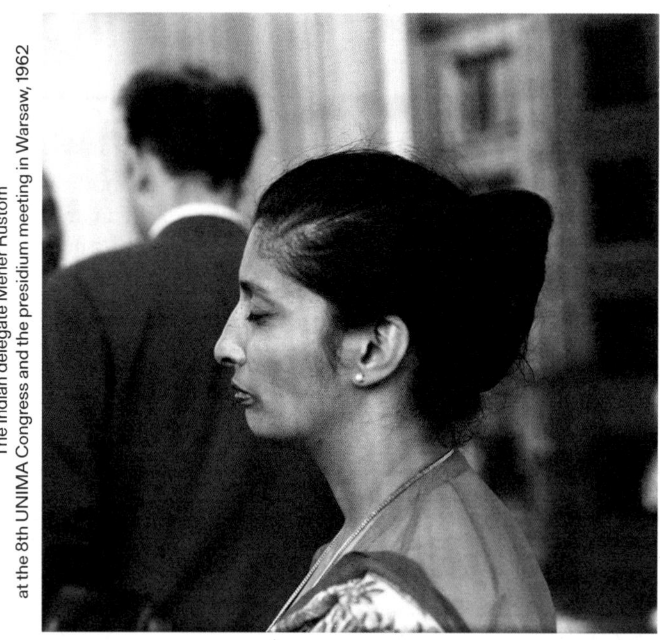

The Indian delegate Meher Rustom at the 8th UNIMA Congress and the presidium meeting in Warsaw, 1962

Die indische Delegierte Meher Rustom Contractor auf dem VIII. UNIMA-Kongress und der Präsidiumssitzung in Warschau, 1962

Aus DDR-Zeiten gibt es Spuren eines intensiven Kontakts zwischen der Abteilung Puppentheater in den Staatlichen Kunstsammlungen Dresden und Meher Contractor (Contractor lebte in dieser Zeit hauptsächlich in Ahmedabad im indischen Bundesstaat Gujarat, wo auch Chetna Vora und ihre Eltern ansässig waren, sie hatten gemeinsame Freunde und berufliche Verbindungen über die Darpana Academy of Performing Arts). Wir haben eines der wenigen noch erhaltenen Exemplare der vom indischen Volkstheaterverband Bharatiya Natya Sangh herausgegebenen Zeitschrift *NATYA* aus dem Winter 1960/61 gefunden, signiert und der Sammlung übermittelt von Meher Contractor.[8] Diese Ausgabe war insofern wichtig, als sie (schon durch ihr verspätetes Erscheinen) die mit dem Erscheinen eines derartigen Periodikums verbundenen Anstrengungen dokumentierte, das nur durch die anhaltende Zusammenarbeit mit Puppentheatern im Ostblock überhaupt möglich wurde. Meher Contractor signierte dieses Exemplar der Zeitschrift persönlich und mit einer Widmung an ihren „lieben Freund Max Jacob mit allen guten Wünschen von Meher Contractor".[9] Spürbar wird hier eine „Politik der Freundschaft", die den Internationalismen, um die es in diesem Band geht, eine weitere Ebene hinzufügte. Meher Contractor trug auch nicht nur sporadisch, sondern über fast 30 Jahre zur Entstehung eines Internationalismus der Puppentheatertraditionen und ihrer modernen Adaption im Ostblock bei.

Etwa 27 Jahre nach dieser Ausgabe von *NATYA* schickte sie einen weiteren Brief mit Datum vom 24. Juni 1987 nach Dresden,[10] diesmal als Vertreterin der indischen Sektion der UNIMA in Ahmedabad:

6. Meher R. Contractor, „Trends in World Puppetry", in: *Sangeet Natak* 43, 1977, S. 60–64, hier S. 60.

7. https://wepa.unima.org/en/meher-rustom-contractor

8. Bharatiya Natya Sangh und Som Benegal (Hg.): *NATYA. Theatre Arts Journal*, 4, Nr. 4, Winter 1960/61: „Puppet Theatre Around the World", SKD, Puppentheatersammlung, Inv.-Nr. 17118.

9. Zu Max Jacob siehe S. 64.

10. Briefwechsel Meher Rustom Contractor – Rolf Mäser. Brief vom 24.6.1987. SKD, Puppentheatersammlung. C14191,8_1 / C14191,8_2.

Dear Rolf,
Thank you very much for the 3 calanders [*sic*] received and your letter with the beautiful card. I will send the calanders to Mr Virmani and Dadi[,] who helped me a great deal during our Festival & meeting.
We were very happy you could come to India, but I wish we had the funds to invite your wife too. Please forgive us for any inconveniences caused to you during your stay with us—it was just a case of mishaps & overlapping performing groups with the Executive Committee.
In fact it was so kind of you to have accomodated [*sic*] yourself to help us out of an embarrassing position. Thank you very much for all your kindness.
About the shadow puppets—Rolf, I will try to send them with anyone going your side of to [*sic*] a UNIMA meeting, as we are not allowed to send leather puppets like that. But I shall remember in future. With my best regards to you & friends in [the] DDR & and your wife.
Sincerely
Meher Contractor

This letter sheds light on many things—not only the politics of friendship with the GDR, but also a profound lived practice of it. At the same time, it is also a historical document, as it highlights how Meher Contractor prepared a new generation of puppet theater artists and experts such as Dadi Pudumjee.[11] There is another long history of connection with Pudamjee and puppet theater in the GDR. In the archive, we find an image announcing a performance of *The Double Shadow*, or *Der doppelte Schatten*, as a collaboration with Gotthard Feustel, head dramaturge of Puppentheater Berlin. The correspondence with Rolf Mäser, director of the puppetry section at the SKD's Museum for Saxon Folk Art and member of UNIMA, stretches over many years and further underlines the profound impact of this friendship on the making of modern puppet theater in India today. As an urtext, we might identify the existence of a German translation of the original English catalog of the *Indian Theatre* exhibition of 1967. This exhibition was organized by the Ministry of Public Education of the Indian Government in New

11. See Claudia Orenstein, "Women in Indian Puppetry: Negotiating Traditional Roles and New Possibilities," *Asian Theatre Journal* 32, no. 2 (2015): 493–517, http://www.jstor.org/stable/24737042.

„Lieber Rolf,
herzlichen Dank für die drei Kalender, die wir erhalten haben, und Deinen Text mit der wunderschönen Karte. Ich werde die Kalender an Herrn Virmani und an Dadi schicken, die mir mit ihrer Teilnahme am Festival und an der Tagung einen großen Gefallen getan haben.
Wir haben uns sehr gefreut, dass Du nach Indien kommen konntest, ich wünschte nur, wir hätten die Mittel gehabt, auch Deine Frau einzuladen. Bitte verzeih allfällige Unannehmlichkeiten während Deines Aufenthalts bei uns – das waren einfach Missgeschicke und zeitliche Überschneidungen zwischen den Aufführungen einiger Gruppen und den Treffen des Exekutivkomitees.
Es war besonders zuvorkommend von Dir, eine eigene Unterkunft zu suchen, um uns aus einer peinlichen Lage herauszuhelfen. Vielen, vielen Dank für Deine Liebenswürdigkeit.
Was die Schattenpuppen angeht – Rolf, ich werde versuchen, sie jemandem mitzugeben, der ein UNIMA-Treffen bei Euch besucht, denn wir dürfen Lederpuppen nicht einfach so versenden. Aber wenn der Zeitpunkt kommt, denke ich daran. Mit den allerbesten Empfehlungen an Dich und Deine Freunde in der DDR & an Deine Frau.
Herzlich,
Meher Contractor"

Dieser Brief erhellt so manches – nicht nur die Politik der Freundschaft mit der DDR, sondern auch, wie sehr sie gepflegt und gelebt wurde. Er ist zugleich ein historisches Dokument und erzählt nebenbei davon, dass Meher Contractor eine neue Generation von Puppenspieler·innen und Wissenschaftler·innen ausbildete, darunter auch Dadi Pudumjee.[11] Auch Dadi Pudumjee verband eine langjährige Zusammenarbeit mit dem Puppentheater der DDR. Im Archiv finden wir dazu ein Bild, das die Aufführung *Der doppelte Schatten* als Gemeinschaftsproduktion mit Gotthard Feustel, dem Chefdramaturgen des Puppentheaters Berlin, ankündigt. Die Korrespondenz mit Rolf Mäser, dem Leiter der Puppenspielabteilung im damaligen Dresdner Volkskundemuseum und Mitglied des UNIMA-Exekutivkomitees, zog sich über viele Jahre und veranschaulicht die große Bedeutung dieser Freundschaft für die Geschichte des modernen Puppentheaters im heutigen Indien.

11. Vgl. Claudia Orenstein, „Women in Indian Puppetry: Negotiating Traditional Roles and New Possibilities", in: *Asian Theatre Journal*, 32, 2015, Nr. 2, S. 493–517, online: http://www.jstor.org/stable/24737042

Delhi. The exhibition was designed and organized by Ebrahim Alkazi and held at the National School of Drama and the Asian Theatre Institute of New Delhi. Alkazi was one of the founding figures of modern theater in India, the second and longest-serving director of the National School of Drama in New Delhi, and a connoisseur and collector of art. In Nehruvian India, his contribution to theater in particular and arts in general is immense.

Such presences among these archival materials denote a *longue durée*.

There is also an "affect note" sent by Meher R. Contractor on December 21, 1967, to Rolf Mäser. She writes:

> Dear Mr Maser and Mrs Maser [*sic*],
> This is just to say I have reached home safely and I meant to write & thank you for all your kindnesses from Panchgani in the hills where I was with my husband—but the earthquake we had upset us all & we were really terrified—but through God's grace we all were safe including my brothers' house where we were—though there was much damage in the town but only a crack and [the] falling of some plaster in our homes.
> I was indeed shocked to hear of Prof Max Jacob's demise & then to crown it I got news that Mrs Cora Baird of [the] U.S.A. also died. What a loss to us puppeteers! Max Jacob was such a fine person besides a puppeteer that the loss is for us all in the world of puppets besides his dear wife Marie.

This fragile letter written on an aerogram (lightweight postal stationery used for sending messages abroad at a preferential rate) is one of the most important examples of how a document can invoke a multilayered memory and gather archival traces. The earthquake recounted in the letter occurred in December 1967 less than 60 km from Panchgani, near the Koyna Dam, a large hydroelectric facility that had been constructed five years previously. It is connected to Panchgani by the Koyna River. The earthquake reached a magnitude of 6.3 on the Richter scale and claimed around two hundred lives. This testimony is of key importance in understanding the impact of anthropogenic activity on natural systems: in this case,

Als „Urtext" könnten wir den Fund einer deutschen Übersetzung des ursprünglich englischsprachigen Katalogs zur Ausstellung *Indian Theatre* von 1967 betrachten. Diese Ausstellung wurde vom indischen Bildungsministerium in Neu-Delhi organisiert und von Ebrahim Alkazi an der National School of Drama und dem Asian Theatre Institute in Neu-Delhi gestaltet. Alkazi war einer der Gründerväter des modernen Theaters in Indien, der zweite und am längsten amtierende Direktor der National School of Drama in Neu-Delhi sowie ein Kunstkenner und -sammler. Sein Beitrag zur Kunst allgemein und besonders zum Theater im Indien Nehrus war enorm.

Solche Funde im Archiv der Puppentheatersammlung der SKD zeichnen die Konturen einer longue durée.

Unter anderem findet sich dieser „Affektvermerk" von Meher Contractor an Rolf Mäser vom 21. Dezember 1967. Sie schreibt:

> „Lieber Herr und liebe Frau Maser [sic],
> nur kurz, um Ihnen mitzuteilen, dass ich wohlbehalten zu Hause angekommen bin. Mir lag daran, Ihnen zu schreiben und zu danken für Ihre Güte während meiner Zeit in Panchgani in den Bergen, wo ich mit meinem Mann gewesen bin, doch das Erdbeben hat uns alle sehr bekümmert & wir hatten schreckliche Angst – Gott sei Dank sind wir alle unversehrt, ebenso das Haus meiner Brüder, in dem wir wohnten – obwohl viele Schäden in der Stadt auftraten, nur ein Riss in der Mauer, und im Haus ist ein bisschen Putz runtergekommen.
> Ich war tief getroffen, als ich von Prof. Max Jacobs Ableben erfuhr & zu alldem kam noch, dass auch Frau Cora Baird in den USA verstorben ist. Was für ein Verlust für uns Puppenspieler! Max Jacob war ein so guter Mensch, ganz abgesehen von seinem Puppenspiel, wir alle in der Welt der Puppen werden ihn vermissen, ganz zu schweigen von seiner lieben Frau Marie."

Dieses Dokument der Zerbrechlichkeit, versandt als Aerogramm (auf sehr dünnem Luftpostpapier für Briefe ins Ausland zu geringerem Porto), ist eines der wichtigsten Beispiele dafür, wie ein Dokument zum Träger vielschichtiger Erinnerung und Archivspuren werden kann.[12] Das Epizentrum des Erdbebens im

12. Briefwechsel Meher Rustom Contractor – Rolf Mäser. SKD, Puppentheatersammlung. C 14191,1_1, C 14191,1_2.

12. This earthquake and the water reservoir are of key interest to researchers even today. Harsh K. Gupta of the CSIR-National Geophysical Research Institute, Hyderabad, Telangana, India, writes about this in his 2021 paper, "Koyna, India: A Very Prominent Site of Artificial Water Reservoir–Triggered Seismicity."

seismicity triggered by artificial water reservoirs.[12] It also draws attention to an active contest between the destructive mechanisms of modernity and indigenous practices. As Meher Contractor recounts in her letter, the earthquake fortunately did not cause any major damage. Yet, the reference to the earthquake is also key to understanding that the earth, the mountains, and the water are also connected and in play when we think of the politics of friendship between India and the GDR. This politics cannot be read in anthropocentric terms only, and a "leak" such as this letter helps to underline this.

Her mention of German puppet theater stalwart Max Jacob, who had been president of UNIMA since 1957, is also moving. Jacob is known for the "Kasperhaus" he had set up in the small town of Hohnstein in Saxony in the 1930s and the Hohnsteiner Theater he established in Hamburg after the war. He died in 1967. That Meher Contractor should take note of the passing of a German puppet theater director illustrates how closely related UNIMA chapters were at this time and how they contributed to progress. The picture in the SKD archive taken in Leningrad in 1964, just three years before the death of Max Jacob, captures one last occasion when all of the world's major puppet theater directors appeared together. Among them was Cora Baird, the famous Jewish puppeteer from America who also died in 1967 and is remembered by Meher Contractor in the same letter. Baird had

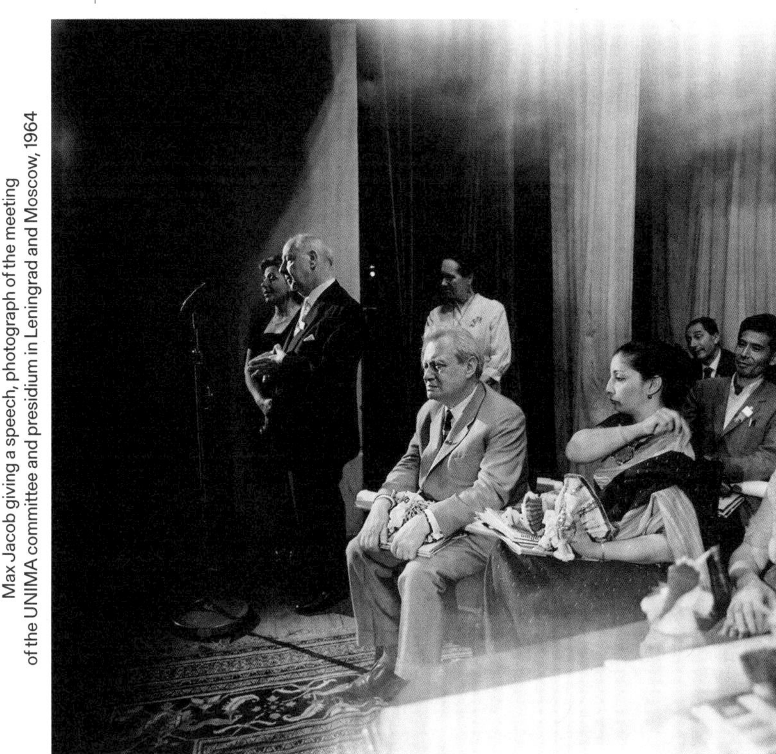

Max Jacob giving a speech, photograph of the meeting of the UNIMA committee and presidium in Leningrad and Moscow, 1964

Max Jacob hält eine Ansprache, Aufnahme von der Kommissions- und Präsidiumssitzung der UNIMA in Leningrad und Moskau, 1964

Dezember 1967, von dem im Brief die Rede ist, befand sich keine 60 Kilometer von Panchgani entfernt in der Nähe eines erst fünf Jahre zuvor erbauten großen Wasserkraftwerks. Der Fluss Koyna verbindet Panchgani mit der Talsperre. Das Erdbeben erreichte eine Stärke von 6,3 auf der Richter-Skala und forderte rund 200 Menschenleben. Dieser Bericht vermittelt eindringlich die Auswirkungen anthropogener Veränderungen auf natürliche Systeme; in diesem Fall wurden die seismischen Erschütterungen durch künstliche Staubecken ausgelöst.[13] In den Blick gerät so der scharfe Konflikt zwischen den destruktiven Mechanismen der Moderne und indigenen Praktiken. Wie Meher Contractor in ihrem Brief berichtet, verursachte das Beben zum Glück keine größeren Schäden. Zugleich wird aus der Bezugnahme auf das Beben auch klar, wie die Erde, die Berge und die Gewässer miteinander verbunden sind und welche Bedeutung sie zum Beispiel auch für die Politik der Freundschaft zwischen Indien und der DDR haben konnten. Denn diese Politik der Freundschaft lässt sich nicht allein in anthropozentrischen Begriffen deuten, und ein „Leck" wie dieser Brief kann dazu beitragen, das ins Bewusstsein zu rufen.

Berührend auch Meher Contractors Erwähnung von Max Jacob, einem Urgestein des Puppentheaters und UNIMA-Vorsitzender seit 1957. Jacob ist bekannt für das Kasperhaus, das er in den 1930er Jahren in der sächsischen Kleinstadt Hohnstein gründete, sowie für das nach dem Krieg in Hamburg aufgebaute Hohnsteiner Theater. Er starb 1967. Dass Contractor der Tod eines deutschen

13. Bis heute interessiert sich die Forschung für dieses Erdbeben und die Staubecken. Von Harsh K. Gupta vom CSIR-National Geophysical Research Institute in Hyderabad, Telangana, Indien, stammt folgender Text dazu: „Koyna, India: A very prominent site of artificial water reservoir-triggered seismicity", in: *Journal of Earth System Science*, 131, 2022, 30, online: https://www.ias.ac.in/article/fulltext/jess/131/0030

been an acclaimed puppeteer for twenty-eight years when she established the first repertory theater for puppets that was accepted as a member by the Actors' Equity Association, in 1965, together with her husband Bil Baird. The Bil Baird Marionette Theater continued to run for another nine years after Cora's death, under the auspices of the American Puppet Arts Council, a nonprofit organization she had founded to promote puppetry as an art form in the United States. Through her tours in India, Afghanistan, and Nepal for the US Information Agency, and her work on puppet theater, she became a close acquaintance of Meher Contractor's.

There is an early letter (sent on August 16, 1968, from 1, Kautilya Marg in New Delhi to Rolf Mäser) sent by the Trade Representation of the German Democratic Republic in India. Trade relations between the GDR and India were established before India's official recognition of East Germany in 1972. The year 1972 was a landmark year, and a major turning point in the relationship between India and the GDR. Bangladesh became a new country through Indira Gandhi's and India's active involvement in 1971, and the GDR was the third country in the world (after Bhutan and India) to recognize it officially (Bhutan and India on December 6, 1971, and the GDR on January 11, 1972). It is also important to note that trade relations with West Germany (FRG) focused on extractive industries such as an oil production facility in Gujarat or a Krupp steel plant on Indigenous land in Rourkela, while East Germany was always the preferred intellectual partner with figures such as Professor Jürgen Kuczynski, who produced an account of the history of labor and the economy in modern India for the East German Academy of Sciences.[13] We have this note relating to Meher Contractor that comes from long before the establishment of embassies in 1972. At the time, simple exchanges of cultural products had to be carried out via the two countries' trade missions, which was often made difficult by bureaucracy. The note says:

> Dear Mr. Maser [*sic*]!
> Mrs. R. Contractor, India, sent us the enclosed exposed film to forward to you. In the same shipment there were also some other small items made of paper, fabric, and wire. Unfortunately, we received it all in a condition that

13. Vir Bahadur Singh, ed., *Economic History of India (1857–1956)* (Allied Publishers, 1965), https://archive.org/stream/in.ernet.dli.2015.122253/2015.122253.Economic-History-Of-India-1857-1956_djvu.txt.

Puppentheaterdirektors naheging, veranschaulicht, wie eng damals die Beziehungen zwischen den nationalen UNIMA-Sektionen waren und wie sie gemeinsam die Entwicklung vorantrieben. Ein Foto im Archiv der SKD, das nur drei Jahre vor Max Jacobs Tod 1967 in Leningrad aufgenommen wurde, fängt einen der letzten Momente ein, als die wichtigsten Puppentheaterdirektor·innen der Welt gemeinsam in der Öffentlichkeit auftraten – unter ihnen auch die berühmte jüdische Puppenspielerin Cora Baird aus Amerika, die ebenfalls 1967 starb und an die Meher Contractor im selben Brief ebenfalls erinnert. Cora Baird war bereits 28 Jahre lang als gefeierte Puppenspielerin tätig gewesen, als sie 1965 mit ihrem Mann Bil Baird das erste Repertoiretheater für Puppen gründete, das von der Actors' Equity Association als Mitglied aufgenommen wurde. Das Bil Baird Marionette Theater hielt den Betrieb nach Coras Tod noch neun Jahre aufrecht, nicht zuletzt dank der Unterstützung durch den American Puppet Arts Council, den Cora Baird zur Förderung des Puppenspiels als Kunstform in den Vereinigten Staaten gegründet hatte. Im Zuge ihrer Tourneen durch Indien, Afghanistan und Nepal im Auftrag der United States Information Agency sowie iher Publikationen zum Puppentheater wurden sie und Contractor enge Vertraute.

Ein früher Brief (vom 16. August 1968) ging vom Sitz der Handelsvertretung der Deutschen Demokratischen Republik in Indien, Kautilya Marg Straße Nr. 1, Neu-Delhi, an Rolf Mäser in Dresden / Radebeul.[14] Handelsbeziehungen zwischen der DDR und Indien wurden schon vor der offiziellen Anerkennung der DDR durch Indien 1972 geknüpft. Das Jahr 1972 war ein Wendepunkt in den politischen Beziehungen zwischen den beiden Ländern. Bangladesch wurde infolge der Kriegsbeteiligung Indiens unter Indira Gandhi 1971 zu einem eigenen Land und die DDR der dritte Staat in der Welt (nach Bhutan und Indien), der es formell anerkannte (Bhutan und Indien am 6. Dezember 1971, die DDR am 11. Januar 1972). Wichtig zu wissen ist auch, dass Indiens Wirtschaftsbeziehungen zur Bundesrepublik Deutschland sich auf Rohstoffindustrien wie eine Ölförderanlage in Gujarat oder ein Stahlwerk von Krupp auf indigenem Land in Rourkela konzentrierten, während die DDR stets der bevorzugte Partner für den intellektuellen Austausch war, nicht zuletzt dank Persönlichkeiten wie Jürgen Kuczynski, der für die Akademie der Wissenschaften in der DDR eine Darstellung zur Arbeits- und Wirtschaftsgeschichte des modernen Indien verfasste.[15] Es gibt eine Notiz, Meher

14. SKD, Archiv der Puppentheatersammlung, Brief vom 16. August 1968, unterzeichnet von Somburg, Handelsvertretung der DDR in Indien, an Rolf Maser, Dresdner Volkskunstmuseum und Puppenmuseum, Dresden – Radebeul, Dokumentnummer 755.

15. Jürgen Kuczynski, *Die Geschichte der Lage der Arbeiter unter dem Kapitalismus*, Bd. 27a: *Die englischen Kolonien*, Berlin: Akademie-Verlag 1965. Ein Teil des Indien-Kapitels erschien unter dem Titel „Conditions of Workers (1880–1950)" auch in Indien in: Vir Bahadur Singh (Hg.), *Economic History of India: 1857–1956*, Bombay u. a.: Allied Publishers Private Ltd. 1965, S. 609–637, online: https://archive.org/details/in.ernet.dli.2015.122253

did not allow it to be forwarded to you. We have told Mrs. R. Contractor about the situation.
Further steps to be taken with the film were evidently discussed with you.

Another small but important piece of information is noted at the bottom of this letter: *Telegram address*: *Havdin New Delhi.* It allows us to keep track of all the telegrams that were sent to the Trade Mission of the GDR. This small telegram address becomes an important marker for finding all the telegrams sent by the GDR representatives in India and is thus a major source of information. These documents are also multidirectional, since we can also derive information from them on addresses that do not exist anymore. For example, although Meher Contractor sent a letter dated January 15, 1972, from Nowroji Vakil Compound in Ahmedabad, there are no traces of this compound to be found today. Thus, the material presence of such places in the form of an address makes further research possible that can help recover these historical locations and their memory. In the letter, addressed to the editor of *Arbeitsgemeinschaft für das Puppenspiel*, she writes:

> To
> The Editor
> Pupper Theatre Sammlung [*sic*],
> STAATLICHE, DRESDEN
> Barkengasse 6
> 99122 Radebeul 4, DDR
>
> Dear Sir,
> Thank you for so kindly sending me regularly the arbeitsgemein schaft für das puppenspiel [*sic*] and the New Year Greetings. I wish all the best to your and all our friends in Germany a very Happy New Year [*sic*].
> I am enclosing a report of our last year's work which may be useful for your journal.
> With best wishes,

Contractor betreffend, die aus einer Zeit lange vor Eröffnung der Botschaften 1972 stammt. Zu dieser Zeit musste selbst der simple Austausch von Kulturgütern über die beiden Handelsniederlassungen abgewickelt werden und wurde durch deren bürokratische Schwerfälligkeit oft behindert. In dem Vermerk heißt es:

> „Lieber Herr Maser [sic],
> Mrs. R. Contractor, Indien, übersandte uns beiliegenden belichteten Film zur Weiterleitung an Sie. In der gleichen Sendung waren auch einige weitere Kleinigkeiten aus Papier, Stoff und Draht. Leider war alles bei Erhalt in einem Zustand, der eine Weiterleitung an Sie nicht zuliess. Wir haben Mrs. Contractor davon unterrichtet. Offenbar war mit Ihnen die weitere Verfahrensweise mit dem Film abgesprochen.
> Mit freundlichen Grüssen!
> Somburg"

Ein weiteres wichtiges Detail findet sich am Ende dieses Briefes: „Telegrammadresse: Havdin New Delhi". Mit diesem Hinweis kommen wir im Archiv Telegrammen auf die Spur, die an die Handelsniederlassung der DDR gerichtet waren. Bei systematischem Durchforsten der Bestände im Archiv der Puppentheatersammlung erschließen sich dadurch viele Mitteilungen, die an die damaligen Vertreter der DDR in Indien gingen, und somit eine wichtige Quelle zur politischen Geschichte. Die Dokumente geben zudem Hinweise in verschiedene Richtungen, da wir daraus auch Informationen über heute nur noch schwer zuzuordnende Adressen erhalten. Beispielsweise schickte Meher Contractor einen auf den 15. Januar 1972 datierten Brief vom Norwoji Vakil Compound in Ahmedabad, einem Gebäude, von dem heute keinerlei Spuren mehr zu finden sind. Dass solche Orte nun immerhin eine konkrete Präsenz in Form ihrer Anschriften erhalten, eröffnet die Möglichkeit, in weitergehenden Recherchen eventuell diese historischen Orte und ihre Geschichte zutage zu fördern. In diesem Brief an den Herausgeber der Arbeitsgemeinschaft für das Puppenspiel schreibt Meher Contractor:

> „An
> Die Redaktion

Sincerely,
Meher R. Contractor
(Mrs. Meher R. Contractor)
Hon. Director,
Puppet Section
DARPANA ACADEMY, AHMEDABAD

Thus, in the seemingly official documentation and notes, we can find traces of the archives that refer to what is missing, to something that leads to a historical encounter.

These relations are fragile and vulnerable. They are associated with worries as well as with a sense of solidarity and are part of an emerging struggle to make the institutional boundary lines porous.

One such example is a handwritten letter by Meher Contractor to Rolf Mäser:

Herr Rolf Mazer [*sic*]
Director Puppet Section
Dresden Museum of Folkarts
Dresden. G. D. R.

Dear Herr Mazer [*sic*],
On February 18th this year I sent you 8 coloured slides of my puppet plays for the Television Centre here[;] since I have received no acknowledgement from you of these, I am worried as they cost me a lot of money and I can not recapture these scenes again. I had sent them by airmail & registered post. I shall be only to [*sic*] glad if you can just drop me a line to say you have received them & relieve my anxiety & so I can complain to the post. Henryk Jurkowski writes you all had a very nice UNIMA meeting in Dresden and it must have been interesting meeting all friends again. I am glad to hear also some concrete points were realised.
With best wishes to you & Frau Mazer & all friends in [the] GDR.

Puppentheater Sammlung,
STAATLICHE, DRESDEN
Barkengasse 6
99122 Radebeul 4, DDR

Sehr geehrter Herr,
danke für Ihre Freundlichkeit, mir regelmäßig die ‚Arbeitsgemeinschaft für das Puppenspiel' zuzusenden und für Ihre Neujahrsgrüße. Ich wünsche Ihnen allen das Beste und all Ihren Freunden in Deutschland ein sehr glückliches neues Jahr.
Ich füge einen Bericht über unsere Arbeit im abgelaufenen Jahr bei, der für Ihre Zeitschrift vielleicht von Nutzen ist.
Mit den besten Wünschen,
herzlich,
Meher R. Contractor
(Mrs. Meher R. Contractor)
Hon. Director,
Puppet Section
DARPANA ACADEMY, AHMEDABAD"

So finden wir unter scheinbar nur offiziellen Schriftstücken und Vermerken in den Archiven auch Spuren, die uns helfen können, Lücken in der Überlieferung zu schließen.

Sie erzählen von fragilen und anfälligen Beziehungen, sie zeugen von Sorgen, von Solidarität und dem Bemühen, die Grenzen zwischen Institutionen durchlässiger zu machen.

Ein Beispiel dafür liefert ein handgeschriebener Brief von Meher Contractor an Rolf Mäser:

„Herr Rolf Mazer [sic]
Leiter der Puppenspielabteilung
Museum für Sächsische Volkskunst Dresden
Dresden. DDR.

Sincerely
Meher Contractor

In the letter written by Rolf Mäser on May 31, 1977 (replying to her letter of May 5, 1977) addressed to Meher R. Contractor at her Shahi Bagh (misspelled as "Shahi Bad" in Mäser's letter) address in Ahmedabad.

Frau
Meher R. Contractor
Shahi Bad [*sic*]
Ahmedabad 380004
Indien
31.5.1977

Dear Mrs. Meher R. Contractor,
Thank you for your letter of May 5, 1977. I am happy to let you know that the slides sent on February 18 arrived with us.
The UNIMA Committee selected one of the slides for the 1979 calendar.
The fee will be paid to you by Henschel Verlag, Berlin. Please let us know which bank the amount is to be transferred to. Specimen copies of the publication will be sent to you once it is published.
I am very sorry that you were unable to be in Dresden for the UNIMA Executive Committee conference.
With kind regards, also from my wife,
Rolf Mäser
Director
Member of the UNIMA Executive.

Sehr geehrter Herr Mazer [sic],
am 18. Februar dieses Jahres habe ich Ihnen acht Farbdias von meinen Puppenspielen für den hiesigen Fernsehsender geschickt. Da ich keine Bestätigung erhalten habe, sorge ich mich, denn sie haben viel Geld gekostet und ich kann die Szenen aus der Erinnerung nicht mehr wiederherstellen. Ich hatte die Aufnahmen per Luftpost und Einschreiben gesendet. Ich wäre Ihnen äußerst dankbar, wenn Sie mir wenigstens eine kurze Nachricht schicken könnten, des Inhalts, dass Sie sie erhalten haben & meine Sorgen unbegründet sind & damit ich mich anderenfalls bei der Post beschweren kann. Henryk Jurkowski schreibt, dass Sie allesamt ein sehr schönes UNIMA-Treffen in Dresden hatten. Es muss sehr interessant gewesen sein, all die Freunde wiederzusehen. Ich freue mich auch zu hören, dass einige konkrete Punkte umgesetzt werden konnten.
Mit den besten Wünschen an Sie & Frau Mazer und an alle Freunde in der DDR.
Herzlich,
Meher Contractor"

In einem Brief vom 31. Mai 1977 antwortet Mäser auf ihr Schreiben vom 5. Mai (wobei er in der Adresse statt Shahi Bagh fälschlich „Shahi Bad" schreibt):

„Frau
Meher R. Contractor
Shahi Bad [sic]
Ahmedabad 380004
Indien
31.5.1977

Liebe Frau Meher R. Contractor!
Ich erhielt dankend Ihren Brief vom 5.5.77 und teile Ihnen mit, daß die Dias (slides) vom 18. Februar bei uns angekommen sind.
Die UNIMA-Kommission hat ein Dia davon für den Kalender 1979 ausgewählt. Das Honorar wird Ihnen dafür vom Henschelverlag Berlin

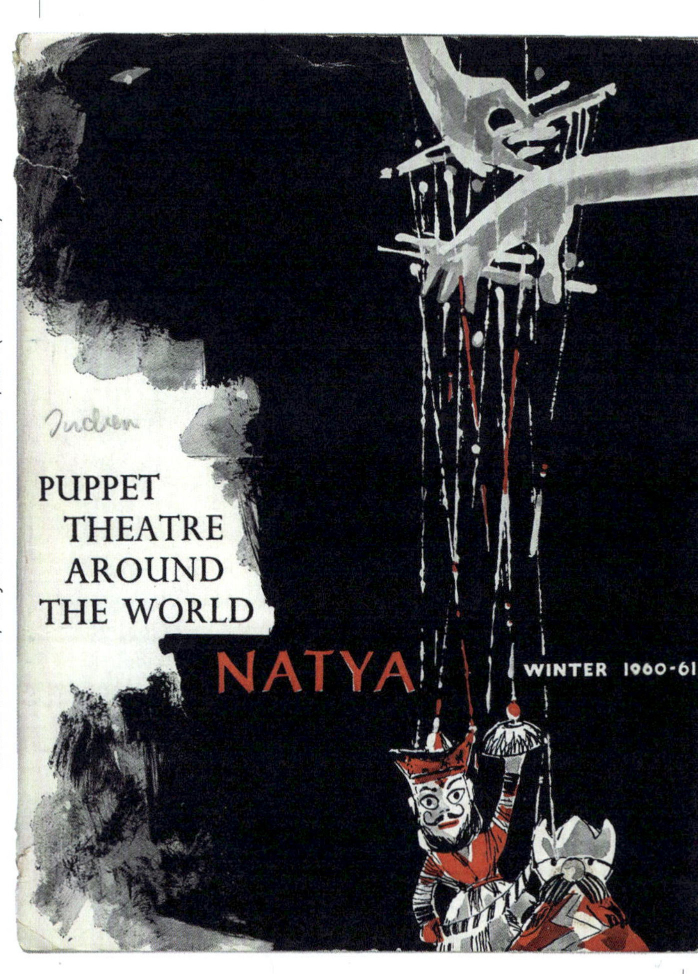

Bharatiya Natya Sangh / Som Benegal (Hrsg.): *Natya. Theatre Arts Journal*, Vol. 4, No. 4, Winter 1960/61: *Puppet Theatre Around the World*

Bharatiya Natya Sangh and Som Benegal, eds., "Puppet Theatre Around the World," *Natya: Theatre Arts Journal* 4, no. 4 (Winter 1960/61)

bezahlt. Bitte teilen Sie uns mit, auf welche Bank der Betrag überwiesen werden soll. Belegexemplare der Publikation gehen Ihnen nach Erscheinen zu.
Wir bedauern sehr, daß Sie nicht in Dresden zur UNIMA-Exekutivtagung sein konnten.
Mit freundlichen Grüßen, auch von meiner Frau, Ihr
Rolf Mäser,
Direktor
Mitglied des Exekutivkomitees der UNIMA."

KRISHNA LAL AND SUSHILA ROHATGI: A REWRITING OF THE UNWRITTEN

Between the years 1984 and 1986, a notable collaboration occurred between India and the GDR in terms of art exchanges that resulted in two exhibitions shared between the Dresden State Art Collections (Staatliche Kunstsammlungen Dresden, SKD) and the National Museum in New Delhi: *Art Treasures from Dresden*, November 18, 1984 – February 10, 1985), an SKD exhibition mounted in New Delhi, and *Treasures of Indian Craftsmanship from the 16th to the 19th Century*, an exhibition from the National Museum put on in the SKD's Albertinum—with the opening held on October 24, 1985, as part of the GDR's Indian Cultural Days. The profound work of professors Doreen Mende and Monica Juneja in studying the potentialities of such exchanges sheds light on their impact on our thoughts on and imagination of internationalism.

My hypothesis argues that there is a need for epistemological measures to counter a marginalization of these cultural exchanges in Western historiography. India–GDR art relations are ignored and sidelined in favor of Indian–German art exchanges that favor the Western hegemony or overemphasize the Cold War as an overarching context whenever this particular period is being referred to. This active pushing to the periphery is ongoing because most of the India–GDR exchanges are recounted from the point of view of male historians, artists, statesmen, and curators, underlining the "rule of the father," as it were. In such accounts, the role of Indian women curators, artists, art managers, and politicians is marginalized or written in such a way that they seem like minor players in the overall scheme. I will attempt to reverse such a historiography by telling the story of Krishna Lal and Sushila Rohatgi.

KRISHNA LAL UND SUSHILA ROHATGI: DAS UNGESCHRIEBENE NEU SCHREIBEN

In den Jahren 1984 bis 1986 kam es auf der Achse des Kunstaustauschs zu einer bemerkenswerten Zusammenarbeit zwischen Indien und der DDR, die zwei Ausstellungen in Dresden und Delhi hervorbrachte: *Kunstschätze aus Dresden* (18. November 1984 bis 10. Februar 1985), eine Ausstellung der Staatlichen Kunstsammlungen Dresden im Nationalmuseum in Neu-Delhi, und *Kostbarkeiten indischer Handwerkskunst des 16. bis 19. Jahrhunderts*, eine Ausstellung des Nationalmuseums Neu-Delhi im Albertinum der Staatlichen Kunstsammlungen Dresden mit Eröffnung am 24. Oktober 1985 im Rahmen der Tage der Kultur Indiens in der DDR. Die eingehende Forschung von Doreen Mende und Monica Juneja zu den Potenzialen solcher Austauschprogramme bringt zur Geltung, was diese für unseren Begriff und unsere Vorstellung vom Internationalismus bedeutet haben.

Meine Hypothese lautet, dass es epistemologischer Maßnahmen bedarf, um der Vernachlässigung dieses kulturellen Austauschs in der westlichen Geschichtsschreibung entgegenzutreten. Die Kunstbeziehungen zwischen Indien und der DDR werden bislang links liegen gelassen, die Rede ist vor allem von solchen, die die westliche Hegemonie bekräftigen und den Kalten Krieg als umfassenden Kontext über die Maßen betonen, wann immer auf diese Jahre Bezug genommen wird. Dieses Abschieben einer anderen historischen Realität an die Peripherie des Geschehens findet statt, weil die meisten Beziehungen zwischen Indien und der DDR aus dem Blickwinkel männlicher Historiker, Künstler, Staatsoberhäupter und Kuratoren geschildert werden und hierbei gewissermaßen die „Herrschaft des Vaters" zum Tragen kommt. In solchen Darstellungen wird die Bedeutung indischer Kuratorinnen, Künstlerinnen, Kunstmanagerinnen und Politikerinnen marginalisiert oder man lässt diese zumindest wie Nebenfiguren im größeren Zusammenhang

1. "Bapu Lives On with Rohatgi Family," *The Times of India*, October 3, 2009, https://timesofindia.indiatimes.com/city/kanpur/bapu-lives-on-with-rohatgi-family/articleshow/5084772.cms.

Dr. Krishna Lal and Sushila Rohatgi did not engage in representational politics. They completely rewrote the political spectrum of transactions between the institutions concerned. I make the case that they were not merely present at the time, but that their presence and input affected every aspect of the making of these exhibitions and left a distinct imprint on every exchange.

I first learned of the presence of Dr. Krishna Lal and Sushila Rohatgi in the archive at the SKD through the help given to me by the institution's archivist Vera Wobad. Again and again, their names would appear on the backs of photographs we viewed. While these archival traces have been overlooked in the past, they seemed to me like conscious choices made by the archivist. It is an example of archival solidarity practice, planting a seed for posterity, beyond institutional constraints and political interests. Here, by reading these images closely, by listening to and feeling them, I will borrow a question posited by Tina M. Campt in her book *Listening to Images*: "What is the place in this archive for images assumed only to register forms of institutional accounting or state management?" I will call this retrieval of images a "transduction of affect."

Sushila Rohatgi was one of the foremost exponents of cultural internationalism in India. A great-granddaughter of the famous anti-colonial revolutionary Madan Mohan Malviya, who also established Banaras Hindu University (BHU), she grew up with Mahatma Gandhi as a frequent visitor to her family home in Kanpur in Uttar Pradesh, where he would stay on visits to the city, as she later recounted in an article.[1] Gandhi planted a tree in the garden that grew strong, as did Sushila herself, in the affectionate nurture of Gandhian values. During her

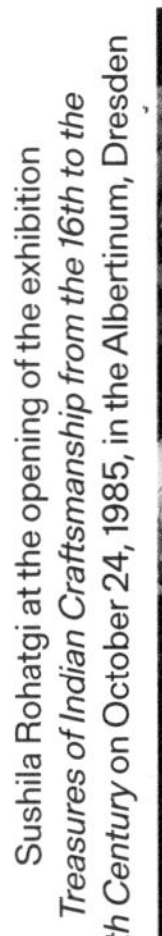

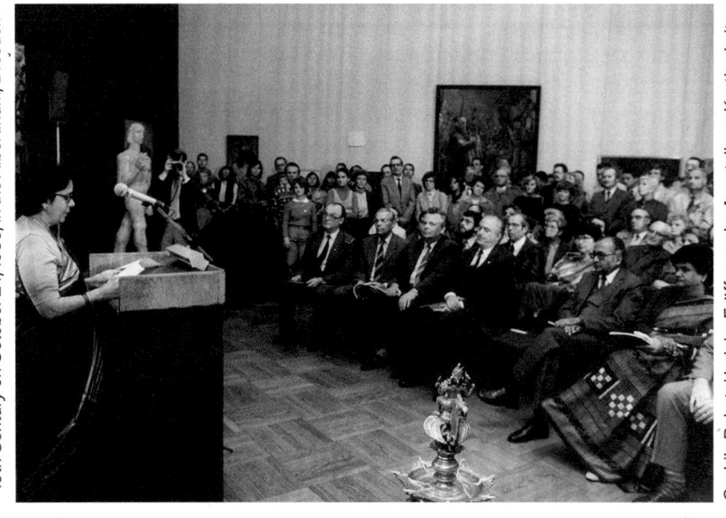

Sushila Rohatgi at the opening of the exhibition *Treasures of Indian Craftsmanship from the 16th to the 19th Century* on October 24, 1985, in the Albertinum, Dresden

Sushila Rohatgi bei der Eröffnung der Ausstellung *Kostbarkeiten indischer Handwerkskunst des 16. bis 19. Jahrhunderts* am 24. Oktober 1985 im Albertinum, Dresden

des Geschehens wirken. Ich werde hier versuchen, einer derartigen Historiografie die Geschichte von Krishna Lal und Sushila Rohatgi entgegenzusetzen.

Krishna Lal und Sushila Rohatgi haben sich nicht mit politischer Repräsentation aufgehalten. Sie haben die politische Bandbreite der Transaktionen zwischen den Beteiligten komplett umgestaltet. Ich behaupte hier, dass beide Frauen in der fraglichen Zeit nicht einfach nur anwesend waren, sondern dass ihre Gegenwart und ihre Beiträge sämtliche Aspekte der Entstehung dieser Ausstellungen geprägt und jedem Austausch unverkennbar ihren Stempel aufgedrückt haben.

Von Krishna Lal und Sushila Rohatgi habe ich zuerst im Archiv der Staatlichen Kunstsammlungen Dresden erfahren, angestoßen durch die Arbeit von Doreen Mende und mit der Hilfe der Archivarin Vera Wobad. Immer wieder tauchten die Namen der beiden auf den Rückseiten von Fotografien auf, die wir uns ansahen. Zwar wurden ihre Spuren im Archiv in der Vergangenheit übersehen, doch dass es sie gab, schien mir ein Resultat bewusster Entscheidungen aufseiten der Archivarin zu sein – ein Beispiel für gelebte Solidarität in der Archivarbeit, eine Saat für die Nachwelt, die trotz institutioneller Beschränkungen und widriger politischer Interessen aufgeht. Indem ich diese Bilder hier genau betrachte, sie sozusagen abhöre und abtaste, gehe ich an sie mit einer Frage heran, die Tina M. Campt in ihrem Buch *Listening to Images* stellt: „Welchen Stellenwert haben in diesem Archiv Bilder, von denen man meint, dass sie lediglich Formen institutioneller Vergewisserung oder staatlicher Verwaltung festhalten?" Ich werde dieses Bergen von Bildern eine „Transduktion von Affekt" nennen.

Auf diesem Bild aus dem Albertinum, aufgenommen am 24. Oktober 1985, sehen wir drei Delegierte des National Museum in Delhi. Die Staatsministerin für Kunst und Kultur der Republik Indien, Sushila Rohatgi, steht am Pult und hält

long life (1921–2011), she witnessed all the changes that took place in India, the independence from territorial colonialism, and the new values of postcolonialism. Throughout, she remained an active leader. She was elected to parliament twice, in 1967 and 1971. In 1985, she became a member of the Upper House of the Indian parliament (the Rajya Sabha) and Union Minister for Education and Cultural Affairs. It was at this time that she visited the Albertinum in Dresden, where she delivered a speech. She was one of the very few women ministers in India (there have been only seventeen since 1952), as we gather from a recent book published by the Upper House: "Since 1952, 17 women members of Rajya Sabha have joined the Council of Ministers in various capacities. While being a member of Rajya Sabha, Smt. Indira Gandhi became the Prime Minister of India. Smt. Lakshmi N. Menon, Smt. Violet Alva, Smt. Jahanara Jaipal Singh, Smt. Nandini Satpathy, Dr. (Smt.) Phulrenu Guha, Kum. Saroj Khaparde, Miss Kumudben Manishankar Joshi, Smt. Margaret Alva, Dr. (Smt.) Sathiavani Muthu, Smt. Sushila Rohatgi, Rajkumari Amrit Kaur, Smt. Renuka Chowdhury, Smt. Kamla Sinha, Smt. Jayanthi Natarajan, Smt. Urmila Chimanbhai Patel and Smt. Sushma Swaraj have held many portfolios and introduced many Bills concerning the issues in which the respective ministries were involved."[2]

It is also quite important that she held these positions at the very beginning of a new phase in Indian politics, in the second and third ministries of Rajiv Gandhi, which included Dr. Sarojini Mahishi, Nandini Satpathy, and Saroj Khaparde. These were turbulent times, with the murder of Indian prime minister Indira Gandhi, widespread communal violence throughout the country that claimed thousands of lives, and a newly sworn-in Rajiv Gandhi (whose address we find in the catalog of the exhibition). Thus, culture was a highly sensitive subject, and as a result the work of Sushila Rohatgi as State Minister of Culture and Dr. Krishna Lal, who essentially pulled the strings at the National Museum for this cultural

2. Rajya Sabha Secretariat, *Women Members of Rajya Sabha* (Rajya Sabha Secretariat, [2003]), 60. The abbreviation Smt. (Shrimati) is an honorific used in Indian languages for adult women, comparable to Ms. or Mrs. in English.

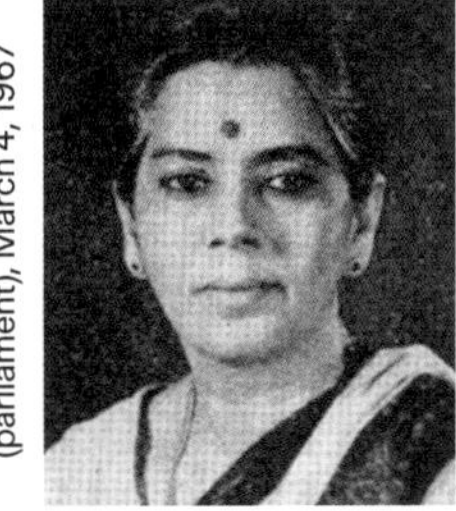

Sushila Rohatgi, former member of Lok Sabha (parliament), March 4, 1967

Sushila Rohatgi, ehemaliges Mitglied des Parlaments (Lok Sabha), 4. März 1967

eine Rede vor geladenen Gästen. Der Direktor des Indischen Nationalmuseums, Laxmi P. Sihare, sitzt in der ersten Reihe neben der Kuratorin seines Hauses, Krishna Lal.

Sushila Rohatgi war eine der wichtigsten Vertreter·innen des kulturellen Internationalismus in Indien. Als Großenkelin des berühmten Freiheitskämpfers Madan Mohan Malviya, der auch die Banaras Hindu University (BHU) gegründet hatte, lernte sie schon in der Kindheit Mahatma Gandhi kennen, der ein häufiger Gast in ihrem Elternhaus in Kanpur, Uttar Pradesh, war. Gandhi kam zu Besuch, wann immer er in der Stadt war.[1] Er pflanzte einen Baum im Garten, der wie Sushila selbst unter der liebevollen Zuwendung im Geiste Gandhis prächtig gedieh. In Ihrem langen Leben wurde Sushila Zeugin all der epochalen Veränderungen beginnend mit der Unabhängigkeit vom territorialen Kolonialismus bis hin zu den neuen Vorstellungen des Postkolonialismus. In all dieser Zeit hatte sie eine führende Rolle. Sie wurde zweimal, 1967 und 1971, ins indische Parlament gewählt. 1985 wurde sie Mitglied der Rajya Sabha, der zweiten Kammer des indischen Parlaments, und Ministerin für Bildung und kulturelle Angelegenheiten auf Unionsebene. In dieser Zeit besuchte sie das Albertinum in Dresden, wo sie eine Rede hielt. Wie wir aus einer neueren Publikation der Rajya Sabha erfahren, war sie eine von sehr wenigen Ministerinnen in Indien (es gab seit 1952 nur 17):

„Seit 1952 sind 17 weibliche Mitglieder der Rajya Sabha in verschiedenen Funktionen in den Ministerrat eingetreten. Smt. Indira Gandhi wurde Ministerpräsidentin von Indien, als sie der Ranya Sabha angehörte. Smt. Lakshmi N. Menon, Smt. Violet Alva, Smt. Jahanara Jaipal Singh, Smt. Nandini Satpathy, Dr. (Smt.) Phulrenu Guha, Kum. Saroj Khaparde, Miss Kumudben Manishankar Joshi, Smt. Margaret Alva, Dr. (Smt.) Sathiavani Muthu, Smt. Sushila Rohatgi, Rajkumari Amrit Kaur, Smt. Renuka Chowdhury, Smt. Kamla Sinha, Smt. Jayanthi Natarajan, Smt. Urmila Chimanbhai Patel und Smt. Sushma Swaraj haben viele Ämter bekleidet und zahlreiche Gesetzesvorlagen auf den Gebieten eingebracht, mit denen ihre jeweiligen Ministerien befasst waren."[2]

1. „Bapu lives on with Rohatgi family", in: *The Times of India*, 3.10.2009, online: https://timesofindia.indiatimes.com/city/kanpur/bapu-lives-on-with-rohatgi-family/articleshow/5084772.cms

2. *Women Members of Rajya Sabha*, Neu-Delhi: Rajya Sabha Secretariat, [2003], S. 60, https://cms.rajyasabha.nic.in/UploadedFiles/ElectronicPublications/Women_Members_Rajya%20Sabha.pdf

exchange, becomes doubly sensitive and crucial. In his memoir, "Cabinet-Making and Unmaking," Bhabani Sen Gupta recounts how the new situation caused widespread instability in the cabinet: "What caught the attention of the nation most was the creation of nodal ministries, an amalgamation of several closely interrelated ministries or departments under one cabinet minister who was to be assisted by several junior ministers each in charge of a particular department. The most conspicuous of these nodal ministries was the innovative Ministry of Human Resources, which was placed under Narasimha Rao, to be assisted by two women, Margaret Alva looking after Youth Affairs, Women and Sports, and a new entrant, Sushila Rohatgi, Education and Culture."[3] The importance of her speech is further underlined when we see the pressure her ministry is put under, with a reshuffle already carried out in May 1986. Her appearance at the Albertinum and her visit to Dresden as part of the exhibition *Treasures of Indian Craftsmanship from the 16th to the 19th Century* sent by the National Museum in New Delhi are special events in this context. Thus, this speech at Albertinum, her visit to Dresden, and this exhibition in general are rare vignettes that allow us to sense and feel her vision. The May 1986 reshuffle brought in twelve new ministers, three of them into the cabinet, and removed nine. Sushila's ministry was under immense pressure, which can be sensed from the viciousness of the comments in the media by people who were unhappy with the changes in the government and unable to accept women as ministers in charge of important portfolios: "Even the prime minister's pet nodal

3. Bhabani Sen Gupta, "Cabinet-Making and Unmaking," *Economic and Political Weekly*, February 6, 1988, 230–33.

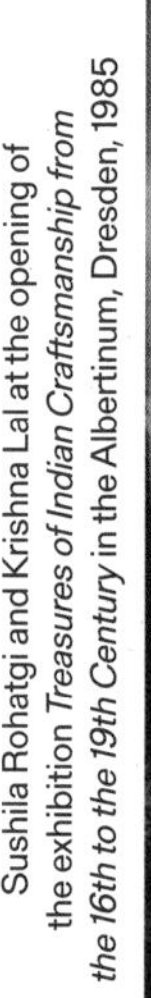

Sushila Rohatgi and Krishna Lal at the opening of the exhibition *Treasures of Indian Craftsmanship from the 16th to the 19th Century* in the Albertinum, Dresden, 1985

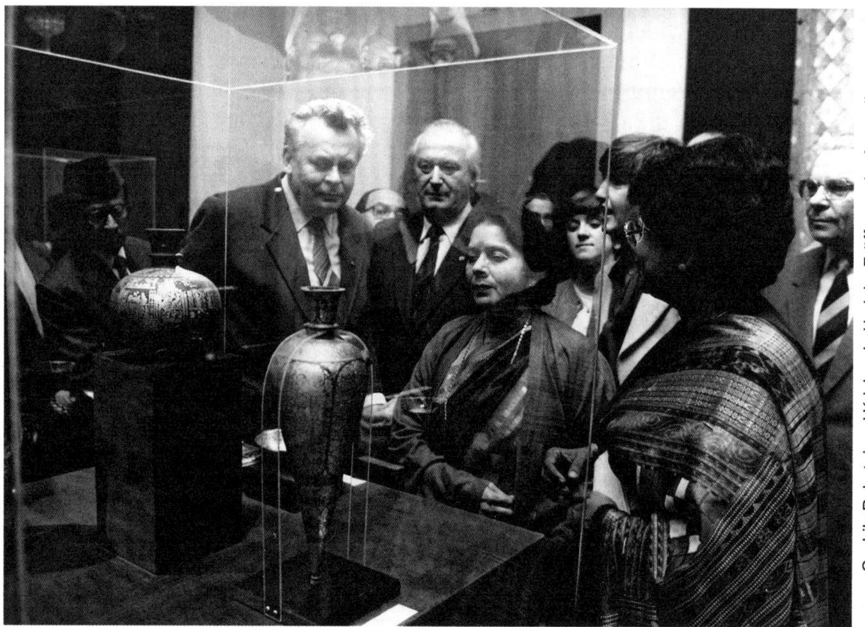

Sushila Rohatgi und Krishna Lal bei der Eröffnung der Ausstellung *Kostbarkeiten indischer Handwerkskunst des 16. bis 19. Jahrhunderts* im Albertinum, Dresden, 1985

Wichtig zu wissen ist auch, dass Rohatgi diese Positionen am Beginn einer neuen Phase der indischen Politik innehatte, nämlich im zweiten und dritten Kabinett unter Rajiv Gandhi und neben Sarojini Mahishi, Nandini Satpathy und Saroj Khaparde. Es waren unruhige Zeiten: Indiens Ministerpräsidentin Indira Gandhi wurde ermordet, überall im Land kam es zu gewalttätigen Zusammenstößen zwischen verfeindeten Lagern, die Tausende Menschenleben kosteten, und mit Rajiv Gandhi wurde ein neuer Regierungschef vereidigt (von dem sich im Ausstellungskatalog ein Grußwort findet). Kultur war unter diesen Umständen ein äußerst heikles Gebiet, und umso mehr Feingefühl erforderte diese Aufgabe von Sushila Rohatgi als zuständiger Staatsministerin sowie von Krishna Lal am Nationalmuseum, die bei diesem Kulturaustausch maßgeblich die Fäden zogen. Der indische Politikwissenschaftler Bhabani Sen Gupta schildert in seinem Aufsatz *Cabinet-Making and Unmaking*, wie die neue Situation das Kabinett durcheinanderbrachte:

„Am meisten staunte die Nation über die Einführung der Nodal Ministries (Knotenministerien), Zusammenschlüsse eng verbundener Ministerien und Abteilungen unter der Führung eines Ministers im Kabinett, der dann die Schlüsselposten mit Junior-Ministern besetzte. Am auffälligsten unter diesen Nodal Ministries war ein fortschrittliches Ministerium für personelle Ressourcen unter Narashimha Rao, dem zwei Frauen assistierten: Margaret Alva, zuständig für den Bereich Jugend, Frauen und Sport, sowie Sushila Rohatgi, zuständig für Bildung und Kultur."[3]

Welches Gewicht Rohatgis Rede hatte, tritt noch deutlicher hervor, wenn wir den politischen Druck bedenken, unter dem ihr Ministerium stand. Bereits im Mai 1986 kam es zu einer Kabinettsumbildung. Ihr Auftritt im Albertinum

3. Bhabani Sen Gupta, „Cabinet-Making and Unmaking", in: *Economic and Political Weekly*, 23, 1988, Nr. 6, 6. Februar, S. 230–233.

ministry was dealt a blow. Sushila Rohatgi who was looking after Education—a huge empire with 7,00,000 [*sic*] institutions in the country ranging from primary schools to higher research bodies, and, above all, the prime minister's pet New Education Policy—was shifted to Power,[4] and her place given to another woman minister of state, Krishna Sahi, who had to begin from scratch."[5]

> During 1985–86 when Smt. Sushila Rohatgi was Minister of State in the Ministry of Education and Culture, she introduced the UGC (Amendment) Bill, 1985. Smt. Margaret Alva as Minister of State in the Department of Youth Affairs and Sports and Women and Child Development in the Ministry of Human Resource Development had introduced very momentous bills on women which were ultimately passed by both the Houses of Parliament and enacted. Some of these are: Dowry Prohibition (Amendment) Bill, 1986, Indecent Representation of Women (Prohibition) Bill, 1986, the Infant Milk-foods and Feeding Bottles (Regulation of Production, Supply and Distribution) Bill, 1986, etc.
> These facts vividly show that both as private members and as members of the Council of Ministers, women members of Rajya Sabha played veritably an important role in taking parliamentary initiatives to highlight several significant issues.[6]

As minister of education, she laid the foundation for the University Grant Commission (Amendment) Bill, which required her to respond to multiple challenges. In the debate that ensued in parliament after the bill was introduced, she addresses some of these important memories, which had an impact on the development of the 1985/86 exhibition and the dealings surrounding it:

> While fulfilling its responsibilities, it is the duty of the UGC [to] give grants. It is not dolling [*sic*] out money. It is not the charity that it is giving. It is carrying out its duty through giving grants and giving grants only to those institutions which have been found fit to receive the grants

4. This refers to the transfer of Sushila Rohatgi to the Department of Power as Minister of State for Energy, an office that she occupied from May 12, 1986, to May 9, 1988. See Wikipedia, "Ministry of Power (India)," last modified November 12, 2024, 10:54 (UTC), https://en.wikipedia.org/wiki/Ministry_of_Power_(India).

5. Gupta, "Cabinet-Making."

6. Rajya Sabha Secretariat, *Women Members of Rajya Sabha*.

und ihr Besuch in Dresden im Rahmen der Ausstellung *Kostbarkeiten indischer Handwerkskunst des 16. bis 19. Jahrhunderts* des Nationalmuseums Neu-Delhi in Dresden sind vor diesem Hintergrund besondere Ereignisse. Sie lassen uns Rohatgis Vision erspüren und erahnen. Die Umbildung brachte 1986 zwölf neue Minister ins Amt, von denen drei dem Kabinett angehörten. Neun der bisherigen mussten gehen. Sushila Rohatgis Ministerium geriet ebenfalls in die Schusslinie, was sich an der Gehässigkeit der Kommentare in den Medien ablesen lässt; sie stammten von Leuten, die mit der Umbildung der Regierung unzufrieden waren und Frauen im Ministerrang bei wichtigen Ressorts nicht hinnehmen wollten.

„Sogar das liebste Knotenministerium des Premierministers geriet unter Beschuss. Sushila Rohatgi, die für Bildung zuständig war – ein Riesenreich mit 700.000 Institutionen im Land, von Grundschulen bis zu hochrangigen Forschungseinrichtungen, einschließlich der dem Premierminister so am Herzen liegenden Neuen Bildungspolitik – wechselte ins Energieministerium. Rohatgis Stelle übernahm eine weitere Staatsministerin, Krishna Sahi, die ganz von vorne beginnen musste."[4]

> „1985/86, als Smt. Sushila Rohatgi Staatsministerin im Ministerium für Bildung und Kultur war, brachte sie eine Vorlage zur Gesetzesänderung in Sachen Hochschulbildung ein (1985). Smt. Margaret Alva hat als Staatsministerin in der Abteilung Jugend, Sport und Frauen wegweisende Gesetzesentwürfe zu Frauenrechten eingebracht, die am Ende von den beiden Kammern des Parlaments verabschiedet wurden. Darunter sind: das Gesetz zum Mitgiftverbot (Änderung) 1986, das Gesetz zur ungebührlichen Darstellung von Frauen (Verbot) 1986, das Gesetz zur Milchnahrung und den Saugflaschen für Kleinkinder (Regulierung von Herstellung, Nachschub und Verteilung) 1986 usw.
> Diese Tatsachen machen deutlich, dass weibliche Angehörige der Rajya Sabha eine bedeutende Rolle beim Voranbringen parlamentarischer Initiativen in wichtigen Themenbereichen spielten."[5]

Als Bildungsministerin leitete sie eine Gesetzesänderung für die University Grants Commission ein, die über Fördermittel im Hochschulbereich entschied – ein Vorhaben, bei dem sie eine Vielzahl von Schwierigkeiten angehen musste. In

4. Gupta, „Cabinet-Making and Unmaking".

5. *Women Members of Rajya Sabha*, S. 60.

> and it is very very necessary that they have to fulfil certain regulations and stipulations before they become entitled to receive these grants. There may be stipulations that they should have the forum like the one suggested in the Gajendragadkar Commission's recommendations or may be that they should have Rs. two crores worth of facilities whether it [is] staff or buildings or something like that.[7] So, we find that 40 of these universities have been established since 1972 and 14 out of them have not yet been declared to be fit to receive assistance. But that does not mean that they are not recognised. The fact is that they have not come up to certain standards. After fulfilling this criterion, they should be entitled to receive the assistance. I would only request the hon. Members from various parties take up this matter with the respective State Governments and see that the fulfilment of these conditions is expedited and the UGC is satisfied and then only the financial assistance that they expect can be given to them.[8]

It is important to note that, as Minister of Culture, her influence extended over a wide range of cultural artifacts, including films. At a time when there was a prevalent fear of censorship, the question of how to treat film and internationalism arose. This would be very important for Chetna Vora and her film *OYOYO* (1980). In a reply to the question of censorship for the films, she answers very lucidly:

> 3604. PROF. K. V. Thomas: Will the Minister of HUMAN RESOURCE DEVELOPMENT be pleased to state:
> (a) the guidelines given for the censorship of films;
> (b) whether the imported films are treated separately from the Indian films;
> (c) whether a senior officer of the grade of Jt. Chairman would be posted in Madras or Cochin to dispose of all cases of censorship not involving policy; and
> (d) whether the films imported would be censored at the port of entry?

7. One crore is a unit of value equal to ten million rupees.

8. *Lok Sabha Debates (English Version): Fourth Session (Eighth Lok Sabha)*, 8th series, vol. 12, no. 21, Tuesday, December 17, 1985 – Agrahayana 26, 1907 (Saka) (Lok Sabha Secretariat, [1985]), 381–82, https://eparlib.nic.in/bitstream/123456789/1386/1/lsd_08_4_17-12-1985.pdf.

der Parlamentsdebatte über den Entwurf nannte sie wichtige Eckpunkte, die auch für die Konzeption und Durchführung der Ausstellung 1985/86 relevant sind:

> „Die Aufgabe der UGC ist die Vergabe von Fördermitteln. Sie verteilt nicht einfach Geld. Die Auszahlung ist keine Mildtätigkeit. Die Kommission erfüllt ihre Pflicht, indem sie Fördermittel vergibt, und zwar nur an solche Einrichtungen, die dafür als geeignet befunden wurden. Es ist im höchsten Maß erforderlich, dass diese gewissen Regelungen und Bestimmungen entsprechen, um Anspruch auf Fördermittel erheben zu können. Das können Bestimmungen sein, dass es ein Forum gibt, wie in den Empfehlungen der Gajendragadkar-Kommission vorgeschlagen, oder dass sie über Betriebsmittel im Wert von 20 Millionen Rupien verfügen, in Form von Stellen oder Gebäuden oder Ähnlichem. Wir stellen fest, dass 40 dieser Universitäten Neugründungen seit 1972 sind und 14 von ihnen bislang nicht als geeignet für den Empfang von staatlicher Unterstützung geführt werden. Das heißt nicht, dass sie nicht anerkannt sind. Tatsache aber ist, dass sie bestimmten Standards nicht entsprechen. Sobald sie diese Kriterien erfüllen, sollten sie ebenso berechtigt sein, Zuwendungen zu erhalten. Ich möchte nur die ehrenwerten Mitglieder verschiedener Parteien bitten, diese Angelegenheit mit den Regierungen des jeweiligen Bundesstaats zu erörtern und dafür zu sorgen, dass die Erfüllung der Förderbedingungen zur Zufriedenheit der Kommission vorankommt, denn nur dann kann die erwartete finanzielle Unterstützung auch an sie ausgezahlt werden.“[6]

Bemerkenswert ist auch, dass Rohatgi als Kulturministerin Einfluss auf eine große Vielfalt von kulturellen Erzeugnissen nahm, auch auf Filmproduktionen. In einer Zeit der Furcht vor der Zensur stellte sich die Frage, wie man aus internationalistischer Sicht mit dem Film umgehen sollte. Das war auch für Chetna Vora und ihren Film *OYOYO* (1980) von großer Bedeutung. Auf die Anfrage bezüglich einer Zensur von Filmen antwortet Rohatgi sehr hellsichtig:

> „3604. Prof. K. V. Thomas: Würde die Ministerin für die ENTWICKLUNG DER HUMANRESSOURCEN freundlicherweise Stellung

6. https://eparlib.nic.in/bitstream/123456789/1386/1/lsd_08_4_17-12-1985.pdf, Sp. 381–282.

THE MINISTER OF STATE IN THE DEPARTMENTS OF EDUCATION AND CULTURE SHRIMATI SUSHILA ROHATGI): (a) and
(b) All films including imported films presented for certification are examined by the Central Board of Film Certification in accordance with the provisions of the Cinematograph Act 1952 and the guidelines issued thereunder. A copy of these guidelines is placed on the Table of the House. [Placed in Library. See No. LT 1942/85]
(c) No. Sir.
(d) There is no such proposal at present.[9]

From May 12, 1986, to May 9, 1988, Sushila Rohatgi was Minister of State for Energy. Even then, she was responsible for strengthening and connecting various areas of education and culture. While contributing immensely to the parliament as a state minister, Sushila constantly worked on her idea of internationalism in the East. The following are examples from the archives that further allow us to identify this internationalism in the India–GDR axis. In the annual report of the Ministry of External Affairs of India for 1985–1986, we find two such records:

> The Vice-President paid an official visit to the German Democratic Republic in November 1985 during which he had talks with Chairman Honecker and Vice Chairman Krenz. The visit provided an occasion for reviewing bilateral relations and leading political issues. The Indo-GDR Joint Commission for Economic, Scientific and Technical Cooperation met in New Delhi in November 1985. The two sides were led respectively by the Minister of Industry, Shri N. D. Tiwari and the GDR Minister of Foreign Trade Mr. H. Solle. The Trade and Payments Agreement for 1986 was signed in New Delhi. The most noteworthy event in cultural relations was the holding of 'Days of Indian Culture in the GDR' in October 1985. The Minister of State for Culture Smt. S. Rohatgi visited the GDR on this occasion.[10]

9. *Lok Sabha Debates (English Version): Fourth Session (Eighth Lok Sabha)*, 8th series, vol. 11, no. 18, Thursday, December 12, 1985 - Agrahayana 21, 1907 (Saka) (Lok Sabha Secretariat, [1985]), 80, https://eparlib.nic.in/bitstream/123456789/3409/1/lsd_08_04_12-12-1985.pdf.

10. "Annual Report 1985-86," Ministry of External Affairs, Government of India (1985-86), 30, https://mealib.nic.in/?2514?000.

zu Folgendem beziehen:
(a) die Zensurrichtlinien für Filme;
(b) ob importierte Filme gesondert von indischen Filmen behandelt werden;
(c) ob ein höherer Beamter des Grades Jt. Chairman in Madras oder Cochin eingesetzt werden soll, der sich um alle Fälle von Zensur außerhalb politischer Belange kümmert; und
(d) ob die importierten Filme am Einfuhrhafen zensiert werden sollen?

STAATSMINISTERIN IN DEN ABTEILUNGEN FÜR BILDUNG UND KULTUR, SHRIMATI SUSHILA ROHATGI:
(a) und (b) Sämtliche zur Genehmigung vorgelegten importierten Filme werden vom Central Board of Film Certification nach den Bestimmungen des Kinematografiegesetzes von 1952 und den darin niedergelegten Leitlinien geprüft. Eine Kopie dieser Richtlinien wird auf dem Tisch der zweiten Kammer ausgelegt [in der Bibliothek, siehe Nr. LT 1942/55].
(c) Nein, mein Herr.
(d) Es gibt zurzeit keine derartigen Vorschläge."[7]

Vom 12. Mai 1986 bis zum 9. Mai 1988 war Rohatgi Staatsministerin für Energie und setzte sich auch hier nachdrücklich dafür ein, verschiedene Bereiche der Bildung und Kultur miteinander zu verbinden. Neben ihrer intensiven parlamentarischen Tätigkeit als Staatsministerin trieb Rohatgi beharrlich ihre Vision vom Internationalismus im Osten voran. Im Folgenden einige Beispiele aus dem Archiv, die diesen Internationalismus auf der Achse Indien – DDR für uns greifbarer machen. Im Jahresbericht des indischen Außenministeriums von 1985/86 finden wir diesbezüglich zwei Einträge:

> „Der Vizepräsident reiste im November 1985 zu einem offiziellen Besuch in die Deutsche Demokratische Republik, wo er mit dem Staatsratsvorsitzenden Honecker und dem Stellvertretenden Vorsitzenden Krenz sprach. Der Besuch bot die Gelegenheit zu einer Bestandsaufnahme der bilateralen Beziehungen und vordringlichen politischen Themen. Die gemeinsame

7. https://eparlib.nic.in/bitstream/123456789/3409/1/lsd_08_04_12-12-1985.pdf, Sp. 80.

11. Ibid, 29.

12. *Rulings and Observations from the Chair, 1952–2000* (Rajya Sabha Secretariat, 2001), 312.

And a second that can help us identify the continuity of her cultural efforts over the longer term:

> A leading event was the decision to hold a Festival of Indian culture in the USSR in mid-1987 to be followed by a Festival of Soviet culture in India in the winter of 1987. Other leading visitors from India to the Soviet Union during this period were the Defence Minister, the Minister of State for Information & Broadcasting Shri N. V. Gadgil and the Minister of State for Culture Smt. Sushila Rohatgi.[11]

Many rules, such as "Paper can be laid on the table anytime," are still in use by the Indian government and the rules are regularly quoted in parliamentary transactions, no matter which party is in power.

> Papers laid on the Table: Papers can be laid on the Table by the Government at any time.
> The Deputy Minister in the Ministry of Finance, Shrimati Sushila Rohatgi laid a copy of the notification regarding enhancement of excise duty on *Khandsari* sugar towards the end of the sitting on 30 April 1974. Shri Rajnarain objected to the laying of papers at any time by the Deputy Minister. The Vice-Chairman said: From the Government side the Minister can place a statement at any time.[12]

We haven't heard the speech that we see her delivering in this image at the Albertinum, but we can get an idea of her sense of humor, which she often used to put things in their place and give a larger meaning to things. Once, while she was Minister of Culture, she was continuously interrupted by two members during a parliamentary session. One was asking about the breaking of idols and another about the stealing of idols from India, after rare statues had been seized by Mathura city police in the state of Uttar Pradesh. This episode is also important in terms of restitution politics in the West today and of how Sushila settled these questions in her own way early on.

> Kommission für wirtschaftliche, wissenschaftliche und technische Zusammenarbeit zwischen Indien und der DDR tagte im November 1985 in Delhi. Die beiden Seiten wurden vom Industrieminister Shri N. D. Tiwari respektive DDR-Außenhandelsminister H. Sölle geführt. Eine Handels- und Zahlungsabwicklungsvereinbarung für das Jahr 1986 wurde in Neu-Delhi unterzeichnet. Im Bereich kultureller Beziehungen waren vor allem die ‚Tage der Kultur Indiens in der DDR' hervorzuheben. Aus diesem Anlass besuchte die Staatsministerin für Kultur, Smt. S. Rohatgi, die DDR."[8]

Der zweite Eintrag vermittelt einen Eindruck von der Kontinuität ihrer kulturpolitischen Bemühungen über einen längeren Zeitraum hinweg:

> „Ein zentrales Ereignis war die Entscheidung, um die Mitte des Jahres 1987 ein Festival der indischen Kultur in der UdSSR zu veranstalten und anschließend eines der sowjetischen Kultur in Indien im Winter 1987. Unter weiteren hochrangigen Besuchern aus Indien in der Sowjetunion waren der Verteidigungsminister, Staatsminister für Information und Rundfunk Shri N. V. Gadgil und Staatsministerin für Kultur Smt. Sushila Rohatgi."[9]

Zahlreiche Verfahrensregeln wie das „jederzeit mögliche Auslegen von Schriftstücken auf dem Tisch" werden im indischen Parlament bis heute gepflegt und in den Sitzungsprotokollen regelmäßig erwähnt. Auch Regierungswechsel änderten daran nichts:

> „Auslegen von Schriftstücken: Schriftstücke können jederzeit von der Regierung auf dem Tisch ausgelegt werden.
> Die stellvertretende Finanzministerin Shrimati Sushila Rohatgi legte zum Ende der Sitzung vom 30. April 1974 die Abschrift einer Mitteilung bezüglich einer Erhöhung der Steuer auf Khandsari-Zucker aus. Shri Rajnarain protestierte gegen das Auslegen von Schriftstücken durch die Vizeministerin. Der stellvertretende Parlamentsvorsitzende hielt fest: Als Vertreterin der Regierung kann die Ministerin jederzeit eine Verlautbarung in dieser Weise platzieren."[10]

8. *Annual Report 1985–86, Ministry of External Affairs, Government of India*, https://mealib.nic.in/?2514?000?

9. Ebd.

10. *Rulings and Observations from the Chair, 1952–2000*, Neu-Delhi: Rajya Sabha Secretariat 2001, S. 312.

13. *Lok Sabha Debates (English Version): Fourth Session (Eighth Lok Sabha)*, 8th series, vol. 11, no. 13, Thursday, December 5, 1985 – Agrahayana 14, 1907 (Saka) (New Delhi: Lok Sabha Secretariat, [1985]), 28, https://eparlib.nic.in/bitstream/123456789/2965207/1/lsd_08_04_05-12-1985.pdf.

> SHRIMATI KRISHNA SAHI: Is the hon. Minister aware that after theft these rare and priceless idols are being smuggled out of the country and that the quantum of such smuggling has increased over the last five years? Will the hon. Minister state the reasons for this?
> SHRIMATI SUSHILA ROHATGI: Such theft and smuggling do take place. But the figures relating to the centrally protected monuments which we have with us do not show that there has been any increase in such cases over the last one year. On the contrary there has been some decline in this regard. We have the figures with us in this ragard [*sic*] and a vigil is being kept on it, but the smuggling is going on in spite of these efforts. The public also will have to extend their cooperation in this endeavor. We are considering to raise the fine and the term of imprisonment which is six months for the present, for those who indulge in smulging [*sic*] and violation of law and do not get their registration done.[13]

The Chairman of the House interrupted and she gave a sharp retort:

> SMT. SUSHILA ROHATGI: Sir, I seek your protection. Sir, is the question relating to breaking of idols or stealing of idols?
> MR. CHAIRMAN: Whatever you want to answer, you can answer. If you look at the Chair and answer, you won't be diverted.
> SMT. SUSHILA ROHATGI: It is only because I am directly looking at you that I am seeking your protection, Sir.
> MR. CHAIRMAN: I am really grateful to you.[14]

In the various archival instances that we find in the SKD in-house archive, the name of Dr. Krishna Lal, deputy director of the National Crafts Museum in New Delhi, appears again and again on various administrative forms—signing a long list of objects that has been meticulously examined or a memo on the trip or creating specifications of the object and suggesting edits. The changes she made and the way she held such a large-scale discussion together attest to her deep commitment

Wir kennen den Wortlaut der Rede nicht, die wir Rohatgi auf dem Foto im Albertinum halten sehen, doch es gibt Belege für ihren Witz, durch den es ihr oft gelang, die Dinge ins Verhältnis und in einen umfassenderen Zusammenhang zu setzen. So wurde sie in ihrer Zeit als Kulturministerin während einer Parlamentssitzung fortwährend von zwei Abgeordneten unterbrochen. Einer stellte Fragen zur Zerstörung von Heiligenbildern, ein anderer zum Diebstahl von Heiligenfiguren aus Indien. Anlass war, dass im Staat Uttar Pradesh kostbare Statuen von der Stadtpolizei in Mathura sichergestellt worden waren. Diese Episode ist auch mit Blick auf die heutige Restitutionspolitik in westlichen Ländern bemerkenswert. Umso interessanter, wie Rohatgi schon am Beginn ihrer Amtszeit mit diesen Fragen umging.

> „SHRIMATI KRISHNA SAHI: Ist der ehrenwerten Ministerin bewusst, dass diese kostbaren und unbezahlbaren Heiligenbilder nach dem Diebstahl außer Landes geschmuggelt werden und dass die Zahl solcher Entwendungen in den letzten fünf Jahren stetig gestiegen ist? Vermag die ehrenwerte Staatsministerin Gründe dafür zu nennen?
> SHRIMATI SUSHILA ROHATGI: Ein solcher Diebstahl und Schmuggel findet in der Tat statt. Doch die Zahlen bezüglich der wichtigsten geschützten Denkmäler, über die wir verfügen, lassen keinerlei Zunahme solcher Fälle im Verlauf des letzten Jahres erkennen. Im Gegenteil sind sie etwas zurückgegangen. Wir haben die Zahlen parat und das Problem im Auge, dennoch und trotz dieser Mühen geht der Schmuggel weiter. Auch die Öffentlichkeit wird sich zu mehr Zusammenarbeit mit den Behörden bereit finden müssen. Wir erwägen, die Geldstrafen zu erhöhen und auch die Haftstrafen, die gegenwärtig sechs Monate für jemanden betragen, der sich in Schmuggel und Bruch des Gesetzes ergeht und sich seiner Festsetzung entzieht."[11]

Der Parlamentsvorsitzende unterbrach sie, und sie reagierte schlagfertig:

> „SMT SUSHILA ROHATGI: Mein Herr, ich bitte um Ihren Schutz. Zielt die Frage auf die Zerstörung oder den Diebstahl von Heiligenbildern?
> VORSITZENDER: Worauf immer Sie antworten wollen, antworten Sie.

11. https://eparlib.nic.in/bitstream/123456789/2965207/1/lsd_08_04_05-12-1985.pdf, Sp. 28.

to her role and her expertise on the subject. While preparing the catalog, she went to great lengths to get the most precise description of craft products from a huge geographical area, with an immense variety of object samples, many of them on display in the 2024 exhibition at the Albertinum *Till the Sun Rises*.

It is probably also good to read this account of her journeys after this brief visit to the Albertinum in 1986. Now retired from the National Museum of India in Delhi, Dr. Krishna Lal, together with her daughter, owns and runs a craft-based art gallery in Delhi that goes by the name of Krishnayan.

The gallery's website formerly included the following biography: "Since retiring from the National Museum, Mrs. Lal has been devoting her time and energy to artists from remote parts of India and is bringing these traditional designs of India rendered in the non-traditional medium of textiles and art objects to the mainstream.

Mrs. Lal studied at Aligarh Muslim University and has a Diploma in Museography from France. She has explored museums and presented papers at international conferences across the globe. At the National Museum, she has coordinated several national and international exhibitions.

Her literary and research work includes catalogs on *Bidriware in the National Museum Collection, New Delhi*; *Indian Decorative Arts*, published in German and Russian; and *Phulkari: From the Realm of Women's Creativity*. Mrs. Lal was honored for her work on Phulkari by Prime Minister Manmohan Singh's wife Mrs. Gursharan Kaur.

14. *The House Laughs: An Anthology of Wit and Humour in the Rajya Sabha* (Rajya Sabha Secretariat, 2015), 78, https://cms.rajyasabha.nic.in/UploadedFiles/ElectronicPublications/The_House_Laughs.pdf.

Ausstellung des Nationalmuseums New Delhi anläßlich der Tage der indischen Kultur in d. DDR

501/
198513
F 1520

24. 10. 1985
Eröffnung der Sonderausstellung „Kostbarkeiten indischer Handwerkskunst des 16. bis 19. Jahrhunderts" im Albertinum, 2. Obergeschoß (Georg-Treu-Platz-Trakt)
Frau Sushila Rohatgi, Staatsministerin für Erziehung und Kultur der Republik Indien, bei der Eröffnungsansprache.
1. Reihe von links:
1) Prof. Bachmann, Generaldirektor
2) Oswin Forker, Sekretär f. Wissenschaft, Volksbildung u. Kultur der SED-Bezirksleitung Dresden
3) Günther Witteck, Vorsitzender des Rates d. Bezirkes Dresden
4) Kurt Löffler, Staatssekretär im Ministerium f. Kultur d. DDR
5) Dr. L. P. Sihare, Direktor des Nationalmuseums New-Delhi
6) Krishna Lal, stellv. Direktorin der Kunstgewerbesammlung des Nationalmuseums New Delhi

ADN-ZENTRALBILD

Back of a photo of Sushila Rohatgi at the opening of the exhibition *Treasures of Indian Craftsmanship from the 16th to the 19th Century* on October 24, 1985, in the Albertinum, Dresden

Rückseite eines Fotos von Sushila Rohatgi bei der Eröffnung der Ausstellung *Kostbarkeiten indischer Handwerkskunst des 16. bis 19. Jahrhunderts* am 24. Oktober 1985 im Albertinum, Dresden

Wenn Sie zum Vorsitzenden schauen, während sie antworten, werden Sie nicht abgelenkt.
SMT. SUSHILA ROHATGI: Gerade weil ich Sie gerade direkt ansehe, mein Herr, bitte ich um Ihren Schutz.
VORSITZENDER: Das rechne ich Ihnen hoch an."[12]

Auf Dokumenten im Hausarchiv der SKD erscheint immer wieder der Name von Krishna Lal, der stellvertretenden Leiterin des National Crafts Museum in Neu-Delhi, nicht zuletzt auf allerhand Verwaltungsformularen. In einem Fall unterschrieb sie eine peinlich genau geprüfte lange Liste mit Objekten, in einem anderen einen Vermerk zu einer Reise. Anderswo machte sie Detailangaben zu den Objekten und schlug Textänderungen vor. Diese Änderungen und die Art und Weise, in der Lal einen Kulturtransfer dieser Größenordnung steuerte, zeigen nicht nur, wie sehr sie dabei in ihrer Rolle aufging, sondern beweisen auch ihre Sachkompetenz. Bei der Arbeit am Katalog scheute sie keine Mühe, möglichst präzise Beschreibungen der Handwerkskunst aus einem großen Kulturraum mit einer enormen Vielfalt an Ausstellungsstücken zustande zu bringen. Etliche von diesen werden auch in der Ausstellung *Bis zum Sonnenaufgang* im Albertinum 2024 gezeigt.

Aufschlussreich sind wahrscheinlich auch die folgenden Angaben über ihre Zeit nach dem kurzen Gastspiel im Albertinum von 1986. Seit ihrer Pensionierung und ihrem Abschied vom Indischen Nationalmuseum in Delhi betreibt Krishna Lal mit ihrer Tochter eine Galerie für Kunsthandwerk in Delhi mit dem Namen Krishnayan.

12. *The House Laughs, an Anthology of Wit and Humour in the Rajya Sabha*, Neu-Delhi: Rajya Sabha Secretariat 2015, S. 78, online: https://cms.rajyasabha.nic.in/UploadedFiles/ElectronicPublications/The_House_Laughs.pdf

Her latest publication is *Kantha: Poetry Embroidered on Cloth*, which is the catalog of the Kantha Collection of IGNCA, and her book *Cosmetics and Its Impact on Indian Art* is being prepared for publication. Mrs. Lal has spent over fifty years in the field of decorative arts and textiles. She is a decorated officer of the government of India and has received several accolades for her work both while serving at the National Museum and after her retirement. She has received a commendation from India's first prime minister, Shri Jawaharlal Nehru. She has been featured on national television and in several publications."

In her earlier work *Image Matters*, Tina M. Campt discusses familial images and their relationship with affect. This helps us to understand the affective encounters that we find in these images of Sushila Rohatgi and Dr. Krishna Lal in the SKD archives. Campt writes: "How do such images *register*? To ask how these photos register is to attempt to catalog both a sensibility and a range of sensory affects they display and evoke in others. Family and the forms of filiation and affiliation, linkage and belonging that family evokes constitute a crucial sensibility that registers in these images at multiple sensory and affective levels. It is a sensibility that begins with vision and sight, with *what we see*, but it certainly does not end there."[15]

It is in such affiliations and familiar affectivity that continuities between the work of Chetna Vora, Sushila Rohatgi, and Dr. Krishna Lal established themselves.

15. Tina M. Campt, *Image Matters: Archive, Photography, and the African Diaspora in Europe* (Duke University Press, 2012), 13.

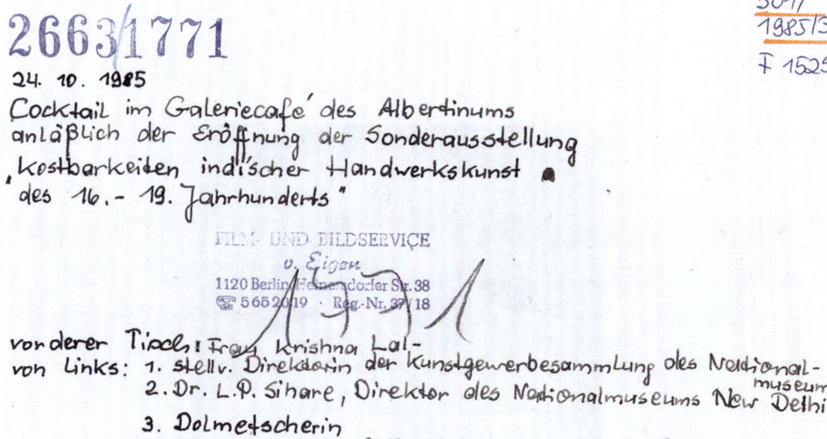

2663/1771

501/
1985/3
F 1525

24. 10. 1985
Cocktail im Galeriecafé des Albertinums
anläßlich der Eröffnung der Sonderausstellung
„Kostbarkeiten indischer Handwerkskunst
des 16.–19. Jahrhunderts"

FILM- UND BILDSERVICE
v. Eigen
1120 Berlin, Heinersdorfer Str. 38
565 20 19 · Reg.-Nr. 37/18

vorderer Tisch: Frau Krishna Lal –
von links: 1. stellv. Direktorin der Kunstgewerbesammlung des Nationalmuseums
2. Dr. L.P. Sihare, Direktor des Nationalmuseums New Delhi
3. Dolmetscherin
4. Staatsministerin f. Erziehung u. Kultur der Republik Indien Sushila Rohatgi (verdeckt)
5. Kurt Löffler, Staatssekretär im Ministerium f. Kultur der DDR

Record of the various participants at the opening of the exhibition *Treasures of Indian Craftsmanship from the 16th to the 19th Century* in the Albertinum, Dresden, on the back of a photograph, 1985

Zeugnis verschiedener Teilnehmer bei der Eröffnung der Ausstellung *Kostbarkeiten indischer Handwerkskunst des 16. bis 19. Jahrhunderts* im Albertinum, Dresden, auf der Rückseite eines Fotos, 1985

Auf der Website der Galerie waren folgende biografische Angaben zu finden: „Frau Lal widmet ihre Zeit und Kraft Künstler·innen aus entlegenen Teilen des Landes und überträgt traditionelle Muster und Entwürfe Indiens in nicht traditionelle Medien wie Textilien und Kunstobjekte für ein breiteres Publikum.

Sie studierte an der Aligarh Muslim University und hat in Frankreich einen Abschluss in Museografie erworben. Sie hat überall in der Welt Museen studiert und wissenschaftliche Vorträge gehalten. Im Nationalmuseum hat sie eine Reihe nationaler und internationaler Ausstellungen koordiniert.

Zu ihren Forschungsarbeiten und Publikationen gehören Kataloge zum Bestand an Bidriware (Metallarbeiten aus Karnataka) in der Sammlung des Nationalmuseums, Beiträge zu angewandter indischer Kunst in deutscher und russischer Sprache sowie *Phulkari: From the Realm of Women's Creativity*. Für ihre Forschung zur Phulkari-Stickerei wurde sie von Gursharan Kaur, der Gattin von Ministerpräsident Manmohan Singh, ausgezeichnet.

Ihre jüngste Veröffentlichung ist *Kantha: Poetry Embroidered on Cloth*, der Katalog zur Kantha Collection des Indira Gandhi National Centre for the Arts. Demnächst erscheint der Band *Cosmetics and Its Impact on Indian Art*. Frau Lal hat mehr als 50 Jahre im Bereich der angewandten Kunst und Textilgestaltung gearbeitet. Sie hat als Bedienstete des indischen Staates Ehrungen erhalten und wurde für ihre Arbeit im Nationalmuseum, auch nach ihrer Pensionierung, nachdrücklich gelobt, unrer anderem von Indiens erstem Ministerpräsidenten Shri Jawaharlal Nehru. Sie selbst und ihre Arbeit waren Gegenstand im indischen Rundfunk und in mehreren Publikationen."

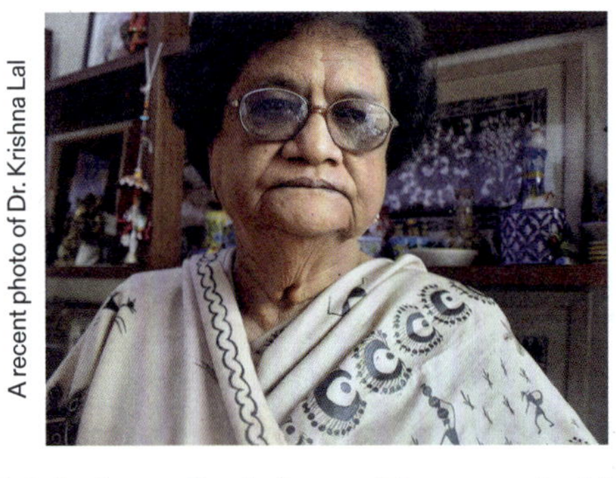
A recent photo of Dr. Krishna Lal

Ein aktuelles Bild von Krishna Lal

Tina M. Campt beschäftigt sich in ihrem Buch *Image Matters – Archive, Photography, and the African Diaspora in Europe* (2012) mit Familienfotos und ihrem Bezug zum Gefühlsleben. Dieses Buch hilft uns, die Affektbegegnungen in den Fotos von Sushila Rohatgi und Krishna Lal im Archiv der SKD zu beschreiben. „Wie prägen sich solche Fotos uns ein?", fragt Campt:

„Diese Frage zu stellen, heißt zugleich, eine Palette von Empfindungen und Sinneseindrücken zu inventarisieren, die solche Fotos zeigen und in anderen erzeugen. Familienbande und die Formen von Kindschaft und Abstammung, von Verwandtschaft und Zugehörigkeit, die mit der Familie einhergehen, sind elementare Empfindungsweisen, und sie schlagen sich in diesen Bildern auf vielen Ebenen der Sinne und Affekte nieder. Diese Welt der Empfindungen beginnt mit dem Sehen und mit dem, was wir sehen, aber sie endet gewiss nicht damit."[13]

Solche Zugehörigkeiten und Affekte der Vertrautheit bildeten den Rahmen, in dem Kontinuitäten zwischen den Lebenswerken von Chetna Vora, Sushila Rohatgi und Krishna Lal entstehen konnten.

13. Tina M. Campt, *Image Matters: Archive, Photography, and the African Diaspora in Europe*, Durham, NC: Duke University Press 2012, S. 13.

THE GEOPOLITICS OF EXHIBITING AS A PROBLEM-SPACE: A SEALED ENVELOPE FROM 1985

Doreen Mende

DIE GEOPOLITIK DES AUSSTELLENS ALS PROBLEMRAUM, ERLÄUTERT ANHAND EINES VERSIEGELTEN UMSCHLAGS AUS DEM JAHR 1985

This essay[1] is a reflection on the exhibition *Art Treasures from Dresden* from the Old Masters Picture Gallery of the Dresden State Art Collections (Staatliche Kunstsammlungen Dresden, SKD) at the National Museum in New Delhi in 1984/85, with a particular focus on the curatorial knowledge facilitating the geopolitics of exhibiting during the global Cold War. What can we learn from it, specifically in dealing with an institutional awareness, about the collections' complex knowledge systems at the thresholds of art, exhibition making, art historical research, and histories of imperialism and war? How can we approach this assemblage through a critical post-communist horizon in a postwar *global East* that is documented in the archive of the SKD? How did an exhibition in 1985, which operated within a geopolitical context between the German Democratic Republic (GDR) and India, deal with colonial legacies of modernity, and how did it resonate in a modernity of state-structured internationalism? It would be ignorant to believe that a worldview aligned with state-socialist principles (as they existed in the GDR) in the context of the global Cold War could have overcome the racial violence of friendship—i.e., a friendship aligned with strategies of what Quinn Slobodian called "socialist chromatism."[2] Thus, describing such modernity cannot be easily analyzed through a moral distance that makes a judgmental distinction between good and bad. In the words of David Scott, what if we consider the exhibition in hand as a "problem-space" that instigates reflection and a set of methodologies to think with—full of contradictions and challenges—rather than a problem that could somehow be solved? Because a "problem-space" is "an ensemble of questions and answers around which a horizon of identifiable stakes (conceptual as well as ideological-political stakes) hangs. That is to say, what defines this discursive context are not only the particular problems that get posed as problems as such (the problem of 'race,' say), but the particular questions that seem worth asking and the kinds of answers that seem worth having."[3] The concept of "problem-space" as a figure of thought shall guide us through the following analysis of the exhibition as a network of practices to navigate a curatorial research within the political pressures of state socialism during the Cold War. A subtle variety of implications may be drawn from the set of questions that oscillate between the cultural diplomacy, curatorial

1. I would like to thank Monica Juneja and Eva Bentcheva for inviting me to present this research at the conference "Lessons Learned? Transcultural Perspectives in Curating and Pedagogies," which was held at the SKD's Japanese Palais (Japanisches Palais), July 14–16, 2022, as part of the 2022 *Transcultural Academy "Towards a Worlded Public,"* conceptualized by the Heidelberg team of the international research group Worlding Public Cultures: The Arts and Social Innovation (WPC).

2. Quinn Slobodian, "Socialist Chromatism: Race, Racism, and the Racial Rainbow in East Germany," in *Comrades of Color: East Germany in the Cold War World*, ed. Quinn Slobodian (Berghahn, 2015).

3. David Scott, *Conscripts of Modernity: The Tragedy of Colonial Enlightenment* (Duke University Press, 2004), 4.

Dieser Essay entfaltet einige Überlegungen zur Ausstellung *Art Treasures from Dresden*, veranstaltet 1984/85 von der Gemäldegalerie Alter Meister der Staatlichen Kunstsammlungen Dresden im Indischen Nationalmuseum in Neu-Delhi. Insbesondere geht es mir hier um ein kuratorisches Wissen, das in der Zeit des Kalten Krieges die Geopolitik des Ausstellens von Kunst begünstigte. Was können wir daraus über die Komplexität der Wissenssysteme einer Sammlung im Grenzbereich von Kunst, Ausstellungsgestaltung und kunsthistorischer Forschung, aber auch im größeren Zusammenhang einer Geschichte von Imperialismus und Krieg lernen? Wie können wir daraus ein entsprechendes institutionelles Bewusstsein entwickeln? Wie uns dieser Gemengelage in einem kritischen postkommunistischen Horizont und im Kontext des globalen Nachkriegs-Ostens annähern, der im Archiv der Staatlichen Kunstsammlungen Dresden dokumentiert ist? Wie ging eine Ausstellung von 1985, die unter den damaligen geopolitischen Rahmenbedingungen im Austausch zwischen der DDR und Indien stattfand, mit dem kolonialen Erbe der Moderne um, und welche Resonanz erzeugte dies innerhalb einer Moderne staatlich gegründeter Internationalismen?

Es wäre unbedarft zu glauben, dass eine den Grundsätzen des Staatssozialismus gehorchende Weltanschauung (wie sie in der DDR bestand) im globalen Kalten Krieg die Rassengewalt der Freundschaft – also einer Freundschaft nach den strategischen Maßgaben dessen, was Quinn Slobodian „sozialistischen Chromatismus" genannt hat[1] – jemals wirklich überwunden hätte. Eine so geartete Moderne zu beschreiben, gelingt mithin nicht aus der moralischen Distanz des Urteilens zwischen Gut und Böse. Wenn wir nun aber, um es mit David Scott zu sagen, die fragliche Ausstellung als einen „Problemraum" betrachten, der eine Reflexion darüber anstößt und einige dafür geeignete Methoden bereithält? Der uns in Widersprüche verstrickt und uns Rätsel aufgibt, statt eben nur ein Problem zu behaupten, das sich irgendwie lösen ließe? Ein „Problemraum" wäre demnach „ein ganzes Bündel von Fragen und Antworten, um die herum sich ein Horizont feststellbarer (begrifflicher ebenso wie ideologisch-politischer) Interessen und Anliegen abzeichnet. Bestimmend für den Diskurskontext sind, mit anderen Worten, nicht nur die besonderen Probleme, die sich als Probleme per se stellen (etwa das Problem der ‚Rasse'), sondern besondere Fragen, die es wert scheinen, gestellt zu werden, sowie Antworten, die die Mühe wert sind."[2] Der Begriff des „Problemraums" soll uns als Gedankenfigur durch die nun

1. Quinn Slobodian, „Socialist Chromatism: Rase, Racism, and the Racial Rainbow in East Germany", in: ders. (Hg.), *Comrades of Color. East Germany in the Cold War Wold*, New York: Berghahn 2015, S. 23–39.

2. David Scott, *Conscripts of Modernity: The Tragedy of Colonial Enlightenment*, Durham, NC: Duke University Press 2004, S. 4.

intelligence, and geopolitical alliances connecting India (at the time of Indira Gandhi) with the GDR through memories, promises, and failed attempts at anti-colonial worldmaking. It constitutes what could be considered a *modernity otherwise* that is similar to a *knowledge otherwise*—i.e., a knowledge that might have remained sealed for decades, in this case literally: When I started my research on this exhibition, which I also chose as an initial point of entry as head of research at the SKD into the vastness of the institution's historical (un)consciousness, there were envelopes full of documents in the archive that had not been opened since they were sealed—most likely by the curator—in 1985. Soon after embarking on the research, my interest was drawn to the curator, the art historian Annaliese Mayer-Meintschel.

The exhibition *Art Treasures from Dresden* shown at the National Museum, Janpath, in New Delhi from November 18, 1984, to February 10, 1985 was curated by Mayer-Meintschel, a specialist in Dutch and Flemish painting of the fifteenth to eighteenth century who had worked at the SKD since 1955. In 1963, she became custodian of the Old Masters Picture Gallery and was its director from 1969/70 until 1991. Colleagues described her as a resolute, charismatic, and independent intellectual who was not a member of the SED (Socialist Unity Party), the ruling party in the GDR's system of state socialism.[4] One could only maintain a position of power in a state museum through fearlessness, social intelligence, and an excellent international reputation as a scholar-cum-custodian of the works of artists like Belotto, Rubens, Brueghel, Rembrandt, Van Dyck, Dürer, Cranach, and Titian. *Art Treasures from Dresden* in New Delhi encapsulates her methods, vocabularies, and tactics.

4. I would like to thank Harald Marx, Uta Neidhardt, and Thomas Rudert for their input.

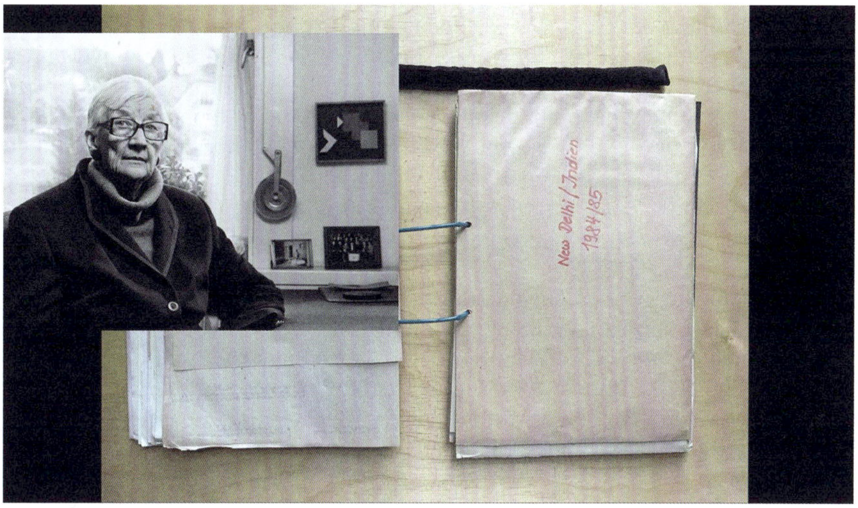

Annaliese Mayer-Meintschel (1928–2020), director of the Old Masters Picture Gallery in Dresden from 1968 to 1991, curator of the exhibition *Art Treasures from Dresden*, 1984, National Museum, New Delhi, and cover of the archival folder SKD 02/GGAM 189, Staatliche Kunstsammlungen Dresden

Annaliese Mayer-Meintschel (1928–2020), von 1968 bis 1991 Direktorin der Gemäldegalerie Alte Meister Dresden, Kuratorin der Ausstellung *Art Treasures from Dresden*, 1984, Nationalmuseum, Neu-Delhi, und Deckel der Archivmappe SKD 02/GGAM 189, Hausarchiv Staatliche Kunstsammlungen Dresden

folgende Analyse leiten. Wir betrachten darin die Ausstellung als ein Netzwerk von Praktiken, mit denen sich kuratorische Forschung unter den politischen Zwängen des Staatssozialismus im Kalten Krieg betreiben ließ. Daher können die Fragen, die sich daraus ergeben, auch fortführen von jener nach der graduellen Vereinnahmung beim Jonglieren zwischen Kulturdiplomatie, kuratorischer List und geopolitischer Bündnistreue, wie sie zwischen Indien (zur Zeit Indira Gandhis) und der DDR unter anderem in Gestalt von Erinnerungen, Verheißungen und Versuchen und Irrtümern antikolonialer Weltschöpfung wirksam wurden. Diese Praktiken ergeben insgesamt etwas, das man eine *andersartige Moderne* in Anlehnung an ein *andersartiges Wissen* nennen könnte, das heißt an ein Wissen, das andernfalls womöglich noch Jahrzehnte unter Verschluss geblieben wäre – in diesem Fall übrigens durchaus im engeren Wortsinn: Als ich mit meinen Recherchen für diese Ausstellung begann, die ich auch zum Ausgangspunkt für mein Eintauchen in die Weiten und Tiefen des historischen (Un-) Bewussten dieser Institution als neue Forschungsleiterin an den SKD machte, gab es im Archiv Umschläge voller Dokumente, die seit dem Verschließen vermutlich durch die Kuratorin im Jahr 1985 niemand geöffnet hatte. Es dauerte nicht lange, bis ich mich für diese Kuratorin zu interessieren begann.

Die Ausstellung *Art Treasures from Dresden* im National Museum, Janpath, Neu-Delhi, vom 18. November 1984 bis 10. Februar 1985 wurde von der Kunsthistorikern Annaliese Mayer-Meintschel kuratiert, einer seit 1955 in den SKD tätigen Spezialistin für die niederländische und flämische Malerei des 15. bis 18. Jahrhunderts. Ab 1963 war Mayer-Meintschel Kustodin der Gemäldegalerie Alter Meister und seit 1969/70 deren Direktorin. Kolleg·innen beschreiben sie als eine resolute, charismatische und freisinnige Intellektuelle, die nicht der Sozialistischen Einheitspartei Deutschlands angehörte.[3] Unter diesen

3. Ich danke Harald Marx, Uta Neidhardt und Thomas Rudert für diese Hinweise in persönlichen Gesprächen.

5. "Modalitäten des Leihvertrages sind mit mir oder Mitarbeitern der Galerie nicht besprochen worden." Archive number 02/GGAM/89 SKD archive [my translation].

The SKD's in-house archive contained all kinds of documents that help to reconstruct the conditions of the making of the exhibition, outlining an exhibition history: correspondence between Mayer-Meintschel and the SKD's general director, *Hausmitteilungen* (in-house memos) in the age before emails, agreements/negotiations with ministries and between the National Museum in New Delhi and the SKD, lists of art works, revised lists of art terminology, insurance budgets, letters, floor plans, catalog concepts and drafts, telegrams, travel plans, itineraries, authorizations for police protection to secure the "art treasures" in transit, visa and transit visa regulations for paintings and people alike, from Dresden to Amsterdam via West Germany through to their arrival in New Delhi, and back again. For example, the *Agreement* (filed in the folder 02/GGAM 189) comprises a nine-page document explicating in fifteen points the precise conditions of realizing *Art Treasures from Dresden* in New Delhi and a five-page appendix with a list of works in three languages: English, Hindi, and German. In brief, the agreement indicates (a) geopolitics across a divided world during the global Cold War, when the route traveled by the artworks is mapped out from Dresden to Copenhagen (passing through West Germany) by truck, and from Amsterdam to New Delhi by plane, accompanied by art historians from Dresden, including Mayer-Meintschel, and on the way back from New Delhi by Dr. A. S. Bisht and others ; (b) the agreement also indicates the political economy of the exhibition with regard not only to the insurance value of 40,700,000 Swiss Francs (which also shows how the political economy was involved in the geopolitics of exhibition infrastructures) but also to the organization of a police escort for the lender's commissioners from Dresden to Copenhagen and back "undertaken by the lender, providing police protection." In the legal documents, we can also see the "art treasures" being recategorized as "artworks." In an internal memorandum by Mayer-Meintschel to the museum's general management, the curator notes: "Modalities of the loan agreement have not been discussed with me or the gallery staff."[5] This is indicative of Mayer-Meintschel's clarity in holding her ground as a director of one of the GDR's most important historic art collections. However, it is the sheer variety of documents that makes the complex infrastructure of exhibition making visible.

Umständen eine Machtposition in einem staatlichen Museum zu erreichen und zu halten, erforderte Unerschrockenheit, soziale Intelligenz und einen hervorragenden internationalen Ruf als Wissenschaftlerin und Kustodin der Werke von Bellotto, Rubens, Brueghel, Rembrandt, van Dyck, Dürer, Cranach und Tizian. *Art Treasures from Dresden* in Neu-Delhi stellte Mayer-Meintschels Methoden, ihr Vokabular und ihre Taktiken exemplarisch unter Beweis.

Das Hausarchiv der SKD enthält alle Arten von Dokumenten, anhand deren sich die Entstehungsbedingungen dieser Ausstellung und ihr Verlauf rekonstruieren lassen: Schriftverkehr zwischen Mayer-Meintschel und dem Generaldirektor der SKD, Hausmitteilungen aus einem Zeitalter vor der E-Mail, Vereinbarungen und Verhandlungen mit Ministerien sowie zwischen dem National Museum in Neu-Delhi und den SKD, Listen von Kunstwerken, überarbeitete Listen kunsthistorischer Begrifflichkeiten, Versicherungssummen, Briefe, Grundrisse, Konzepte und Entwürfe für den Katalog, Telegramme, Reisepläne und -routen, Genehmigungen für den Polizeischutz zur Sicherung der „Kunstschätze" auf dem Transportweg, Visa- und Transitvisabestimmungen für Gemälde wie für Personen und die Reise von Dresden über Westdeutschland und Amsterdam nach Neu-Delhi und wieder zurück. Beispielsweise umfasst das Agreement (abgelegt in Ordner 02/GGAM 189) eine neunseitige Erörterung in 15 Punkten zu den genauen Bedingungen, unter denen *Art Treasures from Dresden* in Neu-Delhi stattfand, sowie einen fünfseitigen Anhang mit einer Werkliste in drei Sprachen: Englisch, Hindi und Deutsch. Die Vereinbarung enthält Einzelheiten über (a) die grenzüberschreitende Geopolitik in einer vom Kalten Weltkrieg gespaltenen Welt, insofern hier die Reiseroute der Kunstwerke von Dresden nach Kopenhagen (durch Westdeutschland) im LKW und von Amsterdam nach Delhi im Flugzeug und in Begleitung von Mayer-Meintschel und anderen Kunsthistorikern aus Dresden sowie auf dem Rückweg von Dr. A.S. Bisht und anderen (n. n.) festgelegt ist; (b) die politische Ökonomie der Ausstellung angesichts nicht nur eines Versicherungswertes von 40 700 000 Schweizer Franken (der zudem auf das Gewicht der politischen Ökonomie in der Geopolitik des Ausstellungsbetriebs hinweist), sondern auch der Aufstellung einer Polizeieskorte für die Beauftragten des Leihgebers auf dem Weg von Dresden nach Kopenhagen und zurück „auf Betreiben des Leihgebers, der für den Polizeischutz sorgt". Wir können in den Rechtsdokumenten

It was most likely Mayer-Meintschel herself who had carefully closed the sealed envelopes in the archive. During my visit, the archivist Vera Wobad and I opened them. The first envelope contained press clippings from Indian newspapers, such as a *Times of India* article by the poet and scholar Keshav Malik.[6] Another article by Babatosh Chakraborty in the *National Herald* with the title "GDR for closer economic ties" also included a short report on the exhibition, and the illustrated magazine Saptahik Hindustan published a review. Furthermore, the folder contained an invitation card to an official reception of the Ministry of Cultural Affairs with the general director of the National Museum, Mr. Laxmi Prasad Sihare, season's greetings by the Polish sculptor Fredda Brilliant and her husband, the British writer Herbert Marshall, as well as the exhibition booklet in English and Hindi.[7] The second envelope, a few pages further on in the folder, contained the actual floor plan of the exhibition in Gallery 1.F.F. with the entrance and exit all in one hall space. Mayer-Meintschel's profound knowledge of art history as a methodology allowed her to mobilize beyond ideologies of state-socialism, as it existed in the GDR, toward a transnational European approach to culture. While this approach builds on a moment in world history when "art treasures" defined art history as a discipline, it also employs (art) history as a method to undermine the hegemony of state socialism. Mayer-Meintschel clearly fosters a transnational or, more precisely, a European approach (which would be critically seen as Eurocentric today) to the exhibition when she writes in her curatorial opening address to the Indian prime minister:[8] "When selecting the pictures for the exhibition, we tried to let something of the magnificence and richness of the collection be expressed. We also wanted to show

6. Keshav Malik (1924–2014) was a prominent Indian poet, art and literary critic, arts scholar, and curator of postindependence India who assisted Jawaharlal Nehru.

7. In the conversation after presenting this paper, Monica Juneja pointed out the relevance of Laxmi Prasad Sihare (1929–1993), whose research instigated an Indian modernity through his work on art history and institutional vision. Fredda Brilliant (1903–1999) was a Polish sculptor and actress, born in Łódź, Poland. She sculpted some of the greatest figures of her time, including Jawaharlal Nehru, V. K. Krishna Menon, Indira Gandhi, US President John F. Kennedy, and Buckminster Fuller.

8. Most likely Rajiv Gandhi, although the name of the prime minister is not mentioned in the documents.

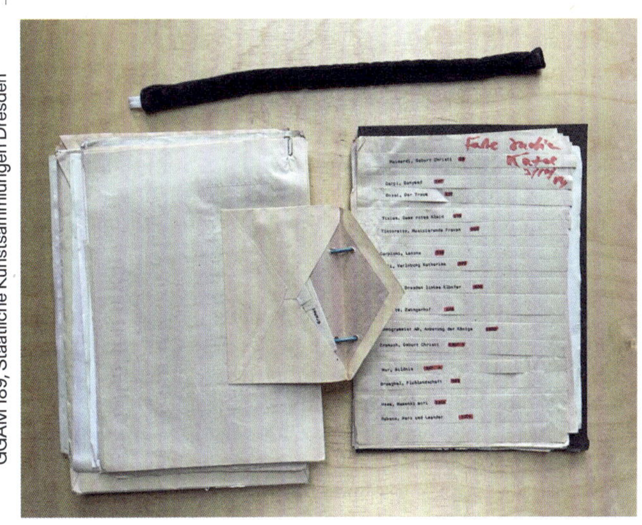

Editing of the catalog *Art Treasures from Dresden*, 1983/84, archival folder SKD 02/ GGAM 189, Staatliche Kunstsammlungen Dresden

Aus der Arbeit am Katalog *Art Treasures from Dresden*, 1983/84, Archivmappe SKD 02/ GGAM 189, Staatliche Kunstsammlungen Dresden

auch eine Umdeutung der „Kunstschätze" zu „Kunstwerken" beobachten. In einer Hausnotiz von Mayer-Meintschel an die oberste Verwaltungsebene des Museums schrieb die Kuratorin: „Modalitäten des Leihvertrages sind mit mir oder Mitarbeitern der Galerie nicht besprochen worden"[4] – womit Mayer-Meintschel deutlich den Anspruch anmeldete, als Direktorin einer der wichtigsten Kunstsammlungen der DDR in solchen Angelegenheiten mitzureden. Und allein schon die Fülle verschiedenartiger Dokumente lässt die komplexe Infrastruktur hinter dem Werden dieser Ausstellung erkennen.

Mit größter Wahrscheinlichkeit war es Annaliese Mayer-Meintschel selbst, die die Dokumente in Umschläge gesteckt, verschlossen und sorgfältig im Archiv verwahrt hat. Während meines Besuchs dort öffnete ich sie gemeinsam mit der Archivarin Vera Wobad. Der erste Umschlag enthielt Presseausschnitte aus indischen Zeitungen, darunter einen Artikel des Dichters und Gelehrten Keshav Malik in der *Times of India*.[5] Ein weiterer Artikel von Babatosh Chakraborty im *National Herald* mit dem Titel „DDR für engere wirtschaftliche Zusammenarbeit" beinhaltete einen kurzen Bericht über die Ausstellung, und die Illustrierte *Saptahik Hindustan* brachte eine Kritik. Enthalten war des Weiteren eine Einladungskarte zum offiziellen Empfang im indischen Ministerium für kulturelle Angelegenheiten mit dem Generaldirektor des Nationalmuseums Laxmi Prasad Sihare,[6] eine Grußkarte der polnischen Bildhauerin Fredda Brilliant[7] und ihres Ehemanns, des britischen Schriftstellers Herbert Marshall, und die Ausstellungsbroschüre auf Englisch und Hindi. Im zweiten Umschlag, ein paar Einlagen weiter im selben Ordner, fand sich der finale Grundriss der Ausstellung in Saal 1. F. F. mit einem Ein- und Ausgang in derselben Halle. Mayer-Meintschel betrieb ihre Ausstellungspolitik auch außerhalb des eigenen Landes und des sozialistischen Einflussbereichs und somit jenseits der Kontrolle des Einparteienstaates DDR.

4. Hausarchiv SKD 02/ GGAM/89.

5. Keshav Malik (1924–2014) war ein im unabhängigen Indien bekannter indischer Dichter, Kunst- und Literaturkritiker, Kunstwissenschaftler und Kurator sowie persönlicher Assistent von Jawaharlal Nehru.

6. Im Gespräch über eine vorherige Version dieses Textes erläuterte mir Monica Juneja den Stellenwert von Laxmi Prasad Sihare (1929–1993), dessen kunstgeschichtliche Forschung und Vision von Institutionen der Kunst grundlegend für die indische Moderne waren.

7. Fredda Brillant (1903–1999) war eine polnische Bildhauerin und Schauspielerin. Sie stammte aus Łódź und schuf Skulpturen einiger ihrer größten Zeitgenossen – darunter Jawaharlal Nehru, V. K. Krishna Menon, Indira Gandhi, US-Präsident John F. Kennedy und Buckminster Fuller.

the unique profile of the Dresden Galleries. In doing so, we have tried above all to trace the relationship between the art of the North and the South of Europe—that fruitful dialogue which began in the fifteenth century and continued into the eighteenth century. It forms the background to the content of our exhibition. It was a time of upheaval in which the whole of Europe was gripped by intellectual, religious, and social movements, and art began to break free from the medieval world of the imagination, leading to a new experience of reality. The culture of the Italian Renaissance was exemplary. The earliest example in the exhibition is by [Bastiano] Mainardi."[9]

Mayer-Meintschel clearly distances herself from nation branding and state socialism. She speaks as a Europeanist, as a humanist. She speaks of "social movements" that "break free from the medieval world." And she speaks as an art historian, for whom the past is an object of study rather than a vehicle for political interests in the present. She insists on the utmost historiographic precision and refuses any state-socialist appropriation of the art of the Renaissance. Her art-historical reasoning seems to consider the history of the Renaissance—which is precisely the moment when "a new world view" begins to form by means of European-imperial competition and colonial domination[10]—to be a closed book. In her position as the director of a state museum in the GDR, history and the knowledge of history are epistemic weapons against (a) nation branding, (b) political instrumentalization, and (c) any structural and political limitations facing an independent researcher. The exhibition and its publication included internationally renowned pieces such as *The Birth of Christ* (1520) by Lucas Cranach the Elder, *Justitia* (1544) by Battista Dossi, *Elector Moritz of Saxony* (1578) by Lucas Cranach the Younger, etc.[11] While their relevance to art history is undisputed, their visual grammar emerged in the age of the formation of Eurocentric cultural imperialism, when art became a channel for camouflaging, silencing, denying, and rendering invisible the colonial extraction of gems such as the Emerald Cluster from the Chivor-Somondoco mine in Colombia on display in the historic Green Vault, the transatlantic trade routes that also involved Saxony under Elector Augustus the Strong, the presence at the royal court in

9. My translation of the original German text (below).

10. Vera Lawrence Hyatt and Rex M. Nettleford, eds., *Race Discourse and the Origin of the Americas: A New World View* (Smithsonian, 1995).

11. The exhibition publication *Art Treasures from Dresden (German Democratic Republic)* was published by the National Museum, New Delhi, and edited, most likely, by Annaliese Mayer-Meintschel with contributions by Harald Marx and Angelo Walther. The prefaces by Rajiv Gandhi and Erich Honecker indicate the political function of the exhibition, along with contributions by Laxmi P. Sihare and Manfred Bachmann. The publication was dedicated to Indira Gandhi, who had just passed away. It consists of sixty-two pages, printed in four colors by R. K. Wadhwa at Thomas Press (I) Ltd., Faridabad, Haryana, India, with "sole distributors: Publications Divisions, Patiala House, New Delhi." The imprint lists the main protagonists and functions of 341 employees of the National Museum.

Als Hebel dafür dienten ihr ihre profunden kunsthistorischen Kenntnisse. Sie nutzte bei ihrem Vorgehen einerseits einen günstigen Moment der Weltgeschichte, in dem „Kunstschätze" noch die Kunstgeschichte als Wissenschaft bestimmten, andererseits aber auch die (Kunst-) Geschichte als Methode, um die Hegemonie des Staatssozialismus zu unterlaufen. Mayer-Meintschel begünstigte ganz klar ein nationenübergreifendes, eigentlich: gesamteuropäisches Herangehen an die Ausstellung (das heute wohl als eurozentrisch kritisiert würde), etwa wenn sie in ihrer kuratorischen Eröffnungsrede an den indischen Ministerpräsidenten[8] schreibt: „Bei der Auswahl der Bilder für die Ausstellung haben wir uns bemüht, etwas von der Großartigkeit und dem Reichtum der Sammlung anklingen zu lassen. Es sollte auch jenes einzigartige Profil der Dresdner Galerie gezeigt werden. Dabei haben wir versucht, vor allem die Beziehungen zwischen der Kunst des Nordens mit dem Süden Europas, jenen fruchtbaren Dialog, der im 15. Jahrhundert begann und bis ins 18. Jahrhundert wirkte, nachzuvollziehen. Er bildet den inhaltlichen Hintergrund unserer Ausstellung. Es war dies eine Zeit des Aufbruchs, in dem ganz Europa von geistiger, religiöser und sozialer Bewegung erfasst wurde und sich die Kunst aus der mittelalterlichen Vorstellungswelt zu lösen begann, zu einem neuen Wirklichkeitserlebnis führte. Vorbildlich war die Kultur der italienischen Renaissance. Das früheste Beispiel in der Ausstellung stammt von [Bastiano] Mainardi."

Mayer-Meintschel distanzierte sich erkennbar von den Beschränkungen eines nationalen Kulturerbes und vom Staatssozialismus. Aus ihren Worten spricht das Bekenntnis einer Humanistin zu Europa. Sie nennt „gesellschaftliche Strömungen", die „sich von der Welt des Mittelalters lösen". Und sie ergreift das Wort als Kunsthistorikerin, für die die Vergangenheit ein Gegenstand der Erforschung und kein bloßes Instrumentarium politischer Interessen in der Gegenwart ist. So besteht sie auf äußerster historiografischer Genauigkeit und verweigert sich jeder staatssozialistischen Vereinnahmung der Kunst der Renaissance. Ihr kunstgeschichtlicher Ansatz erfasst anscheinend die Geschichte der Renaissance als einen abgeschlossenen Moment, in dem sich „eine neue Weltsicht"[9] im Zuge des europäischen imperialen Wettstreits um koloniale Vorherrschaft behauptete. In ihrem Amt als Direktorin eines staatlichen Museums in der DDR dienen ihr die Geschichte und ihre Kenntnis als Waffen des Wissens wider (a) die nationale Markenpflege, (b) politische Indienstnahme und (c) jede strukturell-politische Beschränkung ihrer Arbeit als unabhängige Wissenschaftlerin.

8. Sehr wahrscheinlich Rajiv Gandhi, obwohl der Name des Ministerpräsidenten in den Dokumenten nicht genannt wird.

9. Vera Lawrence Hyatt und Rex M. Nettleford (Hg.), *Race Discourse and the Origin of the Americas: A New World View*, Washington und London: Smithsonian Institution Press 1995.

Dresden of enslaved men such as Tuskee Stannaki of the Muscogee people in North America, or the presence of an unnamed black boy in the background of the painting of *Kurprinz Friedrich August von Sachsen* (1714) by Hyacinthe Rigaud in the Old Masters Picture Gallery. Mayer-Meintschel touches upon the entanglement between imperialist fantasies and art when she continues to speak about the collections in Dresden:

> It was not only the urge at the time to acquire large collections and the joy of beauty per se that inspired the creation of picture galleries—it also resonated with the political need for the absolutist ruling sovereign of the baroque era to project power.[12]

How can we reveal an exhibition history—of East Germany in alliance with India—that does not merely celebrate the archival find but acknowledges the charismatic curatorial wisdom shown by Mayer-Meintschel in rejecting state ideology and political instrumentalization? And how can we practice a transculturality today without perpetuating the structural ignorance of an "apocalyptic millenarian drive" that started in 1492 and created a seemingly irreversible program of racial, environmental, and social injustice through European colonization, supported throughout by art as its visual lubricant?[13]

Despite all the colonial imperialist modernity that existed before the foundation of the GDR in 1949, I stand by this *otherwise*, which introduces a differential principle with regard to the logics of capitalist enlightenment. This underpins my idea of addressing *Art Treasures from Dresden* as a "problem-space" that helps me to conceptualize the exhibition as a modernist technology of worldmaking and allows me to speak about the exhibition through the troubling entanglements of coloniality, "social movements," and internationalism. It invokes what David Scott calls "a context of argument and, therefore, one of *intervention*." For Scott, "a problem-space necessarily has a *temporal* dimension or, rather, is a fundamentally temporal concept. Problem-spaces alter historically because problems are not timeless and do not have everlasting shapes. In new historical conditions old questions may

12. My translation of the original German text (below).

13. Sylvia Wynter, "1492: A New World View," in Hyatt and Nettleford, *Race Discourse*, 24.

Die Ausstellung und die diese begleitende Publikation beinhalteten weltberühmte Werke wie die *Geburt Christi* (um 1520) von Lucas Cranach, die *Allegorie der Gerechtigkeit / Justitia* (1542/43) von Battista Dossi, das Bildnis des Kurfürsten *Moritz von Sachsen* (1578) von Lucas Cranach dem Jüngeren und so weiter.[10] Während ihre Bedeutung für die Geschichte der Kunst unumstritten ist, bildete sich die visuelle Grammatik dieser Werke im Zeitalter des aufkommenden eurozentrischen Kulturimperialismus heraus, als die Kunst zu einem Medium wurde, in dem sich koloniale materielle Extraktionen von Schätzen wie der im historischen Grünen Gewölbe ausgestellten Smaragdstufe aus der Mine Chivor-Somondoco in Kolumbien tarnen, verschweigen, leugnen und unsichtbar machen ließen. In diesen Zusammenhang gehört auch die Tatsache, dass die transatlantischen Handelswege Sachsen unter Kurfürst August dem Starken einbezogen, dass sich am Hof in Dresden versklavte Männer wie Tuskee Stannaki vom nordamerikanischen Volk der Mocogee aufhielten oder dass im Hintergrund eines Bildnisses von August dem Starken (1714) von Hyacinthe Rigaud in der Gemäldegalerie Alter Meister ein ungenannter Schwarzer Junge erscheint. Auch Annaliese Mayer-Meintschel berührt dieses Ineinanderlaufen von imperialistischen Vorspiegelungen und Kunst in ihren Ausführungen über die Dresdner Sammlungen: „Es war nicht nur der Drang der Zeit, große Sammlungen anzuschaffen und nicht nur die Freude am Schönen schlechthin, sondern es entsprach dem politischen Repräsentationsbedürfnis des absolutistisch herrschenden Fürsten der Barockzeit, Bildergalerien anzulegen."

Wie können wir nun eine Ausstellungsgeschichte – Ostdeutschlands im Bund mit Indien – zum Vorschein bringen, die nicht einfach nur die eigenen Archivfunde feiert, sondern auch die kuratorisch-charismatische Weisheit einer Annaliese Mayer-Meintschel anerkennt, sich der Staatsideologie und politischen Instrumentalisierung zu entziehen? Und wie können wir heute mit einer Transkulturalität vorgehen, ohne zugleich die Ignoranz gegenüber jenem „utopisch-millenarischen Drang"[11] fortzuschreiben, der 1492 einsetzte und mit der europäischen Kolonisation unter Nutzung der Künste als visuelles Schmiermittel ein unüberwindliches Schema rassischen, ökologischen und gesellschaftlichen Unrechts schuf?

Trotz all der kolonial-imperialistischen Moderne, die schon lange vor Gründung der DDR 1949 bestand, ist es dieses *Andersartige*, auf dem ich insistiere, dieses Einbringen eines sich von der Logik der kapitalistischen Aufklärung

10. Der Ausstellungskatalog *Art Treasures from Dresden* (DDR) wurde vom National Museum in Neu-Delhi publiziert. Herausgeberin war mit größter Wahrscheinlichkeit Annaliese Mayer-Meintschel unter Mitwirkung von Harald Marx und Angelo Walther. Die Grußwörter von Rajiv Gandhi und Erich Honecker vermitteln einen Eindruck von der politischen Funktion der Schau, ebenso die Beiträge von Laxmi P. Sihare und Manfred Bachmann. Gewidmet wurde der Band der eben erst verstorbenen Indira Gandhi. Er umfasst 62 Seiten im Vierfarbdruck von R. K. Wadhwa beim Verlag Thomas Press (I) Ltd., Faridabad, Haryana, Indien. Als „Alleinvertrieb" ist die „Publications Division, Patiala House, New Delhi" angegeben. Das Impressum führt zahlreiche Akteur·innen und die Zuständigkeiten von 341 Mitarbeiter·innen im National Museum an.

11. Sylvia Wynter, „1492: A New World View", in: Hyatt und Nettleford (Hg.), *Race Discourse and the Origin of the Americas*, S. 5–57, hier S. 24.

lose their salience, their bite, and so lead the range of old answers that once attached to them to appear lifeless, quaint, not so much wrong as irrelevant."[14]

The anthropologist Johannes Fabien suggests that "geopolitics has its ideological foundations in chronopolitics."[15] For our case study, the exhibition *Art Treasures from Dresden* as "problem-space" is situated within geopolitics, which cannot be separated from its temporal dimensions. I will conclude with three points that posit a chronopolitics of problem-space as constitutive of a specific transcultural curatorial dimension—namely, a geopolitics of exhibiting.

First, *Art Treasures from Dresden* at the National Museum in New Delhi suggests a curatorial chronopolitics. Mayer-Meintschel mobilizes a research methodology that approaches history as an argument for a European narrative of

14. Scott, *Conscripts of Modernity*, 4.

15. Johannes Fabian, *Time & the Other: How Anthropology Makes Its Object* (Columbia University Press, 1983), 144. I would like to thank Kodwo Eshun for pointing me to the author and this specific quote. On the concepts of chronopolitics, environment, decolonization, and art, see also T. J. Demos, *Radical Futurisms: Ecologies of Collapse, Chronopolitics, and Justice-to-Come* (Sternberg Press, 2023); Elizabeth Freeman, "Time Binds, or, Erotohistoriography," *Social Text* 23, nos. 3–4 (Fall–Winter 2005), in which Freeman elaborates on the politics of the erotic as a method of queering time and dismantling the chrononormative order that Fabian discussed as "imperial time." For a more precise insight into current debates on the politics of time in the postcolonial condition, see Musab Younis, "Race, the World and Time: Haiti, Liberia and Ethiopia (1914–1945)," *Millennium* 46, no. 3 (2018): 352–70.

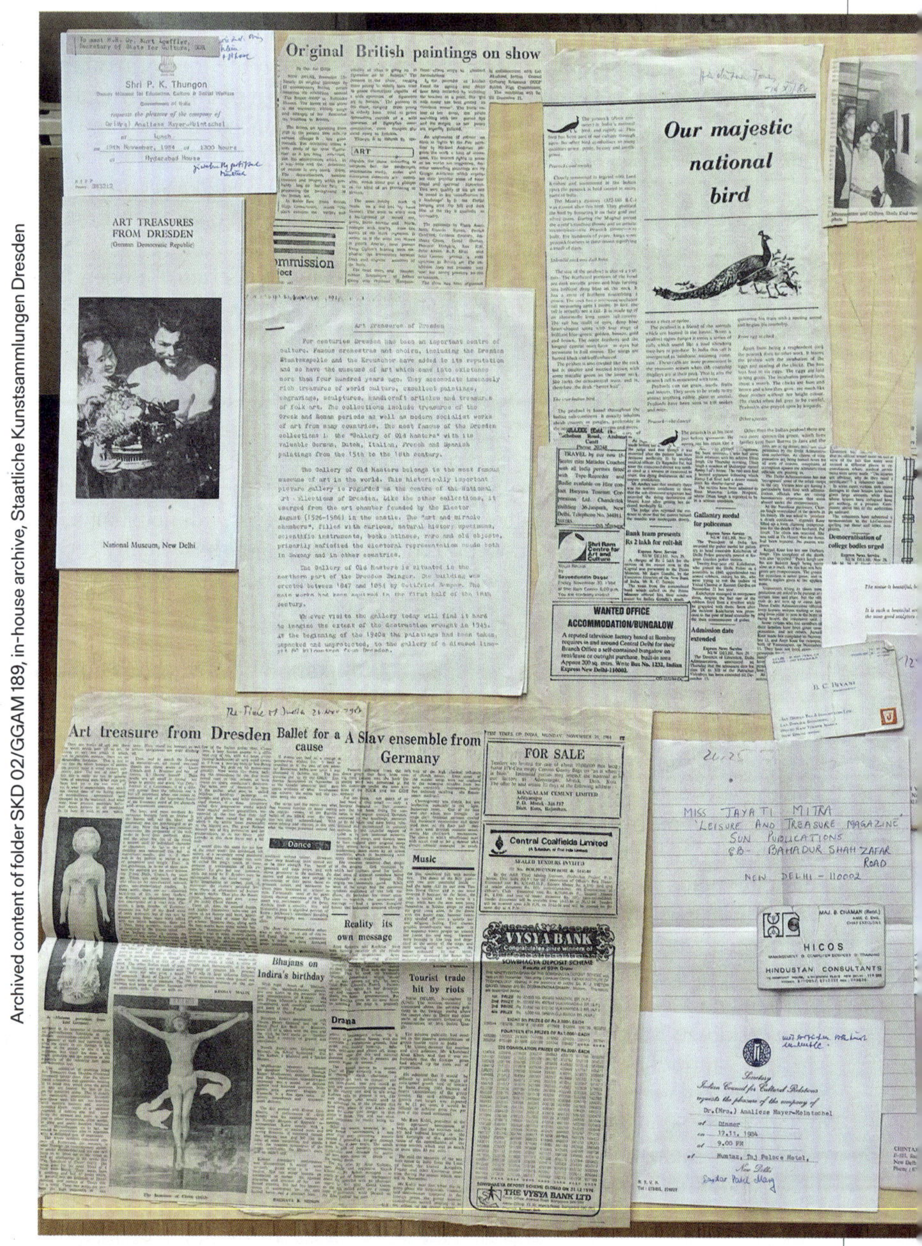

Archived content of folder SKD 02/GGAM 189, in-house archive, Staatliche Kunstsammlungen Dresden

absetzenden Differenzprinzips, das meinen Vorschlag zum Umgang mit *Art Treasures from Dresden* als einem „Problemraum" ausmacht. Es hilft mir, die Ausstellung als eine der Moderne zugehörige Technik der Weltschöpfung zu begreifen und anhand der verstörenden Verstrickungen von Kolonialismus, „gesellschaftlichen Bewegungen" und Internationalismus über sie zu sprechen. Es bringt ins Spiel, was Scott „einen Kontext des Streits, mithin der Einmischung"[12] nennt.

Für Scott hat „ein Problemraum notwendig eine zeitliche Dimension beziehungsweise ist grundsätzlich ein zeitliches Konzept. Problemräume ändern sich historisch, weil Probleme ebenso wenig zeitlos sind wie die Formen, die sie annehmen. Unter neuen historischen Umständen können alte Fragen ihre Brisanz, ihren Biss verlieren, und gehen darin der Parade alter, einst daran geknüpfter Antworten voraus, die nun ebenfalls leblos, schrullig, weniger falsch als vielmehr unerheblich wirken."

12. Scott, *Conscripts of Modernity*, S. 4.

16. Annaliese Mayer-Meintschel, introductory address, November 8, 1984, Hausarchiv SKD 02/GGAM 189.

the Dresden collections and strongly refuses and resists political instrumentalization by a one-party state that regards history as a tool for cultural state diplomacy and state-owned cultural property. It might seem like a closure of history, yet, in a state museum of a nondemocratic state, history becomes a weapon against political instrumentalization by the state. The flip side of this is that Mayer-Meintschel's approach maintains modernity's white ignorance and imperial silence—a silence that we would also find at the Rijksmuseum in Amsterdam or the Metropolitan Museum in New York. Contrary to its claims of anti-imperialist friendship and internationalism, the GDR proved no exception.

Second, there is a chronopolitics within the in-house archive that speaks through two envelopes that have been sealed for more than thirty-five years.

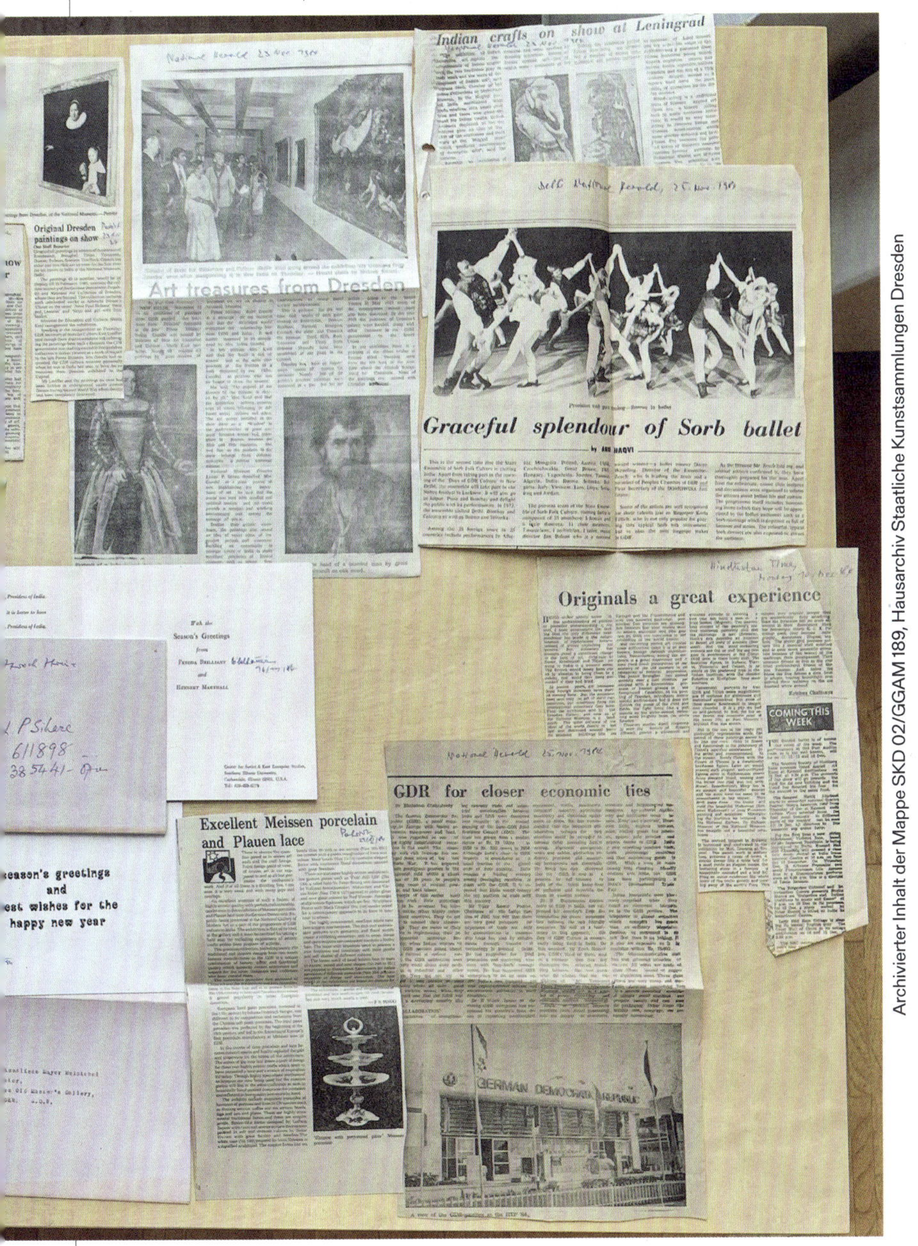

Archivierter Inhalt der Mappe SKD 02/GGAM 189, Hausarchiv Staatliche Kunstsammlungen Dresden

„Geopolitik", meint der Ethnologe Johannes Fabian, „hat ihre ideologische Grundlage in Chronopolitik".[13] Denn auch unsere Fallstudie, die Ausstellung *Art Treasures from Dresden* als „Problemraum", verortet sich in einer bestimmten geopolitischen Gemengelage und ist nicht ablösbar von ihrer zeitlichen Dimension. Ich werde abschließend drei Merkmale einer Chronopolitik des Problemraums anführen, die mir konstitutiv für eine spezifisch kulturübergreifende kuratorische Dimension scheinen, das heißt für eine Geopolitik des Ausstellens von Kunst:

Erstens lässt *Art Treasures from Dresden* eine kuratorische Chronopolitik erkennen. Annaliese Mayer-Meintschel bringt eine Methode in Anschlag, die Geschichte als ein Argument für eine europäische Erzählung der Dresdner Sammlungen erschließt und sich der politischen Instrumentalisierung durch den Einparteienstaat beharrlich verweigert, wie sehr dieser Staat seinerseits die Geschichte als Instrument staatlicher Kulturdiplomatie und Kulturerbe im Staatsbesitz betrachten

13. Johannes Fabian, *Time & the Other. How Anthropology Makes its Object,* New York: Columbia University Press 1983, S. 144. Ich danke Kodwo Eshun für den Hinweis auf den Autor und insbesondere dieses Zitat. Zum Begriffsfeld von Chronopolitik, Umwelt, Dekolonisation und Kunst siehe T. J. Demos, *Radical Futurisms: Ecologies of Collapse, Chronopolitics and Justice-to-Come,* Berlin: Sternberg Press 2003, und Elizabeth Freeman, „Time Binds, or, Erotohistoriography", in: *Social Text,* 23, 2005, Nr. 3–4 (84–85), S. 57–68, die die Politik des Erotischen als eine Methode zum Queering der Zeit und Auseinandernehmen jener chrononormativen Ordnung beschreibt, die Fabian „imperiale Zeit" nennt. Eine genauere Erörterung aktueller Debatten zur Politik der Zeit in der Postkolonialität findet sich bei Musab Younis, „Race, the World and Time: Haiti, Liberia and Ethiopia (1914–1945)", in: *Millennium,* 46, 2018, Nr. 3, S. 352–370.

Unearthing them should not necessarily imply a great archival discovery—the joy of any researcher's ego. Instead, their sealedness seems symptomatic of the systemic silence of an exhibition history as curatorial knowledge that we can trace in the precise insights into contemporary debates on the politics of time in the postcolonial condition: documents, internal memos, notes, the forms of salutation in letters—Mayer-Meintschel starts her internal and external correspondence without the standard opening of "Genosse" (Comrade) and conclusion of "sozialistischer Gruß" (With socialist greetings), a tiny yet important detail of independence that I value and cherish. Furthermore, mobilizing history allows Mayer-Meintschel to speak of "intellectual, religious, and social movements and art [that] began to break free from the medieval world of the imagination, leading to a new experience of reality," thus critiquing absolutist sovereignty.[16] It drafts a social history of art that is closer to realism and, thus, to a future-oriented making of society in the present.

And third, opening the sealed envelopes in the in-house archive reveals a geopolitical dimension to exhibiting that is specific to a state-socialist museum, as Monica Juneja helped me to understand: no museum in Western Europe or North America in 1985 would have loaned and sent "art treasures" from their collections to New Delhi—ostensibly for insurance and security reasons, although this camouflaged the ongoing coloniality of research through the hegemony of access. The documents in the sealed envelope offer an insight into the negotiations between the SKD and the National Museum in New Delhi as partners. The contract has been translated from German into Hindi and English and is signed in all three languages. Today, SKD contracts are signed exclusively in German.

If "geopolitics has its ideological foundations in chronopolitics," as quoted above, the exhibition of works from the Old Masters Picture Gallery in Dresden at the National Museum in New Delhi constitutes a (post)socialist geopolitical condition suggesting a form of art-based internationalism situated between state politics, history as transnational power, the colonial legacies of art history—which turned to the politics of friendship in the context of communism's promise in the global Cold War—and people's (researchers') microsocial skills that continue to

mag. Das kann den Eindruck einer Verweigerung vor der Geschichte überhaupt erwecken, doch tatsächlich wird hier im staatlichen Museum eines undemokratischen Staates die Geschichte zur Waffe gegen staatlich-politische Instrumentalisierung. Die Kehrseite ist, dass Mayer-Meintschels Herangehen am weißen Unwissen und imperialen Schweigen der Moderne festhält – einem Schweigen, das wir ebenso im Rijksmuseum in Amsterdam oder im Metropolitan Museum in New York vorfinden. Ungeachtet ihres Anspruchs auf antiimperialistische Freundschaft und internationale Solidarität bildete die DDR hierin keine Ausnahme.

Zweitens gibt es eine Chronopolitik auch im Hausarchiv. Sie äußert sich in Gestalt zweier Umschläge, die dort mehr als 35 Jahren ungeöffnet lagen. Dass wir darauf gestoßen sind, sollte nicht so sehr als großartiger Archivfund und Wonne für das forschende Ego gelten. Eher wirkt diese Verschlossenheit wie das Symptom eines Schweigens mit System in einer Ausstellungsgeschichte als Geschichte kuratorischen Wissens, dessen Umrisse sich in den treffenden Einsichten gegenwärtiger Debatten über die Politik der Zeit in der Postkolonialität abzeichnen: Schriften, Hausvermerke, Notizen, Grußformeln in Briefen (Mayer-Meintschel begann ihren internen und externen Briefverkehr ohne die damals übliche Grußformel „Genosse" und endete auch nicht mit einem „sozialistischen Gruß", was ich als winzige, doch bedeutsame Unabhängigkeitsbehauptung sehr schätze). Zudem gelang es Mayer-Meintschel durch ihre Mobilisierung der Geschichte, von „geistiger, religiöser und sozialer Bewegung und Kunst" zu sprechen, die „sich aus der mittelalterlichen Vorstellungswelt zu lösen begann, zu einem neuen Wirklichkeitserlebnis führte", womit sie zugleich jeden absolutistischen Herrschaftsanspruch infrage stellte.[14] Darin zeichnet sich eine Sozialgeschichte der Kunst ab, die näher am Realismus und daher auch am zukunftsorientierten Aufbau einer Gesellschaft in der Gegenwart ist.

Und drittens offenbart uns das Öffnen der verschlossenen Umschläge im Hausarchiv eine geopolitische Dimension des Ausstellungsmachens in staatssozialistischen Museum. Wie Monica Juneja mir zu verstehen geholfen hat, wäre 1985 kein Museen in Westeuropa oder Nordamerika bereit gewesen, „Kunstschätze" aus der eigenen Sammlung an ein Museum in Neu-Delhi zu verleihen und nach Indien zu schicken. Nominell wäre das an Versicherungs- und Sicherheitshürden gescheitert, die jedoch nur ein Fortdauern kolonialer Verhältnisse in der Forschung und das Festhalten an der hegemonialen Verfügung über die Kunst

14. Annaliese Mayer-Meintschel, Einführungsrede am 8. November 1984, Hausarchiv SKD 02/GGAM 189.

resonate in the present. If we follow the archive's utopian margins, which reverberate in communism's orientation to the future, the promise of internationalism offers an imaginary—not so much a thematic focus as a research methodology—that allows us to challenge the political dynamics of a post-1990 world. I regard this *curatorial futurity* as a contribution to ongoing research on the methods and vocabularies of transculturality in curatorial practice.

The Dresden State Art Collections are a direct consequence, if not a technology—both in visual and infrastructural terms—of colonial trade systems, the formation of racial global capitalism, and the imperiality of knowledge long before nation-states formed alliances with or against each other. Yet, I would cherish a *modernity otherwise*, as elaborated earlier, that consciously integrates memories of internationalism with social movements, workers' histories, and the transgression of national orders. Where do its forms of knowledge resonate in our present? Would a curatorial futurity entail a futurity of knowledge that might enable a worldmaking *otherwise*—a society to come?

getarnt hätten. Die Dokumente im verschlossenen Umschlag gewähren Einblick in partnerschaftliche Verhandlungen zwischen den SKD und dem Nationalmuseum in Neu-Delhi. Der Vertrag wurde aus dem Deutschen ins Hindi und ins Englische übersetzt und in allen drei Sprachen unterschrieben. Heute werden Verträge mit den SKD ausschließlich auf Deutsch unterzeichnet.

Wenn Geopolitik, wie oben zitiert, „ihre ideologische Grundlage in Chronopolitik hat", so kennzeichnet die Ausstellung der Dresdner Gemäldegalerie Alter Meister im National Museum in Neu-Delhi eine sehr besondere (post-) sozialistische Gemengelage. Diese stellt sich dar als ein Internationalismus der Kunst im Kräftefeld zwischen Staatspolitik, Geschichte im Sinne einer nationenübergreifenden Macht, kolonialem Erbe der Kunstgeschichte und dessen Neuausrichtung auf eine Politik der Freundschaft im Kontext kommunistischer Verheißungen im Kalten Weltkrieg sowie eine mikrosoziale Geschicklichkeit der Beteiligten, die bis in die Gegenwart nachwirkt. Wenn wir die utopischen Ränder des Archivs und ihren Niederschlag in den Zukunftshoffnungen des Kommunismus erkunden, eröffnet uns das Versprechen des Internationalismus eine Vorstellungswelt – weniger Gegenstand als Forschungsmethode –, mit der wir der politischen Dynamik der Welt seit 1990 entgegentreten können. Ich nenne das eine kuratorische Futurität als Beitrag zur laufenden Erforschung von Methoden und Lexiken des Transkulturellen in der kuratorischen Arbeit. Vernünftigerweise lassen sich die Staatlichen Kunstsammlungen Dresden als ein direktes Resultat, wenn nicht sogar als – visuelle wie infrastrukturelle – Technologie der kolonialen Handelssysteme, der Ausbildung des globalen Rassenkapitalismus sowie des herrischen Wissens in einer Zeit lange vor den ersten Bündnissen zwischen Nationalstaaten mit- oder gegeneinander betrachten. Umso mehr wäre mir an einer *anderweitigen Moderne* gelegen, die bewusst Erinnerungen an Internationalismen mit gesellschaftlichen Bewegungen, Historien der Arbeiterschaft und Verletzungen von Staatsordnungen in Wechselwirkung bringt. Wo finden ihre Formen des Wissens in unserer Gegenwart Widerhall? Würde eine kuratorische Futurität eine Futurität des Wissens mit sich bringen und diese vielleicht eine Weltschöpfung *anderer Art* – eine Gesellschaft, die uns noch bevorsteht?

VINIT AGARWAL is an artist, researcher, and curator, as well as the founder of the Jaipur-based Oralities Research Lab, which houses both a library and an event space. This internationalist project is committed to the transmission of oral knowledge as a medium for the future.

MOSES MÄRZ is a researcher, writer, and mapmaker based in Berlin. He received his PhD from the University of Potsdam for a dissertation on Édouard Glissant's politics of relation. His large-scale hand-drawn research maps trace the history of the struggle against coloniality. März is a principal investigator in the "Collaborations" research unit at the University of Potsdam.

DOREEN MENDE is a curator, theorist, and, since 2021, head of the research department at the Dresden State Art Collections (Staatliche Kunstsammlungen Dresden). Mende is a founding member of the Harun Farocki Institute in Berlin and the European Forum for Advanced Practices and principal investigator (PI) of the research project *Decolonizing Socialism: Entangled Internationalism* (2019–24), funded by the Swiss National Science Foundation.

AARTI SUNDER works with the moving image, writing, and drawing. Her interest lies in technology and our relationship with it—in particular, the study of digital infrastructure. To date, she has focused on contemporary labor practices and the fictional margins of protest, myth, and digital-terrestrial play.

SÓNIA VAZ BORGES is a militant interdisciplinary historian and social and political organizer. She has a BA in modern and contemporary history, politics, and international affairs from Iscte – University Institute of Lisbon and an MA in African history from the Faculty of Humanities at the University of Lisbon. She received her PhD in philosophy from Humboldt University of Berlin and a postdoctoral fellowship from the Center for Place, Culture and Politics (CPCP) at the Graduate Center, City University of New York. Vaz Borges is a researcher at the Humboldt University in Berlin.

VINIT AGARWAL ist Künstler, Forscher, Kurator und Gründer des in Jaipur ansässigen Oralities Research Lab, das eine Bibliothek und einen Veranstaltungsraum umfasst. Dieses internationalistische Projekt hat sich der Weitergabe mündlichen Wissens als Medium für die Zukunft verschrieben.

MOSES MÄRZ lebt und arbeitet als Forscher, Autor und Kartograf in Berlin. Er hat an der Universität Potsdam mit einer Dissertation über Édouard Glissants Politik der Relation promoviert. Seine großformatigen handgezeichneten Forschungskarten stellen die Spuren antikolonialer Kämpfe dar. März ist Principal Investigator der Forschungsgruppe „Collaborations" an der Universität Potsdam.

DOREEN MENDE ist Kuratorin, Theoretikerin und seit 2021 Leiterin des Departements Forschung an den Staatlichen Kunstsammlungen Dresden. Mende ist Gründungsmitglied des Harun Farocki Instituts in Berlin und des European Forum for Advanced Practices sowie Principal Investigator des Forschungsprojekts *Decolonizing Socialism: Entangled Internationalism* (2019–2024), gefördert durch den Schweizerischen Nationalfonds.

AARTI SUNDER arbeitet mit Filmen, Texten und Zeichnungen. Ihr Interesse gilt der Technologie und unseren Beziehungen zu ihr – insbesondere widmet sie sich der Untersuchung digitaler Infrastrukturen. Dabei konzentriert sie sich auf heutige Arbeitspraktiken und die fiktionalen Spielräume und Grenzen von Protest, Mythen und digital-terrestrischem Spiel.

SÓNIA VAZ BORGES ist eine militante interdisziplinäre Historikerin und Aktivistin. Sie hat einen B. A. im Bereich Zeitgeschichte – Politik und internationale Beziehungen am Iscte – Instituto Universitario de Lisboa (Lissabon) und einen M. A. in afrikanischer Geschichte an der Fakultät für Humanwissenschaften der Universität Lissabon erlangt. Sie hat am Institut für Erziehungswissenschaften an der Humboldt-Universität zu Berlin promoviert und als Postdoc am Center for Place Culture and Politics (CPCP) des Graduate Center der City University of New York gearbeitet. Sónia Vaz Borges forscht zurzeit an der Humboldt-Universität.

p. 6: Excerpt from Moses März, *Charting OYOYO*, wax crayon, pencil, and collages on paper, ca. 210 × 300 cm, © Moses März

pp. 13–20: Project *Decolonizing Socialism: Entangled Internationalism*, www.entangledinternationalism.org, 2025

pp. 24–27: *OYOYO*, dir.: Chetna Vora, Film and Television Academy of the GDR, 1980, digitized and restored by the Film University Babelsberg KONRAD WOLF, supported by the Film Heritage Funding Program, financed by the BKM, Länder, and FFA

pp. 28–35: Aarti Sunder, *Object to Abstraction: Panorama of a Song* (Objekt zur Abstraktion: Panorama eines Liedes), graphite on rice paper, 849 × 28 cm, 2023, © Aarti Sunder

p. 36: © Moses März, © SKD, photo: Alexander Peitz

p. 40: Excerpt from Moses März, *Charting OYOYO*, wax crayon, pencil, and collages on paper, ca. 210 × 300 cm, © Moses März

pp. 42–49: installation view, *Till the Sun Rises*, Albertinum, Staatliche Kunstsammlungen Dresden, © SKD, photo: Alexander Peitz

p. 51: *OYOYO*, dir.: Chetna Vora, Film and Television Academy of the GDR, 1980, digitized and restored by the Film University Babelsberg KONRAD WOLF, supported by the Film Heritage Funding Program, financed by the BKM, Länder, and FFA

p. 53: Karl Erich Müller, *Demonstration der KP Indiens* (Demonstration by the Communist Party of India), 1970, watercolors, 426 × 584 mm (sheet), Kupferstich-Kabinett, Staatliche Kunstsammlungen Dresden, inv. no. C 1974-291, © Kupferstich-Kabinett, SKD; photo: Caterina Micksch

p. 54: Press clipping about Karl Erich Müller with his work *The Great Demonstration in New Delhi* from 1979, Archive of the Staatliche Kunstsammlungen Dresden, PA237

p. 56 left: Karl Erich Müller, *Inderin* (Indian Woman), Bombay, 1972, lithograph, 180 × 118 mm (display), 419 × 298 mm (sheet), Kupferstich-Kabinett, Staatliche Kunstsammlungen Dresden, inv. no. A 1974-207, © Kupferstich-Kabinett, SKD; photo: Caterina Micksch

p. 56 right: Karl Erich Müller, *Santhal-Frau* (Santhal Woman), 1972, lithograph, 380 × 280 mm (display); 544 × 427 mm (sheet), Kupferstich-Kabinett, Staatliche Kunstsammlungen Dresden, inv. no. A 1974-204, © Kupferstich-Kabinett, SKD; photo: Caterina Micksch

p. 57 left: Karl Erich Müller, *Kopf eines Gauklers* (Head of a Street Artist), 1972, lithograph, 380 × 280 mm (display); 540 × 427 mm (sheet), Kupferstich-Kabinett, Staatliche Kunstsammlungen Dresden, inv. no. A 1974-206, © Kupferstich-Kabinett, SKD; photo: Caterina Micksch

p. 57 right: Karl Erich Müller, *Bildnis Mahathera N. Jinaratana* (Portrait of Mahathera N. Jinaratana), 1972, lithograph, 385 × 290 mm (display), 543 × 428 mm (sheet), Kupferstich-Kabinett, SKD, inv. no. A 1974-203, © Kupferstich-Kabinett, SKD; photo: Caterina Micksch

p. 59: Carl Schröder, "The presidium on the podium," photograph of the meeting of the UNIMA committee and presidium in Leningrad and Moscow, 1964, acetate roll film negative, exposed and developed, scan, Puppet Theatre Collection, Staatliche Kunstsammlungen Dresden, inv. no. F 41,34, © Karin Schröder. Here we see: Taiji Kawajiri (1914–1994), Sergei Obraszow (1901–1992), Meher Rustom Contractor (1918–1992), Marjorie Bachelder (1903–1997), Max Jacob (1888–1967), Jan Malik (1904–1980), Harro Siegel (1900–1985), Dezső Szilágyi (1922–2010), Maria Signorelli (1908–1992), Jean-Loup Temporal (1921–1983), George Speaight (1914–2005), Jan Bussell (1909–1985), Henryk Ryl (1911–1983), Hans R. Purschke (1911–1986), Henryk Jurkowski (1927–2016), Jože Pengov (1916–1968), and Michail Michailowitsch Koroljew (1913–1983),

p. 60: Carl Schröder, "The Indian delegate Meher Rustom at the 8th UNIMA Congress and the presidium meeting in Warsaw," 1962, acetate roll film negative, exposed and developed, scan, Puppet Theatre Collection, Staatliche Kunstsammlungen Dresden, inv. no. F 39,11, © Karin Schröder

S. 6: Ausschnitt aus Moses März: *Charting OYOYO*, Wachmalstift, Bleistift und Collagen auf Papier, ca. 210 x 300 cm, © Moses März

S. 13-20: Projekt *Decolonizing Socialism Entangled Internationalism*, www.entangledinternationalism.org, 2025

S. 24-27: *OYOYO*, Regie: Chetna Vora, Hochschule für Film und Fernsehen der DDR 1980, Digitalisierung und Restaurierung der Filmuniversität Babelsberg KONRAD WOLF, unterstützt durch das Förderprogramm Filmerbe, finanziert durch BKM, Länder und FFA

S. 28-35: Aarti Sunder: *Objekt zur Abstraktion: Panorama eines Liedes*, Graphit auf Reispapier, 849 x 28 cm, 2023, © Aarti Sunder

S. 36: © Moses März, © SKD, Foto: Alexander Peitz

S. 40: Ausschnitt aus Moses März: *Charting OYOYO*, Wachmalstift, Bleistift und Collagen auf Papier, ca. 210 x 300 cm, © Moses März

S. 42-49: Installationsansicht, *Bis zum Sonnenaufgang*, Albertinum, Staatliche Kunstsammlungen Dresden, © SKD, Foto: Alexander Peitz

S. 51: *OYOYO*, Regie: Chetna Vora, Hochschule für Film und Fernsehen der DDR 1980, Digitalisierung und Restaurierung der Filmuniversität Babelsberg KONRAD WOLF, unterstützt durch das Förderprogramm Filmerbe, finanziert durch BKM, Länder und FFA

S. 53: Karl Erich Müller: *Demonstration der KP Indiens*, 1970, Pinsel in Wasserfarben, 426 x 584 mm (Blatt), Kupferstich-Kabinett, SKD, Inv.-Nr. C 1974-291, © Kupferstich-Kabinett, SKD, Foto: Caterina Micksch

S. 54: Zeitungsartikel über Karl Erich Müller mit seinem Werk *Die große Demonstration in New-Delhi* von 1979. Archiv der SKD, PA237

S. 56 links: Karl Erich Müller: *Inderin, Bombay*, 1972, Lithografie, 180 x 118 mm (Darstellung), 419 x 298 mm (Blatt), Kupferstich-Kabinett, SKD, Inv.-Nr. A 1974-207, © Kupferstich-Kabinett, SKD, Foto: Caterina Micksch

S. 56 rechts: Karl Erich Müller: *Santhal-Frau,* 1972, Lithografie, 380 x 280 mm (Darstellung); 544 x 427 mm (Blatt), Kupferstich-Kabinett, SKD, Inv.-Nr. A 1974-204, © Kupferstich-Kabinett, SKD, Foto: Caterina Micksch

S. 57 links: Karl Erich Müller: *Kopf eines Gauklers*, 1972, Lithografie, 380 x 280 mm (Darstellung); 540 x 427 mm (Blatt), Kupferstich-Kabinett, SKD, Inv.-Nr. A 1974-206, © Kupferstich-Kabinett, SKD, Foto: Caterina Micksch

S. 57 rechts: Karl Erich Müller: *Bildnis Mahathera N. Jinaratana*, 1972, Lithografie, 385 x 290 mm (Darstellung); 543 x 428 mm (Blatt), Kupferstich-Kabinett, SKD, Inv.-Nr. A 1974-203, © Kupferstich-Kabinett, SKD, Foto: Caterina Micksch

S. 59: Carl Schröder: Das Präsidium auf dem Podium, Aufnahme von der Kommissions- und Präsidiumssitzung der UNIMA in Leningrad und Moskau, 1964, Rollfilmnegativ aus Acetat, belichtet und entwickelt, Scan, Puppentheatersammlung, SKD, Inv- Nr. F 41,34, © Karin Schröder. Abgebildet sind: Taiji Kawajiri (1914–1994), Sergei Obraszow (1901–1992), Meher Rustom Contractor (1918–1992), Marjorie Bachelder (1903–1997), Max Jacob (1888–1967), Jan Malik (1904–1980), Harro Siegel (1900–1985), Dezső Szilágyi (1922–2010), Maria Signorelli (1908–1992), Jean-Loup Temporal (1921–1983), George Speaight (1914–2005), Jan Bussell (1909–1985), Henryk Ryl (1911–1983), Hans R. Purschke (1911–1986), Henryk Jurkowski (1927–2016), Jože Pengov (1916–1968), Michail Michailowitsch Koroljew (1913–1983),

S. 60: Carl Schröder: Die indische Delegierte Meher Rustom Contractor auf dem VIII. UNIMA-Kongress und der Präsidiumssitzung in Warschau, 1962, Rollfilmnegativ aus Acetat, belichtet und entwickelt, Scan, Puppentheatersammlung, SKD, Inv- Nr. F 39,11, © Karin Schröder

S. 64: Carl Schröder: Max Jacob hält eine Ansprache, Aufnahme von der Kommissions- und Präsidiumssitzung der UNIMA in Leningrad und Moskau, 1964, Rollfilmnegativ aus Acetat, belichtet und entwickelt, Scan, Puppentheatersammlung, SKD, Inv.-Nr. F 41,19, © Karin Schröder

S. 69: Bharatiya Natya Sangh / Som Benegal (Hrsg.): *Natya. Theatre Arts Journal*, Vol. 4, No. 4, Winter 1960/61: *Puppet*

p. 64: Carl Schröder, "Max Jacob giving a speech, photograph of the meeting of the UNIMA committee and presidium in Leningrad and Moscow," 1964, acetate roll film negative, exposed and developed, scan, Puppet Theatre Collection, Staatliche Kunstsammlungen Dresden, inv. no. F 41,19, © Karin Schröder

p. 69: Bharatiya Natya Sangh and Som Benegal, eds., "Puppet Theatre Around the World," *Natya: Theatre Arts Journal* 4, no. 4 (Winter 1960/61), Puppet Theatre Collection, Staatliche Kunstsammlungen Dresden inv. no. 17118, © SKD

p. 71: Sushila Rohatgi at the opening of the exhibition *Kostbarkeiten indischer Handwerkskunst des 16. bis 19. Jahrhunderts* on October 24, 1985, in the Albertinum, Dresden, Archive of the Staatliche Kunstsammlungen Dresden, FA, 501, folder 3, F1520, r, © SKD

p. 72: Sushila Rohatgi, former member of Lok Sabha (parliament), March 4, 1967; source: https://lssapi.nic.in/MemberProfile/biodata_1_12/1932.gif; author: Government of India

p. 73: Sushila Rohatgi and Krishna Lal at the opening of the exhibition *Treasures of Indian Craftsmanship from the 16th to the 19th Century* in the Albertinum, Dresden, 1985, Archive of the Staatliche Kunstsammlungen Dresden, FA, 501, folder 3, F1521, r, © SKD

p. 78: Back of a photo of Sushila Rohatgi at the opening of the exhibition *Treasures of Indian Craftsmanship from the 16th to the 19th Century* on October 24, 1985, in the Albertinum, Dresden, Archive of the Staatliche Kunstsammlungen Dresden, FA, 501, folder 3, F1520, v, © SKD

p. 79: Record of the various participants at the opening of the exhibition *Treasures of Indian Craftsmanship from the 16th to the 19th Century* in the Albertinum, Dresden, on the back of a photograph, 1985, Archive of the Staatliche Kunstsammlungen Dresden, FA, 501, folder 3, F1525, v, © SKD

pp. 85–89: Folder SKD 02/GGAM 189, © SKD, 2024

Theatre Around the World, Puppentheatersammlung, SKD, Inv.-Nr. 17118, © SKD

S. 71: Sushila Rohatgi bei der Eröffnung der Ausstellung *Kostbarkeiten indischer Handwerkskunst des 16. bis 19. Jahrhunderts* am 24. Oktober 1985 im Albertinum, Dresden, Archiv der SKD, FA, 501, Mappe 3, F1520, r, © SKD

S. 72: Sushila Rohatgi, ehemaliges Mitglied des Parlaments (Lok Sabha), 4. März 1967, Quelle: https://lssapi.nic.in/MemberProfile/biodata_1_12/1932.gif, Governmet of India

S. 73: Sushila Rohatgi und Krishna Lal bei der Eröffnung der Ausstellung *Kostbarkeiten indischer Handwerkskunst des 16. bis 19. Jahrhunderts* im Albertinum, Dresden, 1985, Archiv der SKD, FA, 501, Mappe 3, F1521, r, © SKD

S. 78: Rückseite eines Fotos von Sushila Rohatgi bei der Eröffnung der Ausstellung *Kostbarkeiten indischer Handwerkskunst des 16. bis 19. Jahrhunderts* am 24.10.1985 im Albertinum, Dresden, Archiv der SKD, FA, 501, Mappe 3, F1520, v, © SKD

S. 79: Zeugnis verschiedener Teilnehmer bei der Eröffnung der Ausstellung *Kostbarkeiten indischer Handwerkskunst des 16. bis 19. Jahrhunderts* im Albertinum, Dresden, auf der Rückseite eines Fotos, 1985, Archiv der SKD, FA, 501, Mappe 3, F1525, v, © SKD

S. 85-89: Archivmappe SKD 02/GGAM 189, © SKD, 2024